The

Medieval Warhorse

from Byzantium to the Crusades

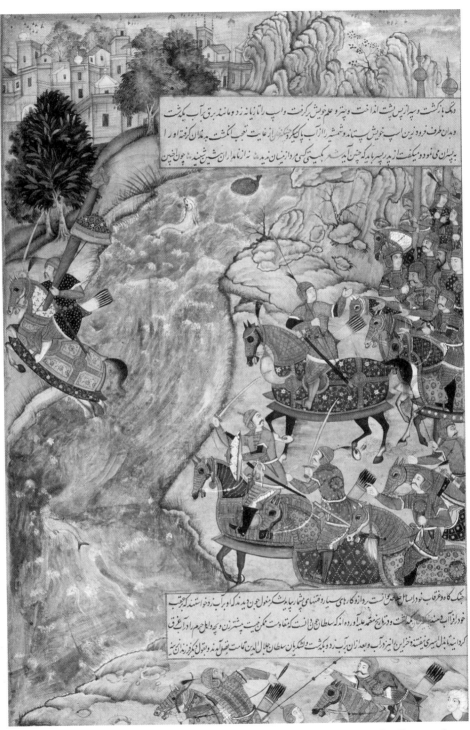

The Khwarazmian Campaign of 1221 (see Chapter Seven). Note the equestrian details – metal, fabric, and leather horse armour, saddlery and shoeing – of the period. (BM 1980. 5–12. 09)

The
Medieval
Warhorse
from Byzantium to
the Crusades

ANN HYLAND

with a Foreword by Michael Prestwich

ALAN SUTTON PUBLISHING LIMITED

First published in the United Kingdom in 1994
Alan Sutton Publishing Limited
Phoenix Mill · Far Thrupp · Stroud · Gloucestershire

First published in the United States of America in 1994
Alan Sutton Publishing Inc · 83 Washington Street · Dover · NH 03820

British Library Cataloguing in Publication Data

A catalogue record for this book is available from the British Library.

ISBN 0–86299–983–9

Library of Congress Cataloging in Publication Data applied for

Endpapers: An early thirteenth-century English Apocalypse (The Master and Fellows of Trinity College, Cambridge, MS R.16.2, f. 23r)

For Hilda and M.K.W.
with thanks

Typeset in 10/12 Times.
Typesetting and origination by
Alan Sutton Publishing Limited.
Printed in Great Britain by
Butler and Tanner, Frome, Somerset.

Contents

Illustrations

The author and publishers would like to thank the following for the loan of and permission to reproduce illustrations:

The Bayeux Tapestry, 5, 32, 34; Bibliothèque Nationale, Paris, 41, 48, 58, 62; M.C. Bishop, 17, 51, 59; The British Library, 16, 23, 25, 33, 36, 37, 38, 39, 40, 47, 49, 53, 55; The British Museum, Frontispiece, 14, 15, 26 (photo supplied by the Bridgeman Art Library), 61; The Master and Fellows of Corpus Christi College, Cambridge, 43, 52, 54, 57; The Courtauld Institute of Art, 50, 56; by courtesy of the Dean and Chapter of Westminster, 4; Edinburgh University Library, 46; from J. Hewitt, *Ancient Armour and Weapons in Europe* (1855), 29, 35; The Mansell Collection, 60; Edward McEwan, 44; the Mongolian Embassy, 45; The Museum of London, 8, 9, 10, 11, 12, 28; National Museum of Wales, 58; Christine Neeson and the British Andalusian Horse Society, 20; R.P. Nicholson, 18p; Österreichische Nationalbibliothek, 19; The Pierpont Morgan Library, New York, 30, 31; Michael Pollock of the Royal Asiatic Society, 45; Royal Commission on Ancient and Historical Monuments of Scotland, 24; Stiftsbibliothek St Gallen, 22; University Museum of National Antiquities, Oslo, Norway, 27.

Maps courtesy of Thames and Hudson.

Illustrations not listed remain the property of the author.

Acknowledgements

I have been helped by many people, not always in an academic or equestrian capacity. In particular I offer my thanks to Professor Michael Prestwich for encouragement, for agreeing to write a foreword and for pointers towards areas of research; and to my veterinary surgeon, Russell Lyon, MRCVS, for discussing aspects of equine veterinary interpretation relevant to medieval horse-management. Frank Brudenell supplied difficult-to-obtain reference material; Caroline Dobson and Dorothy Thurman checked my translations from French; John Clark of the Museum of London discussed equipment with me and helped with illustrations of medieval 'horse furniture'. Edward McEwan helped with a photograph of Mongolian archery and discussed archery techniques. Thanks also to friends who loaned reference books: Shirley Dobson, Bob Gale, Gail Brownrigg, Elizabeth O'Beirne Ranelagh, John Cherry of the British Museum, Dr John Coulston. Dr Mike Bishop, Vivienne Burden, Desmie de Rivaz, Philip Francis and the Mongolian Embassy in London supplied pictures. Ted Moat read the rough draft for flow and structure. Finally I thank Hilda for letting me use her home as a London base during research trips, and my patient equines which took part in practical experiments. My Arabian stallion Nizzolan has showed me the breed's capabilities during the thousands of competitive miles we have ridden together in his lifetime. This made understanding medieval military exploits possible.

Ann Hyland
October 1994

Foreword

The horse was essential to medieval society. Destriers, coursers, rounceys, palfreys and packhorses all had their place in the service of medieval warriors. The most vivid images in the Bayeux Tapestry are not those of the men, who are somewhat caricatured, particularly the English with their moustaches. It is the horses which stand out, proud and elegant, realistically drawn if sometimes implausibly coloured. The knight on foot was formidable enough, but when mounted was capable, so thought the Byzantine emperor's daughter Anna Comnena, of charging through the walls of Babylon itself. Yet although historians readily acknowledge the importance of the horse, and often take with enthusiasm to theories such as that which links the emergence of heavy cavalry and feudal society to the introduction of the stirrup, surprisingly little has been written about medieval horses and the practical problems that they and their management presented. A man such as William Marshall, a chivalric hero who died in 1219, not only knew how to handle a warhorse in battle, but also had the ability to devise an appropriate type of bit for a difficult animal. It requires great practical expertise, such as few historians possess, to understand the problems that faced medieval warriors in dealing with their mounts; Ann Hyland has that expertise, and also the horses on which to try out medieval techniques. The intracacies of different types of harness, the details of saddles, the techniques of riding, the psychology of horses, all have their place in her vivid reconstruction of a lost world of horsemanship. Examination of surviving horseshoes and other equipment yields information on the size of medieval horses; fragments of evidence provide clues as to the different breeds and their capabilities.

The patterns of warfare in the period covered by this book were very varied, but horses provide a common element. The horse played a major role in the destruction of the Roman Empire, and in the preservation of its Byzantine successor. The horses of the nomadic peoples of Central Asia made possible the dramatic conquets by the Avars in the seventh century, and the Mongols in the thirteenth. The latter provide perhaps the most remarkable example of a horse-based society, capable of astonishing expansion and conquest. The horse also played a vital part in the development of the chivalric societies of Western Europe; as this book shows, mounted troops in the hands of Henry II of England made the medieval equivalent of blitzkrieg possible. Cavalry was also essential to the success of Islam, while the Crusades witnessed an intriguing clash between very different equestrian traditions. The mounted knights of the Crusaders provided shock-troops which contrasted strongly with the lighter Moslem cavalry.

One of the most important tasks for the historian is to discover how past societies worked. If the practicalities are not understood, then it is hard to see how the politics and wars can be explained. This book should serve to correct many of the misunderstandings and false assumptions that are bound to arise in a society where the horse no longer plays the vital role it once had.

Michael Prestwich
Pro-Vice Chancellor
University of Durham
August 1994

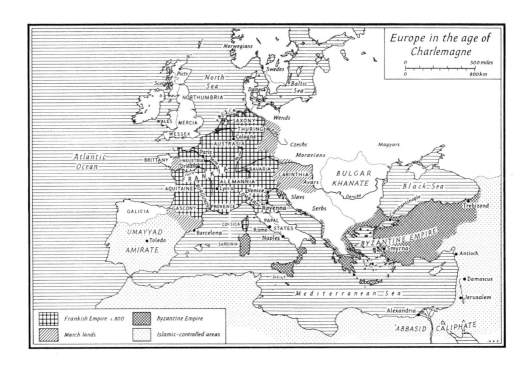

Europe in the age of
Charlemagne

| Frankish Empire c.800 | Byzantine Empire |
| March lands | Islamic-controlled areas |

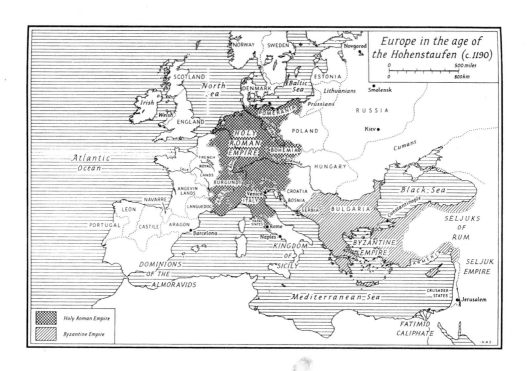

Europe in the age of
the Hohenstaufen (c.1190)

| Holy Roman Empire |
| Byzantine Empire |

Introduction

In the ensuing study of the role of the horse in the medieval period there is no abrupt change from one system of equestrianism to another, but an interleaving set of circumstances that progressed through the so-called fall of the Roman Empire to the early medieval era and culminated in the high medieval period in which the horse became indispensable to the military.

Into this era came a wide variety of equines whose military use made the aggressive policies of land acquisition possible for their owners' incursive armies. A far more detailed picture unfolds than is suggested by phrases such as 'horse-borne' or 'mounted warriors'.

A significant strand of Roman policy was based upon the links forged both with allies and client kingdoms and with Rome's enemies, and it was from this base that the medieval horse culture was to grow and expand. The breeds and types that influenced development were there, as were the forerunners of different systems of mounted warfare and equine management. Of great significance was the construction of horse equipment such as saddles, which permitted a greater degree of military aggression than has been appreciated. The bitting used by Roman cavalrymen, so vital to efficient control, was also the forerunner of later medieval bitting, and of many styles used today.

In the armies of Rome there were large numbers of barbarian soldiers, many of whom were renowned as horsemen. The Eurasian steppe peoples were to afford an ongoing input into cavalry that lasted throughout the medieval period and influenced mounted warfare, most notably the role of the mounted archer.

To the historian many references may lack the full meaning that experience of horses can give. To the horseman who lacks an historian's appreciation, many of these same references do not even register as pertaining to the horse except in the broadest sense. Dual appreciation shows a more complete picture of how an equestrian system has to operate in any age. Some ideas will need rethinking, some can be better explained in the light of what a horse is actually capable of, and there are many great similarities to our modern equestrian methods.

In drawing the threads of equestrian cultures together I have been struck by the similarities between some equestrian peoples and also between the parallel systems of some European and oriental people, especially in the matter of raising the horsed contingents of sedentary populations, and the feudal nature of both the oriental and occidental 'horsed' sections of the military.

Something must be said about why the warhorse went repeatedly into battle.

As a grazier the horse relies on speed to evade an enemy. It is remarkable that he will in certain circumstances face an enemy, and even use aggression against him. Several things govern this. Graziers are not usually aggressive to other species. The horse can be extremely so to his own kind if his territory, grazing area, or mare band is threatened. Aggression often flares into kicking and biting matches that injure both parties. Rather than deterring the fighters pain spurs them on. Several natural vices are evident: rearing and striking with forefeet; biting, often delivered with snakelike speed and precision; and piledriver kicking with hind feet to deliver a crushing and well-aimed blow. The worst fights are between stallions competing for or defending their mares. However, mares and geldings can also be damagingly aggressive.

In European war, stallions predominated; in nomadic cultures, mares and geldings; in settled Islamic populations all were used, with stallions frequently in the front-line heavy cavalry.

Man used the horse's natural proclivities. In a massed charge, herd instinct masked individual animals that might have beat a hasty retreat in a one-to-one conflict. Stallion aggression was useful. Stallions saw other stallions as the enemy, not the riders. Rapid movements in battle incited horses to compete aggressively as individual combats succeeded a charge that had spent itself and lost cohesion. While a blow inflicted in cold blood can immediately rouse the horse to aggression against the rider, wounds received in the height of battle, when adrenalin is flowing and the temper aroused, unless they crippled the horse instantly, would not register until later and then not be appreciated as the result of the earlier conflict. Horses would not initially connect a barrage of long-range missiles with warfare. Therefore they would proceed forward until committed to an assault. A continued barrage meant most armies retreated to re-form.

The Arabic treatises insist that it was vital to build a horse's confidence in his rider, who was exhorted to be judicious with his weapons. A horse trusting his rider will attempt things that others balk at. However, confidence takes time to build. The rider also has to be confident and must be the dominant one in the partnership, though without the need overtly to enforce his will. The rapport between rider and horse stands them in good stead under pressure.

Routs were not always due solely to human weakness. Horses know instinctively if riders are nervous. In battle the horse would not have reasoned why his rider was afraid but would join in any rout without the rider's urging.

Degrees of courage in horses differ, as does aggressiveness in aroused stallions. Horses are complex animals with as many shades to their characters as the men who ride them. The fractious, hard-to-control horse often has a streak of stubbornness that never gives the maximum. Other horses exhibit an extraordinary degree of courage, which is often allied to very amenable and generous natures.

An Arab poet, Abou Bekr ibn Bedr, wrote some verses to his own favourite warhorse Nashuan, who perished in an epidemic of epizootic disease in the Yemen in 1327–8: a fitting tribute not only to Nashuan but to the warhorse in general.

> Thou, O Nashuan, were irreproachable,
>   and without reproach has passed away to those already gone.
> By thy generous nature thou hast endured every test,
>   for endurance is the test of generosity.[1]

ONE

Medieval Equestrian Cultures

THE STEPPE HORSEMEN

The ridden horse facilitated most long-range conquests. The motive force that triggered the movements of steppe peoples was not aggression alone but a pressing need for new grazing grounds for their herds of horses and domestic stock, and the barrier to normal transhumance as other tribes pushed behind them.

Sarmatians appeared regularly from 70 BC until the days of the later Roman Empire; later came the Quadi and Alans,[1] followed by the Huns. Up to the early medieval period, steppe tribes came in a never-ending sequence: Huns, Goths and Visigoths in the fourth century; Huns again in the fifth; Slavs and Avars in the sixth and seventh centuries; Bulgars in the seventh. All depended on the horse, frequently alluded to as a steppe pony though a brief look at some other evidence will show this was an incorrect description. Consequently it is appropriate to make a more rational estimate of the size of equines in the medieval period.

I am not discussing specialist heavy agricultural horses or infusions of carthorse blood into saddle horses, but saddle horses and ponies in general. Ponies and horses are equines that interbreed successfully. An experienced horseman will know if an animal is a pony, a horse, or a first cross. Successive crossings will not be classified so readily. Any breed has a finite upper height limit that no amount of selective breeding will enhance. Crossbreds frequently achieve a larger size than either parent if these are of comparable size. Degeneracy by non-selective breeding, or too close an inbreeding, can result in size reduction. Nowadays horses are generally classified as animals over 14.2 hands high, and ponies as 14.2 hh, or less, a hand being 4 in (10 cm). Should a pony of one of the larger breeds exceed 14.2 hh it does not become a horse. An Arabian, a Barb, or a Thoroughbred which is under 14.2 hh does not become a pony.

Pound for pound, ponies are stronger than horses. Structural differences are also apparent. They are chunkier with coarser bone and usually heavier fleshed than a horse. Their fetlocks carry more hair than those of most saddle horses. These attributes are most noticeable in ponies native to Europe such as the British native ponies, the Austrian Haflinger, the Icelandic pony and the Norwegian Fiord. In Iran the now rare Caspian pony carries less bone, less flesh and less leg hair than a European pony of comparable height, due to evolution, dictates of climate and available herbage, and its oriental ancestry which comes from horse not pony stock.

Horses denied adequate nutrition rarely reach their full genetic potential. Nutrition in Roman times was of a high order and the grains available for feeding carried a higher protein content than most of today's strains.[2] As the Roman cavalry expanded, there was an increasing demand for a horse capable of carrying his own and his rider's armour.[3] Historical evidence for the nutrition theory comes from the cattle industry. Between 1710 and 1785 stock offered for sale at Smithfield meat market in London doubled in weight due to better farming methods and nutrition.[4]

Although it has been thought that most ancient horses were small, skeleton finds have proved otherwise.[5] Also a scrawny, ill-fed horse appears much smaller than a well-fed animal of the same height which has good bone and muscle development. Many Europeans consider anything under 16 hh is small, yet to any stockman a 15 hh animal is more than adequate; the stockier, shorter animal frequently has a larger body mass than his leggier cousin.

With steppe nomad movements efficiency counted, plus the ability to live off the land. Not all steppe animals were small, nor would they all have been of pony breeding, though average size was below that of today's average in managed herds.

As far back as the fifth century BC there is evidence of the horses ridden by early Sarmatian peoples. The Pazyryk grave burials in the Altai mountains of Siberia yielded skeletons and intact hides of horses of two basic types. In *The Frozen Tombs of Siberia* Rudenko says that 'together with small plain herd animals there were thoroughbreds, powerful cantering animals and typical riding horses'. The term Thoroughbred is misleading to contemporary readers, for whom it means a specific breed not then in existence. What is significant is that some of these 'powerful cantering animals' were over 15 hands, some of the body hues had a glint of gold, and also present in the burials were artifacts from Persia.[6] The smaller, coarser animals were around 13.1½ hh, which is not that small a pony. The golden hue is one of the characteristics of today's Akhal Teke horse which stems from an area in Turkmenia that was once part of the Persian Empire. At around the same time in history Herodotus details the numbers and the types of cavalry under Xerxes in his march on Greece.[7] The Persian Nesaean breed was known even then for its remarkable size. Depicted in the Apadana Frieze at Persepolis are heavy, high-crested, muscular horses. In Xerxes' army were Bactrian archers riding their Turanian breed. The interaction of trade with Persia, when allied with the larger skeletal remains at Pazyryk, argues for a wider spread of Persian horses, especially the Turanian, and also that it was not only the massively built Nesaean that had attained considerable height.

Steppe peoples' mounts should not be classified under the umbrella of 'steppe pony' but recognized as a mix of breeds, most with the blood and characteristics of their much earlier central Asian forebears as outlined in the studies of the origins of the early equines conducted by Ewart, Speed, Skorkowski and Ebhardt.[8] Nomadic migratory routes often converged and during the generations of migration stock acquired new characteristics from fresh infusions of blood, as well as hybrid vigour and a possible size increase when an established steppe type made a first cross with local stock. Better, larger animals, often acquired from outside a leader's territory, were reserved for the wealthier cavalry echelons.

PARTHIA, SASSANIAN PERSIA, ARMENIA

With the Parthians and later Sassanian Persians, Rome and Byzantium had a superior huge mounted force to contend with. The Parni, ancestors of the Parthians, originally came from the steppe lands around the Caspian Sea[9] and brought their nomadic equestrian expertise with them. Armenia too had a tradition of horse-breeding for cavalry from Assyrian times onwards, and was later one of Byzantium's recruiting areas. It is from Sargon II of Assyria (721–705 BC) that we first hear of Armenia (Urartu) as a famous horse-breeding nation.[10]

Centuries later Strabo confirms Armenia's equestrian expertise and adds that the Armenians learned their horsemanship and archery from the Medes.[11] They exported a huge yearly contingent of young stock to Persia, and like the Syrians and Albanians also armoured their horses.[12] Until the time of the early crusades Armenia appears frequently in an equestrian context.

Persia had great influence on the dissemination of horses in Asia Minor, with its heavy Nesaean breed, and with the Turanian horses of the Bactrian and Sogdian Satrapies where their best cavalry came from.[13] The lighter Turanian horse was considered a first-rate light cavalry mount and carried the archers famed for their unerring Parthian shot. Rome never conquered the Persians, despite an occasional victory. She did adopt many of their equestrian customs, particularly in barding chargers and utilizing cataphract and *clibanarii* heavy cavalry.[14] Ammianus Marcellinus described the Persian heavy cavalry and indeed seemed highly impressed and rather overawed by the sight of glittering mail-clad horses and riders. Barding could also be of leather.[15]

EUROPE

Of the native early stock of historical Europe we know little that helps us establish what it really looked like. Research has classified the main types, their distribution and basic appearance with the exception of the Turanian horse which Hancar considers was present in the region prior to the Pazyryk burials.[16] This makes sense when one takes into consideration other evidence, including finds of bone, literary allusions, grave goods, and cave paintings which show a refined animal of considerable size. Occasionally a historian or general passed a comment which was recorded: Julius Caesar had an adverse opinion of Germanic horses, which he considered inferior and ill-favoured,[17] but commented favourably on the Gauls' delight in draught horses.[18] These sidelights are useful in confirming certain features, especially as we also know that the Romans admired size in their animals. The Germans, although good horsemen, rode small horses; Caesar's 'inferior' can be accepted as meaning of small stature, because 'ill-favoured' obviously meant of poor conformation. The Gallic draught horses denote a larger, heavier breed. Throughout the Roman era, horses were frequently acquired from conquered and annexed territories where ethnic cavalry units were raised. The countries featuring most strongly after Gaul itself were Spain, Thrace and Pannonia, all with strong equestrian backgrounds, and several with a markedly oriental equine population – Syria, Africa, Palestine, and Moesia each supplying large cavalry contingents.[19] The ethnic units were originally mounted on horses indigenous to their country of origin. Added to this were the barbarian elements that erupted into Europe.

In the fourth century Vegetius Publius Renatus comments on the horses he considers best suited to the military: Hunnish, Thuringian, Burgundian and Frisian. He gives an explicit description of the Hunnish horse. It had a large convex head, staring eyes, a narrow nose, a broad jaw, a strong and stiff neck. Its mane hung down to its knees; it was long-bodied and roach-backed; it had a thick tail, strong cannons and small base (this means it stood over little ground and was very narrow-chested). It had splayed hooves, what we term 'dinner-plate' feet, and hollow flanks. The whole body was angular with a gaunt belly and big bones. Added to this it was thin and notably ugly. On the credit side it had an equable temperament, was calm, endured wounds, learned easily, stood up to work and endured cold and hunger.[20] Quite clearly the Huns did not ride small pony types. They may have started their migrations with animals of fairly small stature, but infusions of new blood had increased the size and non-selective breeding resulted in a less than beautiful beast. Eminently serviceable, though.

The foregoing drawing on horses from the Roman, Persian and nomadic equestrian cultures sets the scene for the ensuing diverse period. The skeins of horsemanship developed according to climate, terrain, national characteristics and usage. The development of equines depended to a great extent on how individual nations valued their wealth in horses, whether seeing the horse as a mere conveyance or as something more, an animal that added to their stature, and as a very important weapon to be used to advantage in war.

The complex picture also shows that medieval warhorses were almost as varied as the breeds we know today.

SADDLERY

From the fifth century BC saddle design underwent technological advances, but the basic shape adhered to two 'bars' of material – stuffed pads, felt, wood, metal, or a combination of these – known as a 'tree' and fitting either side of a horse's spine, joined by an arch, bow, or fork over the withers, termed the pommel, and a cantle over the back. The seat offered varying degrees of comfort and/or security, even without stirrups.

Until recently horsemen and historians accepted that a true saddle with a proper tree did not exist until well into the Christian era. Riding was either bareback or with a blanket – the

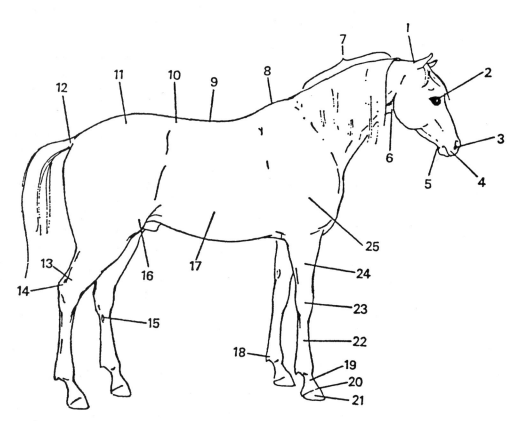

Points of the horse: 1. Poll; 2. Eye; 3. Nostril; 4. Muzzle; 5. Chin groove; 6. Throatlatch; 7. Crest (of neck); 8. Withers; 9. Back; 10. Loins; 11. Point of croup; 12. Dock; 13. Hock; 14. Point of hock; 15. Chestnut; 16. Stifle; 17. Barrel; 18. Fetlock; 19. Pastern; 20. Coronet; 21. Hoof; 22. Cannon bone; 23. Knee; 24. Forearm; 25. Shoulder

Roman *ephippium*, the Greek *ephippion*. This developed into a stuffed pad, as reference to Diocletian's *Edict on Prices* testifies. Specific weights of stuffed 'horse cloths' are priced according to quality.[21]

No exact date can be put to the construction of the first well-designed saddle, but the Pazyryk burials yielded specimens of advanced design and flamboyant decoration. The functional aspects showed that the principles of saddlery were understood as early as the fifth century BC.

The Pazyryk saddles were constructed of two leather cushions with rigid bow arches to the front and rear of each. These were stitched to a felt underpad.[22] Stuffed to maximum capacity they would be quite rigid. Saddle spacers (small wood pronged bars) which joined the cushions together prevented splaying out which could cause pressure on the withers and eventual fistulous withers, rendering the horse temporarily unusable. The functional result was comfortable for the horse, the front and rear bow arches affording some security for the rider.

By the time of Caesar's Gallic wars Roman cavalrymen were riding in saddles, a concession considered effete by the Germans.[23] These saddles, depicted on military carvings, were considered to have been pad saddles; in 1967, however, Dr W. Groenman van Waateringe published leather finds of saddle components from Valkenburg and Vechten, dating to the first century AD, but not until 1984 did it become clear that Roman *alae* used rigid tree saddles with four angled horns for rider security.[24] Listed in Diocletian's *Edict on Prices* is the sum of 500 *denarii* for a military saddle.[25] As the stuffed pad cost 100 *denarii* the military saddle was far more than a pad.

When I first saw the 'Connolly' saddle my immediate reaction was how similar it was to a modern cutting horse saddle. Roman, medieval and western saddles have two main features – a raised fork and cantle – which have identical functions. They keep the rider in the plate, whether threatened by weapon thrust, or by the rapid twistings, turnings and jarring stops of a stock horse working and roping cattle.

I borrowed this saddle to appraise its function, putting one of my own horses through manoeuvres which included the use of throwing and slashing weapons as well as fast starts, stops, wheelings, etc. It became clear that this saddle must have revolutionized cavalry warfare, bringing it to a stage not thought possible until the advent of stirrups.[26] The front horns permitted putting considerably more poundage behind the lance thrust than was possible with a pad saddle. Lateral sword slashes were more effective due to horn security. This model was clearly the prototype for the medieval war and tournament saddles. After a minor change the outward shape showed the continuous front arch and cantle of the early medieval saddle whose tree was crude, being basically two rectangular pieces of wood placed on the horse's back. Such saddles needed a thick pad to alleviate pressures occasioned by lack of a suitably contoured tree. Even today some saddles cause lesions when insufficient or incorrect padding is used. Non-contoured wooden bars continued in use down to current times in some designs. *Man on Horseback* shows a variety of medieval saddles with a multitude of minor variations.[27]

Metal plates that meet in the centre of the cantle indicate the continuous cantle was already in use in the first century AD.[28] The pommel of the Roman saddle raised to accommodate the withers and, flanked by flaring horns, needed a tiny modification, then the whole section was in unbroken form. The fifth-century column of Theodosius II in Constantinople shows that the front arch of the saddle is raised high.[29]

Many of saddlery's innovations stemmed from Asiatic sources and clear representations have come via Chinese art. Excellent examples have survived from the T'ang dynasty (AD 618–906) showing the sophisticated design of the saddle. A seventh-century example from

A small horned Roman saddle

A large horned Roman saddle

Henry V's war saddle. Note the seat raised off the bars, the retaining cantle, and the protection to the lower abdomen afforded by the high pommel

the British Museum shows an Appaloosa horse with a saddle that conformed to its back, the front arch clear of the withers, and cantle encasement for the rider's seat. A statuette from the tomb of Princess Yung T'ai, dating to 706, has stirrups; the rider's thighs are protected by the raised, slightly flaring saddle bow; the enveloping cantle encases both buttock and upper leg giving a very secure seat. It foreshadows the later European saddle with the front arch incorporating complete upper leg protection, the cantle extended upwards and laterally to encase the rider's hips giving security against being butted out of the saddle.

The St Gallen Psalter (*c*. 890–924) shows Carolingian cavalry riding in saddles whose height of pommel and cantle is almost identical with those of the Roman era, the main differences being that front and rear risings were continuous and that the saddles had stirrups.

The Bayeux Tapestry clearly indicates the hard outline of the Norman saddle on a led horse. The saddle has a rigid straight seat and triangular skirts with stirrups hung from the front arch area. The pommel is raised across the withers; the cantle is slightly higher than the pommel. Although the design affords front and rear security, the rider is not secured laterally.

It has been accepted that the medieval knight rode with an almost straight leg in order to deliver a mightier thrust with lance or sword, but this was only part of the reason. The relatively short seats and forward placement of the stirrups forced the rider into that position. There was no room to ride with bent knee. Had the seat length permitted it the rider would not then have been able to use the forward hung stirrup as a stabilizer. When I tried a Roman saddle, which also had a short seat, I found it placed my leg in a straight position and forced me on to my

A detail from the Bayeux Tapestry shows horses wearing typical Norman saddlery. Note the forward hung stirrup

pelvic bones more than does a modern saddle. Given the placing of the medieval stirrup, a rider thrusting downwards stood on his stirrups rather than sat in the saddle.

The comparison of the stirrup placement over the girth area in Moorish and Persian illustrated texts shows that the orientals rode short with bent knee and in a more balanced fashion that allowed the leg to absorb some of a thrust's shock. The European rode stiff-legged, locked rigidly in his saddle which was raised so far off the horse's back that no muscle or back movement of the horse could have been felt. The eastern saddle sat closer to the horse and allowed more subtlety in horsemanship and interaction between horse and rider. Feeling a horse's back movement can alert the rider to any impending malicious move by the horse, enabling him to take counteraction and avert a fall.

Eastern saddlery had no need to develop along the exaggerated lines of European equipment. According to the epic Spanish poem on El Cid, *Poema del Cid*, Catalan saddles from Moorish Spain were flat and loose-girthed, while El Cid and his troopers rode in Galician saddles.[30] On the surface this may not mean much, but the fact that Moors rode in loose-girthed saddles implies superior horsemanship and a total all-up weight that would not be unbalancing, as would be the case in restrictive armour. It also implies use of the more cumbersome war saddle employed by El Cid's troop. These would need girthing far tighter for security. The differences arose due to the type of armour worn and the type of horses used. In El Cid's time plate armour had not been developed though mail was used for the rider (tenth and eleventh centuries). The easterner, though using mail at an earlier date for horse and rider, as described by Ammianus Marcellinus recounting Sassanian Persian customs,[31] and used to some extent in the early Muslim era,[32] rode some horses of lighter build with the inherent strength of oriental breeds coupled with greater intelligence and nimbleness.[33] Europeans had access to and considered they needed heavier cold-blooded breeds.[34] Spain had access to oriental, cold and warm blood stock. Horsemanship in Europe did not make significant advancement until after the close of the medieval period and the rise of the sixteenth-century Italian masters. Although there was certainly skill in riding a destrier, or the lighter-built coursers and rouncies of less affluent knights and men-at-arms, it was a skill depending on punishing action of curb and spur.

Rustam slays a dragon. Note the Persian saddlery and oriental type of horseshoe which covers the whole of the sole of the hoof with the central air hole and nail holes visible

As heavier armour developed, more heavy blood was introduced by horse-breeders, the resulting animals being suitable to carry enormous weights, as well as using their own bulk as battering rams. Unfortunately they also had a pounding gait. The combination of poor action, massed charge tactics and vigorous use of weapons both by the knight and by his opponent delivering blows, called for more solid equipment. Lightweight saddles will not withstand such rigorous dual body movement. However, all changes were gradual and the plate saddle steels and total hip encasement developed in conjunction with fourteenth-century plate armour. A practical aspect of riding in armour is that it is extremely unbalancing, especially when carrying a shield in the rein hand. The addition of stirrups assists in keeping one's balance, but even so if equilibrium is lost a fall is much more likely than if unencumbered with armour.

Although the following legal requirements come from the 1403 Statutes of the Saddlers Company of Limoges they are applicable to saddle construction both earlier and later. They stipulate that the joints of the tree be well glued and reinforced by rivets, and that it should be 'well sinewed above, and below, and that the underneath should be well covered so that the horse's sweat shall not damage the sinews'. This entailed encasing the tree with a web of shredded ox sinews, glueing them on, allowing the glue to cool, applying a second coat and then finishing off with a linen covering.[35] Today's heavy-duty western saddles often have trees covered in rawhide; the effect when rawhide dries and shrinks is similar to the medieval process. Both saddles would be rendered very strong indeed.

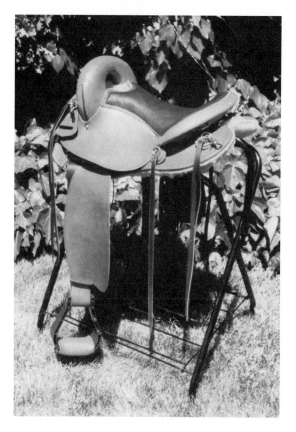

*A modern endurance saddle with raised
pommel and cantle*

One feature that had to be exceptionally strong was the front arch area because excessive stress was placed there by the knight standing in his stirrups and using a weapon. Even greater stress was centred on the stirrup tread and transferred through the leather to the area of attachment to the saddle when the knight used any weapon, particularly in a downward or forward thrusting motion. This pressure bore on the horse's upper shoulder and the edges of the front arch could dig into that region. This argues for use of thick absorbent padding, as although the bars of medieval saddles were large and therefore able to spread weight better than thin bars, they were not sufficiently contoured for individual fit. Today most saddle galls occur in the region of the recessed stirrup bar where pressure becomes localized. To gall a warhorse put him out of action till he healed. A horse suffering back pain may throw his rider and be named 'rogue'. A gall does not have to be open to be painful. Under the laws of Hywel Dda (d. AD 950) galling a horse without rupturing the skin meant a fine of 4 pence; if the gall was raw the fine was quadrupled. The value of a mature palfrey was 120 pence;[36] the fine was thus approximately an eighth of a horse's value, which shows how important it was to keep a working horse sound.

The Saddlers Guild possesses a document attesting to its existence as early as AD 1154, although the organization predates that. In AD 1272 it received its Royal Charter from Edward I. Three years earlier, in AD 1269, the Loriners Guild, which governed the manufacture of bits, spurs and stirrups, had received its Royal Charter.[37] Naturally leatherworkers and tanners worked in close association with saddlers. Tanning had to be of a high order, and tanners were forbidden to tan the less durable thinner hides of sheep, goats, horses and deer for saddles.[38] Cowhide is the best for saddlery, being tough and of varying thickness according to which part of the animal it comes from. Bridle butts, a very expensive leather because of its overall length of up to 7 feet (2.1 m) for the reins, is of top quality, coming from the back and haunch area. Cattlehide does not tear or stretch as much as other, more fragile leathers. Good leather was vital to a knight's safety as a saddle would be only as strong as its weakest part. Preparing harness leather was a year-long process, and in medieval times oak-bark tanning was used, but prior to tanning depilation and cleansing of the hide were needed; dog and pigeon dung was used for this as the enzymes were effective in the process. After tanning came currying: the working-in of oil, fat and tallow rendered from neat beasts (bovines). Consequently the knight's equipment was a very expensive commodity.

The Sire de Joinville, one of King Louis' crusading knights at the siege of Damietta in AD 1249, quotes 800 livres as the cost of re-equipping himself with a horse and armour.[39] Even for the times this was an exorbitant figure indicating the scarcity, and therefore the inflated value, of horses and equipment. A horse 'furnished for war' meant the horse, saddle, bridle, etc., plus any armour he and his rider might carry. The horse might well have been the least valuable part of the package if of a lower grade than destrier.

Civilian saddles were similar to war saddles but without the need for excessively high pommels and cantles. More comfort could be incorporated into the seats and, where not for strictly utilitarian purposes, ornamentation could be very elaborate with silk, velvet, gilding, etc. At the other end of the social scale some medieval folk still rode in stirrupless pad saddles as Sir Henry Crystede related to Froissart after his seven-year sojourn in Irish captivity.[40]

Securing saddles was, in most cases, by means of a single girth attached to the lower part of the tree. As indicated by the girth slot on surviving saddles it was set more centrally than today's girth which is fitted in advance of the outward curve of the horse's belly and gives more security. To counteract the tendency to slide back, breast-collars were used; the haunch harness, which stops the saddle slipping forward on horses with low withers and poor shoulder conformation, was not so common. However, it was used for adornment in fancy outfits to counterbalance the breast-collar. Occasionally a double girth was used, an example being shown in an illustration of the battle of Lincoln (AD 1141) in the *Chronicle of Henry of Huntingdon*. Overgirths were also used, as depicted on St George's picture in the church of San Zeno Maggiore in Verona.

The earliest mention of the stirrup is in a Chinese source dating to AD 477. It had been developing during the fifth century among the nomads of Siberia and the Altai, especially the Juan Juan (Avars). The stirrup was part of the Avar equestrian equipment.[41] The shape of a cast-bronze stirrup of Avar type, in the Ashmolean Museum, Oxford, shows superior design, especially in the wide tread which gave security to bowmen as they rose in their stirrups to shoot. Stirrups are first mentioned in Christian literature in Maurice's *Strategikon*.[42] Gradually they began to appear among different peoples. Those superlative horsemen, the Persians, had adopted it, at least for the nobility, by the mid-seventh century at the latest. A Sassanian silver plate in the Hermitage Museum, St Petersburg, shows a Persian noble using stirrups. He is well balanced as he turns and looses the famous Parthian shot at a springing lion. By AD 651 the Sassanian Persian Empire had fallen when the last king, Yazdegard III, was murdered at Merv.[43] Persia then came under the sway of the Arabs who also used the stirrup. Thereafter stirrups began to appear in western illustrations, one of the earliest being in a Beatus commentary produced around AD 776, showing the Four Horsemen of the Apocalypse. A copy in the British Museum shows all four horsemen using stirrups. By the tenth century stirrups were normal pieces of equipment. Their shape varied, including

An Avar stirrup, found in a dig in London

triangular, round and rectangular shapes, as well as the shape we use today. By the high medieval date most were heavy and box-like. Stirrups gave riders greater stability, and a much improved defensive and offensive capacity. The rider could use them as a brace from which to launch maximum poundage in lance, sword or mace attack. They reduced rider discomfort, especially on a destrier with a pounding gait. In a hunt they must have saved many a fall when horses were following hounds in full cry over rough terrain.

BITTING

Medieval bitting continued the evolution of types existing in the ancient world. Similar bits are used today, but with improvements and an amelioration of severity. There are two basic categories, snaffle bits and curb bits.

Snaffle bits have a less complex action than curbs. They act primarily on the horse's tongue, his lips and the bars of his mouth and lips (bars are the hard gums between molars and incisors and above the tushes). Control is by a direct pull on the rein attached to the ring outside the mouthpiece. Most snaffles are jointed; some have a straight bar; there are variations within the basic type.

Curb bits are potentially harsher. The mouthpiece can be like a snaffle, but the external part consists of a vertical branch of metal above the mouthpiece, and another, usually longer, shank below the mouthpiece to the end of which the rein is attached. A curb chain is attached behind the mouthpiece and fastened so that it lies in the chin groove. When the rein

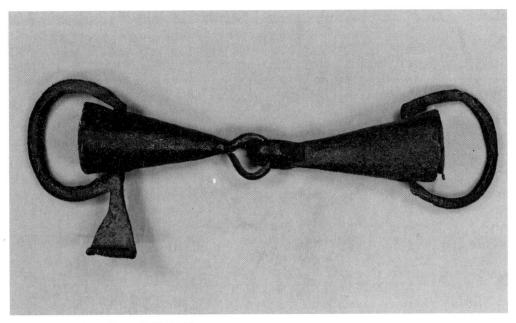

A hollow mouth snaffle, c. 1270–1350

is used the lower shank is pulled backwards, the curb chain tightens, and the upper branch moves towards the horizontal. This puts pressure over the horse's sensitive poll area, the degree governed by the height of the branch above the bit – the longer it is, the more severe. The pressure of the curb chain is dictated by how tightly it is fixed and how long the lower shanks are. A longer shank exerts more pressure; some pressure is imposed by the rotation of the upper branch. The mouthpiece exerts pressure on the corners of the mouth and the tongue if the bit is straight. If it has a port – a U-shaped rising in the middle – this increases severity according to height and width. Some high narrow ports press against the roof of the mouth and pinch the tongue.

Snaffles are used on horses that are easier to control, or when an instant response is not required. Rapid responses would have been essential with warhorses. That such was not always the case we know from Abou Bekr's comment on the large space needed to turn a Frankish horse.[44] This was the result of bad training, coupled with the horse being on the forehand.

Horsemen have always been innovative in designing equipment for controlling horses and this is evident in curb bitting. The bits I have chosen to illustrate are mainly from the Museum of London where John Clark allowed me to examine them. The least severe was a single jointed snaffle with a thick, hollow mouthpiece. This spread pressure over a wide area of the horse's lips, tongue and bars. It was 5¾ in (146 mm) wide and dated 1270–1350. Another snaffle had a mouthpiece 4⅝ in wide (117 mm) with external bars extending below and above it. Each of the sections was roughly triangular; they prevented the bit pulling through the mouth and assisted the turning process; the pulling process was delivered by the rein on one side and the flat sidebars pressed on the other side of the mouth. The mouthpiece was a three-link snaffle 5 in (127 mm) wide which allows more pressure to be put on the bars of the mouth. The centre link had a small smooth disc that could be rotated by the horse's tongue. This kept the jaw relaxed and the mouth moist as the tongue feeling the roller

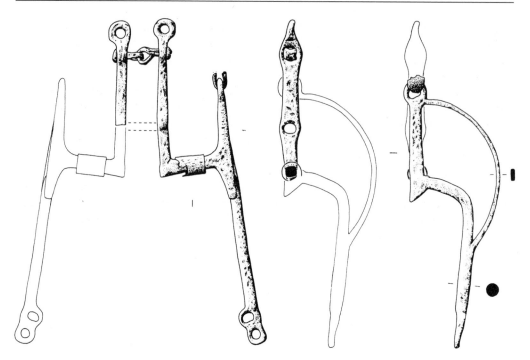

*A severe curb bit with excessively high port and (a fragment of) a metal noseband, c. 1200–30.
(Drawn by Nigel Harriss, Museum of London Archaeology Service)*

encouraged saliva thus keeping the mouth more sensitive. It was dated to the mid-fourteenth century.

Another example was a fragment (about half) of a curb-style bit, dating to 1200–30, with a narrow mouthpiece 4½ in (114 mm) wide and excessively long lower shanks which were attached to the lower part of the cross mouthpiece and would have swivelled freely except for a curved bar which connected the lower shank to the external part of the mouthpiece thus making the shank rigid with pressure operating via the rein on the extremely high port. On the upper part of the port there are two holes through which a bar or chain could be slotted, connecting both sides of the port, but this has not survived. This bit would have exerted much curb chain action on the chin groove and punishing port action on the roof of the mouth. A piece of flat metal encircled the mouthpiece between shank and port. Unfortunately the rest is missing, but had it survived it would have been a noseband as shown by a similar eleventh-century bit in the Musée de Normandie at Caen. This had a metal noseband attached to the mouthpiece on each side of the port which, combined with curb action, would have acted much as a modern mechanical hackamore does on the nose. As the bit rotated and the port acted the noseband would have clamped in a vicelike action. There is a similar bit in the Metropolitan Museum in New York, but although the external parts of this bit were very similar to the London one the mouthpiece was a high ported shape with a transverse bar fixed across the top of the port and extending to the external shanks. The noseband in this instance was fixed to the transverse bar each side of the port. The Metropolitan bit would have sat lower in the horse's mouth, port action would have depressed the tongue, and the nasal control compressed the soft sides of the horse's nose, acting as a hackamore and/or drop noseband to prevent the horse opening his mouth against bit control. A horse with wolf teeth would have found such a bit impossible to wear; today these teeth are removed surgically when they cause problems.

Although exhibiting variations, all three bits were severe curbs with high port and nasal control. I made a mock-up of the Metropolitan bit using a ported rigid shanked western curb, put in the nasal and transverse bar additions and tried it out (gently) to ascertain if my analysis was accurate. It was.

The crude triangular shape shown on many medieval illustrations is thus explained and suggests that this curb, with variations, was common. These bits are ingenious contraptions and show that ways were being sought to enforce rapid control on medieval horses. Other medieval curb bits in the Museum of London catalogue include one that is almost a replica of a modern jointed pelham with rings for two sets of reins for independent snaffle or curb action, or dual action when all four reins were used.[45]

The British Museum has bits from early and later medieval times. Most are snaffles ranging from 4 to 6 in (100 to 150 mm) wide. A particularly interesting snaffle dates to the ninth or tenth century and came from a grave of the Khazar, Saltovo Mayatsk culture, which

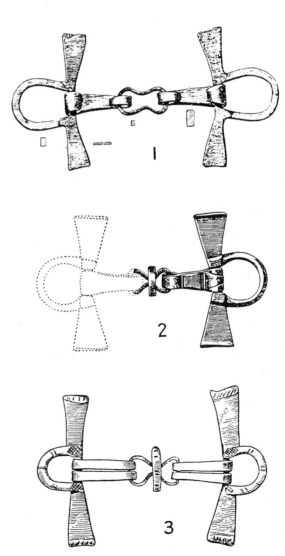

Medieval snaffle bits: 1) an iron snaffle bit; 2) part of a bronze snaffle bit; 3) part of an iron snaffle bit, one cheek piece missing. (From London Museum Medieval Catalogue, *1940)*

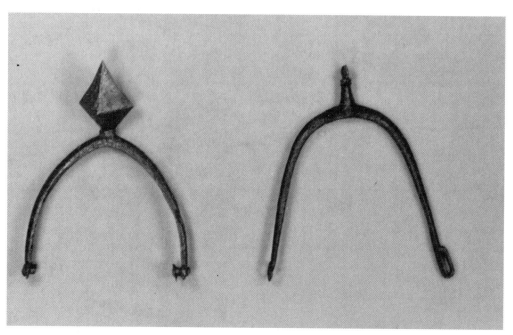

A variety of medieval spurs. The top spur dates to the late fourteenth to early fifteenth century, the bottom two to the twelfth century (left) and the eleventh to twelfth century (right)

puts it nicely into the Magyar period. It is a simple jointed snaffle with cheekpieces extending above and below the bit, but it has a metal slot fixed just below the mouthpiece on each side for attaching a noseband. This would have exerted pressure similar to a Roman snaffle which I had made up in facsimile form and with which I experimented to ascertain its action. Although the mouthpieces vary, the noseband action is the same and prevents the mouth opening. The Khazar bit was at least 5½ in (140 mm) across.[46]

The size of the bit cannot be taken as an accurate indication of the size of the horses as some 15 hh horses need a 5½ in (140 mm) bit while others wear a bit that is an inch (25 mm) narrower. A 5½ in (140 mm) bit can be a perfect fit both for a 14.3 hh horse and for a 16.1 hand animal; my own horses Katchina and Granicus use the same bridle. This is not uncommon.

SPURS

Spurs come in a great variety of styles. The three described are representative of types used from the eleventh to the fourteenth centuries.

The one from the eleventh or twelfth century has four tiny prongs to each spur end, just like a little fork. Although sharp, the prongs could not have penetrated further than the surface of the skin. The lozenge-shaped goad spur from the twelfth century is extremely sharp, but its shape prevented deep entry into the horse's sides. The third spur is 5¾ in (146 mm) long; the business end is a free-moving rowel with eight ¾ in (19 mm) rowels. The shape allowed it to be secured near the top of the rider's heel, which meant the rider's leg did not have to reach up so far to connect. The long shank could rake further back, and also hook underneath a horse's mail, leather, or cloth trapper to connect, although this might be dangerous should the spur become entangled in mail or fabric. It was dated to the late fourteenth century.

TWO

Byzantium and her Enemies

Byzantine military equestrianism cannot be seen in isolation. Many factors affected cavalry operations between the battle of Adrianople in AD 378 and the fall of Constantinople to the armies of the Fourth Crusade in 1204. Byzantium's history was inextricably interwoven with most of the cavalry nations of the medieval period.

Byzantium was heir to the centuries-long Roman improvement in breeding of horses for state, military and civilian use. She also inherited improved cavalry warfare. This had reached large-scale proportions from the time of Emperor Gallienus (AD 253–8) and his successors, particularly Diocletian (AD 284–305) who greatly enlarged both foot and horse.

The empire's agrarian economy was largely geared to producing both the high-class horses themselves and the fodder that maintained them. Many laws in the Theodosian code concern equestrian elements: breeding, acquisition by the military, fodder requisition, use of animals on the *Cursus Publicus*, circus procedure, etc. In the later empire cavalry numbers on the rosters totalled well over 150,000. This was only the tip of the iceberg as youngstock coming along to replace post, state, race, military and civilian animals put an even greater pressure on the finite land resources. Breeds were improved; veterinary medicine was given much prominence. Consequently we have a good picture of the legacy the Byzantines acquired as they moved from the Roman to the medieval period.[1]

By the beginning of the medieval period the Byzantine army had changed. Infantry was no longer the most important arm, though still present in great numbers. The era of the heavy cavalryman arrived in the Christian East centuries before its ascendancy in the West, a process that really began in Gothic Italy and was developed in the eighth century by the Franks.

In the East the horse had long held premier position. The armies of Persia and Armenia, and the constant stream of nomadic steppe-dwellers with which Byzantium had to contend, from the Avars of the sixth to the Seljuks of the eleventh century, were well horsed on animals of many tough indigenous breeds. In between they contended with the Arab incursions of the seventh and eighth centuries. In the eleventh century came incursions of Normans using a heavier animal, which was also prized by that astute Byzantine ruler, Alexius Comnenus I.

The East was rich in horses. Much of this wealth was in Byzantium's realm. Cappadocia, Phrygia and particularly Syria were regions where horse-breeding had been raised to a high degree.[2]

A rapid overview of the equestrian influences that affected Byzantium shows a further variety of equines.

Persia had her famous Nesaean, a heavy, well-muscled and extremely large horse by ancient standards, as the Apadana frieze at Persepolis shows. A reference in official Chinese sources records Persian horses of the first century AD as standing the equivalent of 16 hh,[3] although it does not name them specifically as Nesaean. In the thirteenth century Marco Polo noted that Persia still produced magnificent horses.[4] To a European great size was usually equated with superiority. Neighbouring Armenia also had Nesaean imports, the resultant crosses and her own indigenous breeds. A passage in Xenophon's *Persian Expedition* describes an Armenian breed, smaller than the Persian, but of finer quality.[5]

Frequently literary references and geographical setting, when allied with modern breed descriptions, allow us to pinpoint breeds that exist today, although going by different names. Without specific equestrian knowledge such passages can appear as literary embellishments.

The *Book of Dede Korkut*, estimated to have been compiled in the early fifteenth century, concerns the struggles between the Oghuz Turks and the Pechenegs that took place during the eighth to eleventh centuries.[6] In these struggles the horse has a prominent place. Two breeds are frequently named: the Kazilik, located near Erivan in Armenia, and the Arabian, which had spread rapidly into Anatolia from Arab-dominated territories. The Kazilik is described as black-maned and not an easy ride, needing a skilled horseman to master him.[7] There is also a reference to the yellow coat-colour of foals.[8] The yellow, or dun, coat with black mane points to the modern Akhal Teke.[9] This reference to what must surely be a Turcoman or Turkmene horse shows that this oriental breed spread very rapidly via Turkish incursions into Anatolian and Byzantine spheres. At Aravan near Ferghana rock drawings dating from the first century BC show an oriental type of horse.[10] According to Arabian travel journals of the ninth and tenth centuries the Bactrian horse from Kotal was much prized.[11] Much later, Marco Polo describes the superior horses of Badakshan (Bactria) as possessing great speed, cleverness over tricky going, and immensely hard hooves that needed no shoeing.[12] The Turkmene horse, not then known as such, had a wide geographical spread, largely due to the Persian Empire's cavalry presence in their satrapies of which Bactria and Armenia were two. Ferghana was of course a source for Turkmene stock.

As the horses of Turkmenistan and neighbouring territories were of such importance throughout the whole of the medieval era it is worth noting that the Turkmene had several strains; these became known in later times as individual breeds, each developed by a different Turkic tribe, and the small differences in physique and capabilities owed much to habitat. This can best be illustrated by two modern breeds that have a history spanning several thousand years, the Akhal Teke and the Iomud. Both breeds were raised in the old Soviet Union, under the auspices of the State Research Institute of Horse Breeding, by the Teke and Iomud Turks of Turkmenia. The Akhal Teke is a slightly taller, more refined horse of 14.2 to 15.2 hh; the Iomud is an inch or so shorter (say 25 mm), and has slightly coarser bone. Both breeds are known for speed, great endurance, and ability to perform well in hot and arid conditions. In a twentieth-century feat undertaken by Turkmen riders, Akhal Tekes and Iomuds covered 4,300 km (2,672 miles) in eighty-four days, 1,000 km (620 miles) of it through arid desert with abrasive sand and rock footing, and 360 km (220 miles), covered in three days, over the Kara Kum Desert.[13]

This modern feat highlights one of the main reasons for Turkish success. Neither long distances nor the need to travel fast over inhospitable terrain barred their repeated incursions into Persian and Byzantine territories. Other mounted nomads plagued the Byzantine rulers at different times, especially the Avars and Magyars. The former left little trace, the latter were the precursors of Hungary's famed cavalry.

JUSTINIAN'S WARS

The best source for Byzantium's early medieval period is Procopius of Caesarea, a legal advocate, historian of Justinian's reign (527–65) and from 527 adviser to Belisarius. As Procopius accompanied Belisarius on many campaigns he was an eye-witness of much that he recorded. When not personally present with Belisarius or his contemporary general, the

Two Akhal Teke stallions; the top one is especially lean for racing

eunuch Narses, he recorded details related by reliable witnesses. From his eight books covering the years 527–53 we know how valuable cavalry was to the Byzantine army. The methods of mounting the units and shipping the animals are outlined, and details of cavalry maintenance and subsequent deployment and usage are set down. During these years Justinian's armies fought constantly, although frequently undermanned and underhorsed due to the emperor's niggardliness. Conflict moved from Persia to Africa to Italy, back to Persia and then again to Italy.

Only the Vandalic war had an uninterrupted and short span: Belisarius was sent to Africa in 533, and the following year was awarded a triumph in Constantinople. The Persian problems were inherited and ongoing and cost Byzantium dear, many battles being fought in Justinian's and his successors' reigns, punctuated by short truces, often to free armies to fight on another front. The Gothic war in Italy dragged on for eighteen years.

Procopius leaves us in no doubt that the horse was the important part of the Byzantine army, and that Justinian had his own sizeable stud farms, especially in Thrace.[14]

The Byzantine horsed archer was an expert, capable of loosing arrows from either side of the horse while at full gallop, either shooting a fleeing opponent, or defending himself by a 'Parthian' shot over the horse's rearquarters if he himself was fleeing. The method used was a full draw to the right ear which imparted greater poundage to the arrow.[15] The penetrative quality of Roman equipment used at the battle of Callinicum (AD 531) was due to the adoption of the Hunnic bow and the Mongolian release.[16] The Mongolian release, which uses a thumb lock, is faster, whereas the Mediterranean release, using the fingers to draw, is slower and with an oriental bow the fingers would be crushed.[17] Procopius says the bow used by the Persians at Callinicum was much weaker and the arrows unable to pierce armour, even though the rate of delivery was greater.[18] The mounted Byzantine archers were also armoured with corselets and knee-high greaves. A shield was worn on the shoulder to protect face and neck when shooting.[19] This would have given protection whatever the angle from which the archer shot, the small size of the shield permitting him to shoot his weapon unimpeded. The mounted archer was also expected to fight at close quarters, for which he carried a sword suspended on the left side. Some were also equipped with spears.[20]

Belisarius was about twenty-two years of age,[21] and one of Justinian's bodyguards when the future emperor was still a general. Soon after Justinian's accession in 527 Belisarius was appointed General of the East and ordered to march against the Persians.[22] In 530 his first major battle was fought successfully outside Nisibis near Daras, cavalry playing the significant role on both sides. A large defensive straight trench intersected by a cross-trench was dug by the Romans and a large body of horsemen under Bouzes, and 300 Eruli tribesmen under Pharas, stationed to the left of the straight trench, while on their right outside the trench, at the angle formed by the intersection of the cross-trench, 600 Massagetae Huns under Sunicas and Aigan were set to support Bouzes' and Pharas' horse if they were driven back, the plan being to come in on the Persian flank and get behind them, pinning them between two forces. On the right wing of the Roman trench was stationed a similar formation of horsemen under five different commanders – John, son of Nicetas, Cyril and Marcellus, Germanus and Dorotheus – plus 600 Massagetae under Simmas and Ascan. The centre was formed of forces under Belisarius and Hermogenes, his subordinate commander. Total horse and foot were 25,000 Romans opposing 40,000 Persians.[23] The Persians made the first move, cavalry from their right wing assaulting Bouzes and Pharas who retired to the rear. The Persians did not pursue them for fear of being surrounded, and were in their turn repulsed by the retiring Romans about-facing to counter-attack. In this skirmish only seven Persians fell. No mention is made by Procopius of any Roman dead. The ensuing stalemate was broken and an end brought to the first day's engagement when a

Persian challenged the Romans to individual combat. Andreas, Bouzes' bath attendant, took up the challenge, despatching first one Persian, then another. The brief commentary has a tournament flavour: two chargers galloping against each other, their heads crashing together, each lancer being hurled to the ground as the chargers fell. Andreas being the nimbler of the two leaped to his feet and killed his opponent who was too encumbered to rise.[24] To have two horses colliding is one thing, but for heads to connect frontally shows that at least one rider was inept; presumably the non-military bath attendant, Andreas, had more brawn than brains. Cavalrymen instinctively seek to preserve their mounts, at the same time using weapons effectively, something the Persian was prevented from doing, not being in control of Andreas' horse.

On the second day the Persian forces were augmented by 10,000 men from Nisibis, and after mutual accusations and subsquent exhortations to respective troops the serious fighting began just after noon. Roman troops were arrayed as before; the Persian forces were split, half held in reserve. Heavy losses were inflicted by both sides, archers engaging at closer quarters with spears after arrow supplies ran out. The hard-pressed Roman left was routed, the right-wing Massagetae under Sunicas and Aigan charging to their relief, aided by the concealed 300 Eruli under Pharas attacking and routing the Persian phalanx. Perozes, the Persian *mirranes* or commander, despatched horsemen, including the Immortals, who would have been mounted on the heavy Nesaean warhorses,[25] to the left. Belisarius and Hermogenes countered by ordering Sunicas' and Aigan's 600 horse to join Simmas' and Ascan's Massagetae. To these were added many of Belisarius' men. The centre-line Persians under Baresmanes charged, the Roman centre retreating. The Massagetae stationed in the trench angle came in on the Persian flank, cutting their army in two. When they turned at bay the Romans held their ground, Sunicas killing Baresmanes. The Persians collapsed, and in trying to flee were surrounded by Romans who killed around 5,000, none of the surrounded foot escaping. Daras was the first Roman victory over the Persians for a long time,[26] and from Procopius' pages it is clear that cavalry played a major part.

Belisarius was to continue his heavy use of cavalry throughout his military career. It gave many more victories to Justinian. Only one major defeat occurred under Belisarius'

Coin of c. 550 showing Justinian I on horseback

leadership, against the Persians the following year at Callinicum. Throughout his *History of the Wars* Procopius details cavalry use and touches only lightly on foot soldiers (he is always careful to say explicitly when he means infantry). Many mercenary troops in Byzantine pay were steppe peoples noted for their horsemanship, so mention of them in isolation meant they were mounted, even if not specifically stated as cavalry. Belisarius had a very large personal retinue. After Daras it was enlarged from 1,500 to around 7,000 men.[27] Most came from races known for horsemanship; Procopius often mentions the Goths in Belisarius' *comitatus*, and the Eruli in that of Narses, during the general's successful campaign against the Goths in Italy. Their armour was as described above, and the horses too were armoured.[28] Procopius does not specify details of the horse armour, but this is outlined below from the subsequent reign of Maurice (582–602) who adopted many Avar practices.

The mounted *comitatus* was a force to be reckoned with. Raised and paid by individual commanders, *comitati* were relied on by the emperor to act in the state's interests, but could equally by used against the emperor in an insurrection.

In 533, after a treaty with the Persians released Byzantium to deal with the Vandals in Africa, Belisarius was appointed commander of 10,000 foot and 5,000 horse which set sail for Africa. Two of Belisarius' cavalry commanders, Rufinus and Aigan, a veteran of the Persian wars, were from his personal *comitatus*. In addition to the 5,000 regular cavalry there were 400 Eruli under Pharas, and 600 mounted Massagetae bowmen under Sinnion and Balas. This army was transported in 500 ships, crewed by 20,000 fighting sailors; also aboard was the emperor's gift to Belisarius of 'an exceedingly great number of horses from the royal pastures, which are kept for him [the emperor] in the territory of Thrace'.[29] Remount reinforcements were an important part of military supplies as Amalsuntha, the Gothic queen regent, reminded Justinian when she was negotiating her transference to Constantinople. She had provided 'a multitude of horses to which the final mastery of the enemy was chiefly due'. These horses came from Sicily, long famous for its cavalry and racehorses.[30] The government post horses, under Vandal control, were also surrendered to Belisarius.[31] Collectively this represented a considerable acquisition.

Events in Africa moved rapidly, several mounted skirmishes and larger engagements taking place soon after the landing at Caputvada, which was five days' journey from Carthage where the Vandal army was encamped. The Romans moved onwards at 80 *stades* a day, closing the gap.[32] Soon the Vandal leader Gelimer was begging his brother Tzazon in Sardinia for reinforcements. The Vandal commanders Ammatus and Gibamundas had fallen; the Vandal horses, shipyards, and all Libya and Carthage were held by the Romans, according to Gelimer's letter to his brother.[33] Within three months of the landing, around the middle of December 533, the battle of Tricamarum was fought. Reserving only 500 of the cavalry, Belisarius had sent all the rest ahead under John the Armenian with orders to restrict action to unavoidable skirmishing. He proposed coming up the following day with the other 500 horse and the infantry. The two armies met at Tricamarum 150 *stades* from Carthage.[34]

The battle itself was a pure cavalry engagement for the Romans as Belisarius 'arrived at the opportune moment with his 500 horsemen leaving the infantry advancing at a walk'.[35] Roman tactics were those of enticement, small detachments attacking and retreating several times to lure Vandals out of position. When these failed, the whole Roman force advanced 'turning to flight those before them with no trouble'. The Massagetae Huns, waiting to see which side to back, joined in the harrying. The infantry, arriving soon after the battle, mopped up by attacking the Vandal camp. The Romans lost fewer than 50 men, the Vandals nearer 800.[36] The captured Vandals were subsequently enrolled in five Byzantine cavalry divisions and sent to fight the Persians, except 400 who escaped back to Libya by boat.[37]

Procopius accords the Roman success in the Vandalic wars totally to cavalry when he says

A mosaic from Cathage, c. AD 500, *illustrating a Vandal horseman. Note the branded flank*

the Vandal kingdom was 'completely undone in so short a time by 5,000 men coming as invaders . . . for such was the number of horsemen who followed Belisarius, and carried through the whole war against the Vandals'.[38] He gives no share of victory to the 10,000 infantry. His phrasing suggests that most cavalry were of Belisarius' personal retinue.

Belisarius' next command was to be long drawn out, undermanned and underfunded. In 535 the process of retaking Italy began. The Dalmatian possessions also claimed Justinian's urgent attention. The first successes in the Gothic wars were the taking of Sicily in 535 by Belisarius,[39] and Salones in Dalmatia by Mundus, and later by Constantianus.[40] The war escalated with gains and losses punctuating the next four years till Belisarius' first recall to Constantinople in 540. Naples and Rome were both taken and garrisoned in 536.[41] Rome proved harder to keep. Vitigis, the Gothic king, assembled a huge army, said to have been 150,000 strong, mostly heavy cavalry with men and horses clad in armour.[42] Belisarius too relied heavily on cavalry, a 1,000-strong force being sent to the Milvian bridge to reconnoitre Vitigis' camp site. The Goths had already crossed the river and a cavalry engagement ensued; Belisarius was a target, marked out by his bald-faced, dark grey horse who was so well trained that he manoeuvred out of trouble, rapidly answering Belisarius' aids and enabling his rider to despatch Goth after Goth. Procopius describes the horse as 'very experienced in warfare' and says he 'knew well how to save his rider'. The Romans drove the Goths back on their infantry, who in turn forced the Romans back, and aided by their cavalry chased the Romans back to Rome. As it was dark the defenders refused to open the Salarian gate, forcing the Romans to turn and fight; in the darkness the Goths, thinking Roman reinforcements had arrived, turned and fled.[43]

Once the Romans were back in Rome, water shortages threatened all, particularly the precious horses 'which were indispensable to them'.[44] In conducting the relief of Rome from the year-long Gothic siege, horses were much to the fore. Barbarian cavalry, consisting of 1,600 Huns, Sclaveni and Antae, under Martinus and Valerian, arrived to add to the Roman garrison cavalry which in frequent sallies picked off a total of 4,000 Goths. Even when Vitigis retaliated in kind the Roman success rate remained high, around 1,000 Goths falling in two similar attacks.[45]

Belisarius was quick to accord Roman successes to his cavalry: practically all the Romans and the Huns are good mounted bowmen, but not a man among the Goths has had practice in this branch, for their horsemen are accustomed to use only spears and swords, while their bowmen enter battle on foot and under cover of the heavy armed men. So the horsemen [Goths] unless the engagement is at close quarters have no means of defending themselves against opponents who use the bow . . . as for the footsoldiers, they can never be strong enough to make sallies against men on horseback.[46]

The quick sallies continued successfully, but the general was being pressured for a decisive battle, especially as some of the Roman infantry, newly mounted on captured booty horses, had reached an efficient standard of horsemanship.

The ensuing battle initially went to the Romans, the Goths fleeing to their camp; there, however, many Romans and a 'greater number of horses' were destroyed, and on seeing this the Gothic right-wing cavalry seized the advantage and charged, routing the Roman cavalry who fled to the fortifications of Rome.[47] Thereafter the skirmishing tactics resumed; in all, sixty-seven encounters occurred during the siege, with more to follow as the second year of the war drew to a close.[48]

Belisarius put far more faith in his cavalry than in his infantry. Horses were valuable booty, and were trained where possible to a high degree. They were much needed as losses from injury were heavy. However, their use entailed logistical problems, fodder and water especially being required in huge quantities. Mention is made of grazing areas; Terracina (Regate), 280 *stades* (about 28 miles) from Rome, had good pasture.[49] This meant that not only fortifications but all the surrounding countryside had to be under Roman control. Periodic reinforcements, always heavily weighted in cavalry, were sent from the emperor.[50] As fast as they arrived detachments of cavalry were assigned to places distant from Rome.[51] However, there were never enough reinforcements to allow Belisarius to proceed with rapid subjugation of the Goths.

In 538 Narses the Eunuch arrived as joint commander in Italy bringing with him a 5,000-strong contingent of regular soldiers and 2,000 Eruli tribesmen under Visandus, Aluith and Phanetheus.[52] A critical situation arose when John, formerly under Belisarius but a friend of Narses, refused to act without specific orders from Narses. The delays in troops going to the aid of Liguria and Milan forced surrender to the Goths, who then razed the city.[53]

Narses was recalled in 539,[54] Belisarius in 540.[55] He served another term as General in the East fighting against Chosroes before being reposted to Italy in 544 for another five-year term.[56] Totila was now king of the Goths.[57] He claimed that at the beginning of the war the Goths had held all the fortresses in Italy and possessed an 'overabundance of horses and weapons',[58] and that from the long drawn-out wars with Belisarius their numbers had been reduced from 200,000 to 5,000.[59] The Goths had reasserted and re-equipped themselves in the interim during the succession of commanders appointed after Belisarius. They had denuded the rich island of Sicily of 'a vast number of horses and other animals and stripped the land of grain and its other crops'.[60]

It was left to Narses in his second and final term in Italy to defeat the Goths decisively. This he did in a two-year campaign. Appointed in 552 and well equipped with money and men, and by implication their horses,[61] he made a delayed arrival in Italy after an overland journey plagued by inroads of Huns,[62] and not until 553 was he ready to engage the Goths.[63]

The two armies met at Taginae. Narses was well equipped with Roman and barbarian cavalry, a huge contingent of mercenary Lombards 5,500 strong including their fighting servants, and 2,000 Eruli under Philemuth, plus a great number of Huns and Persians and 400 Gepids.[64] Narses did not rely as much on cavalry as had Belisarius, only 1,500 retaining their horses and being stationed on the extreme left wing at an angle. Their orders were that 500 might give aid if needed by the infantry; the remaining 1,000 were to get behind the enemy thus trapping them between two forces. The rest were dismounted, 8,000 Roman bowmen on both wings, and all the barbarians in the centre.[65] Totila's exhortation to his troops denigrated the barbarians, saying mercenaries would not risk death for money.[66] Procopius echoed the sentiment, saying the dismounting was to prevent desertion and easy flight.[67]

Battle preliminaries had already gone Narses' way, 50 infantry holding a strategic hill and repeatedly repulsing mounted Goths, killing many horses and panicking others by the noise of clashing shields.[68] A challenge to single-mounted combat likewise went to the Romans, Anzales, one of Narses' spearmen, despatching his assailant by a spear-thrust through the side, avoiding injury himself by adroit horsemanship.[69] Totila, magnificently arrayed in gold-plated armour, gave a marvellous display of horsemanship mounted on a very large horse, executing figures of eight at the gallop, the while hurling his javelin aloft, catching it and switching it from hand to hand, and while the horse was in motion going through a repertoire of intricate callisthenics.[70]

But for all the bravado Roman discipline and arms told. The Goths had placed their infantry behind the cavalry to help if the horses were pushed back, but the Gothic horse charged recklessly, were encircled by the crescent of dismounted Roman bowmen on the wings, and lost vast numbers before they could even reach the Roman centre.[71] Although the fight continued till evening, the end was not in doubt. As many as 6,000 Goths fell; many were taken prisoner and later executed. Totila, taking flight, was pursued and mortally injured by Asbadus, a Gepid.[72]

Within months of Taginae the remnants of the Gothic army under Teias met Narses again at Mons Lactarius, and, strangely for two forces known for their cavalry, the entire bitter battle was fought on foot.[73] This battle effectively ended the Goth presence in Italy, and Narses allowed them to depart.[74]

Only in his last major battle did Narses use cavalry to any great extent. It decided the day. They met the incursive Alammanic and Frankish infantry host at Casilinum near Capua in 554. Narses' centre was of heavy-armed regular infantry and his wings highly trained, fully armoured cavalry, armed with bows, javelins and lances. This time cavalry constituted the greater portion of his army. Shooting into the dense enemy mass they inflicted massive damage before charging repeatedly as the enemy ranks thinned and began to break formation. Casilinum was a massacre, those Franks who escaped the harrying being drowned in the River Volturno or killed by the Italians.[75]

Belisarius had brought cavalry to a peak. Narses had made critical use of it. In the reign of Maurice (582–602) it was *the* arm.

THE STRATEGIKON

The Strategikon of the Emperor Maurice details how the horse was equipped, cared for, allocated rations, and used on the march, in formation, and in the hunt.

The *Strategikon* is dated to the latter part of the reign of the Emperor Maurice or immediately after, during the reign of Phocas (602–10).[76] Although its authorship, by the emperor, has not been conclusively proved,[77] prior to his accession Maurice had considerable military experience. The treatise covers all aspects of warfare in a concise, easily understood text intended as a guide for senior army officers. It is clear that the basic Byzantine unit was the cavalryman.[78] Instructions concerning horses show that the author understood their psychological and physiological make-up. Several passages express concern about their general welfare,[79] conservation of their energy,[80] and the adverse effects on them of becoming too excited.[81]

The Byzantines' attitude to warfare was different from that of many of their undisciplined nomadic enemies, and from the haphazard attitude to military engagements shown by some western medieval European armies. Strategy was all-important. To win a war by diplomacy or failing that, skirmishes and raids, was preferable to engaging in a pitched battle.

BYZANTINE CAVALRY BASICS: HORSE AND MAN

Most cavalry consisted of archers who trained first on foot, then on horseback. They could shoot in either the Roman or Persian manner, that is, using either a thumb lock or a finger release, the former adopted from the Huns.[82] The Hunnic method afforded a faster delivery. Practice was to be carried out on a fast-moving horse, preferably on a route march to conserve the horse's energy, and the rider should shoot both straight ahead and to the rear, both to right and left. Speed and dexterity were vital, the archer being expected to shoot, replace his strung bow in its case, grasp and manipulate the spear carried on his back, replace it, and once again take up his bow.[83] He needed a level-headed horse who did not quicken once the reins were slackened,[84] nor as the rider shifted his position for the various releases. Above all, whether the rider was loosing arrow, lance, javelin or spear, the horse had to keep a straight course, an even pace, and a lowered head and neck to facilitate the rider's aim.

The full panoply of the higher-ranking Byzantine cavalrymen consisted of ankle-length hooded mail coat, gorget, small plumed helmet, bow and bowcase, covered quiver for thirty to forty arrows, two cavalry lances of Avar type, and sword. In his baldric the soldier carried an awl and a file for on-the-spot mending of gear and sharpening of weapons. His clothing consisted of a roomy tunic, fixed at the knee when riding (this helped to prevent the pinch and chafe of stirrup leathers), which suggests a garment rather like trousers. The outer covering was a large felt cloak, both for wet weather and to mask the gleam of mail when on patrol. It also gave some protection against arrows.

The horse's tack consisted of a saddle with stirrups, a thick saddle pad, a good-quality bridle, a capacious saddle bag to carry three or four days' iron rations, and spare bowstrings.[85] No doubt other essentials were also carried, such as hoof picks, strips of leather thonging for saddlery and personal gear repair, etc., plus some food for the horse along with the soldier's own rations, and a lasso with a thong and a pair of hobbles. Wicker cages were provided for carrying mail coats when not in use. During battle or when on a raid one of these containers was attached behind the saddle of the soldier's charger to protect the mail coat against the elements, and so that the soldiers could unburden themselves when they were not needed.[86]

The thick saddle pad protected the horse's back from saddle sores and pressure galls, which could have put it out of action, and also gave some protection against arrows or other weapons.

The horse was hobbled before it was turned loose, permitting it to move about slowly, in a shuffling or hopping manner, so it was easily caught and never got too far away from its rider or the camp herder. The lasso facilitated easy recapture when needed, as well as when plundering and capturing booty horses. It was very useful for jerking a fleeing rider from the saddle, or tripping a fleeing horse, according to the dexterity of the man wielding it. The Turks and Mongols also used lassos.[87] It was expected that most cavalrymen had their own servants, the worst paid sharing one servant between four men. The same applied to pack animals carrying provisions and personal impedimenta.[88]

Horses were purchased by the army,[89] usually during the winter so they would be trained and ready for spring offensives. Presumably the purchased animals were in addition to those raised at the imperial stud farms. We have seen that imperial herds were located in Thrace in Justinian's day.[90] In the time of Valentinian and Valens the state owned a stud in Phrygia,[91] and under Arcadius and Honorius there are records of Hermogenian and Palmatian studs in Cappadocia, as well as other, less prized imperial herds.[92] Other acquisitions were by capture of booty horses, along with arms and armour.

General training of animals is not described but the precise details of cavalry drills show chargers were schooled to a reasonably high degree; a green horse with minimal basic education could not have manoeuvred skilfully enough to maintain his allotted place in the ranks. Stress is frequently laid on this, it being expressly forbidden for a cavalryman to charge out ahead of his company in a show of bravado.[93] Punishment for this was execution.[94] The only specific order regarding training of horses is that all animals should become accustomed to working at speed in all types of terrain: open, level country, the cavalry ideal; hills; rough ground; 'thick' ground (which may mean either holding or wooded ground). Climbing and descending hills was to be done rapidly. The former needed a very fit horse, the latter an extremely well-balanced one. Practice sessions were conducted in such terrain, each man in a cavalry unit galloping back and forth over whatever ground lay in his path.[95] This gave practice not only in negotiating rough and/or steep going, but in holding a straight course, which in turn assured an archer or lancer a good aim when in battle. Individual control of a spirited horse is often difficult enough, but in a very large group which is then expected to maintain ranks while charging either in close order at the trot, and even more so in open order at the gallop, it is extremely difficult, although in the latter case horses fanned out as the intent was to pursue the fleeing enemy for a distance of about a mile. At other times a close order chase at the gallop was conducted, and this needed considerably more horsemanship.[96]

UNITS AND FORMATIONS

The basic cavalry unit was the *bandon* or *tagma* with an approximate strength of 300 men, although numbers could be as low as 200 or as high as 400 men. Its immediate commanding officer was the tribune or count. *Tagmas* were grouped into larger formations called *moiras* or *chiliarchies* comprising 2,000 to 3,000 men under a *moirarch*; these in turn were massed into a *meros* consisting of three *moiras* under a *merarch* or *stratelates*. The senior officer was the *strategos*, or general, and his second-in-command the *hypo-strategos*, or lieutenant-general. The *moiras* were grouped into equal-sized *meroses*, each *meros* ideally being between 6,000 and 7,000 men with the centre *meros* under the *hypo-strategos*. Excess numbers were deployed outside the *meros* to support the second line as flank and rear guards, or as ambushers to attack the enemy's rear. To avoid the enemy making an accurate head count *tagmas* were not to be of a standard size.[97] Lower-ranking *tagma* officers were *hekatontarchs* in charge of 100 men, the most senior being the *ilarch* or second-in-command to the tribune; the *dekarchs* over ten men, the *pentarchs* over five, and the *tetrarchs* over four, plus two file guards to each ten-man unit. These five men were to be the better archers and swordsmen.[98]

At battle stations the Byzantines drew up their cavalry in two or three lines, according to total army numbers, as did the Avars and Turks from whom tactics were adopted. The *Strategikon* decries the old system of the Romans and the current one of the Persians which staked all on a single-line frontal assault.[99] The new formation gave a more compact array with the distances between the first-line *meroses* just sufficient to keep each contingent separate while allowing each horse room for unhindered marching. Flank guards marched close in until near the enemy when they moved off to a bowshot's distance.[100] With the equipment used in the Byzantine army, the flight distance of an arrow is 300 yd (275 m); effective range 250 (230 m); accurate target range 133 (120 m); armour-piercing range 100 (90 m).[101]

The second line marched a mile to the rear, their *meroses* a bowshot's distance apart. Close to the enemy the distance between first- and second-line troops was closed up to four bowshots, enabling the second line to give support to the first if necessary. To the rear of the flanks of the second line *tagmas* were stationed to guard it at a bowshot's distance.[102]

In battle the front line was the combat line, the second (and third if also present) the support troops. In each line the *meroses* kept a gap wide enough for any troops pushed back to retire through them on to the rear of the second line where they could regroup and come again.[103] In each *meros* troops consisted of one-third assault troops on the flanks, preferably made up of archers, and two-thirds defenders in the centre.[104] In the event that the Byzantine charge was successful at the first attempt the assault troops were meant to pursue the enemy as far as their camp, the defenders coming up steadily in formation to provide backup if the enemy wheeled and counter-attacked, allowing the assault troops to regroup. If a whole *meros* was pushed back, its orders were that it retire for a distance and then at a shout of command turn and attack again. If after two such attempts they were still being worsted they retired behind the advancing second line where they could again regroup.[105]

Great use was made of flanking manoeuvres, attacks on the enemies' rear positions, encirclements and ambushes.[106] All these moves can be conducted most expeditiously from horseback. Indeed, throughout the treatise the accent is on cavalry, the author maintaining that without cavalry 'it is impossible to confront the enemy with any degree of safety'.[107] It is not until the final book of the treatise that infantry is even mentioned. This chapter also deals with mixed formations of cavalry and infantry, the accent being on cavalry, particularly in the 'formation called convex'.[108]

The Roman army had always been prepared to learn from other nations and to adapt and adopt any useful practices. Maurice was no exception. He devotes a lengthy book of the *Strategikon* to the *Characteristics and Tactics of Various Peoples*. These include the Persians; Scythians, among whom Maurice included Avars, Turks and Hunnish peoples; Franks, Lombards, Slavs and Antes.[109]

THE PERSIANS

Although Maurice condemned Persians for cunning and servility he recognized their martial qualities of foresight, skill, bravery and resourcefulness. The Byzantines had learned to respect Persians over several decades of warfare, not to be finally settled until 628 in the reign of Heraclius (610–40).

In Maurice's day the Persian armies were mostly of mail-clad mounted bowmen, also armed with swords. Lacking lancers, who needed level open country where the charge could maintain cohesion and the horses' speed could be used effectively to increase the impact, the Persians sought to engage in broken country where their archers fired rapidly while galloping surefootedly over rough ground. Consequently the Byzantine general was advised to seek plains country for an engagement and exploit the Persians' weaknesses, knowing they would withstand neither a close-packed charge of lancers nor a frontal assault of disciplined infantry delivering hand-to-hand combat, but would instead turn and flee. If the Byzantines were repulsed and their line turned, their reprise was to be on the Persian flanks and rear, as in pursuit the Persians kept their line evenly ordered.[110]

In view of the recurrent wars with the Persians it would appear that Maurice's thinking was somewhat blinkered and he saw the Persians in a rather optimistic light. Heraclius was to see them differently.

NOMADIC PEOPLES

In writing of nomadic peoples, particularly Turks and Avars, Maurice's advice is far more detailed. Although some of their tactics resemble the Persians', such as fighting over rough going, devastating mounted archery and cutting off enemy supplies, other aspects showed them as more versatile and relentless in battle, and in pursuit of a routed enemy. Horses were their most prized possessions, every man being a proficient rider from childhood. Consequently warfare was conducted almost exclusively from horseback, Maurice even saying these people were uncomfortable on foot.[111]

THE AVARS

Avars had a vital impact on the way the use of the warhorse progressed as they are credited with introducing the stirrup to Europe. This revolutionized cavalry shock tactics, which in turn made it desirable to breed a heavier horse to maximize the added power.

In the mid-sixth century a revolt by the Turkish subjects of the Juan Juan, the people controlling the Altaic and Siberian territories, destroyed their power and drove the remnants out of Asia; they became known as the Avars, a Turkish word meaning exiles.[112] They appeared in the Caucasus in 557 as aggressors against the Alans who sought Byzantine protection. A year later the Avars sent an embassy to Justinian requesting gifts, money and land to settle on. Appearing satisfied with only the first of their demands, which included saddles and bridles and other costly gifts, they concluded an alliance with Justinian, agreeing to fight his enemies.[113]

The Avars took their alliance to mean free rein in the empire's lands, rapidly subjugating the peoples of the lower Danube and heading towards the Thracian plains to which they were temporarily denied access by being prevented from crossing the Danube. On the accession of Justin II in 565 another Avar embassy arrived, again requesting tribute, which was denied. Not to be gainsaid the Avars pressed on, allied with the Lombards, to defeat the Gepids, seized the latter's Dacian and Pannonian lands and in turn forced the Lombards out of Pannonia.[114]

By 568 the Avars had overrun the Älfold where they had ideal grazing grounds to maintain their herds of horses and other livestock. Here they stayed for over two centuries. Once masters of the Älfold the Avars were a constant threat to their former 'allies' who nevertheless still used them when pressured by the Slavs erupting over the Danube, eager to escape Avar domination. In 578 the Byzantines transported 60,000 Avar horsemen under their Khagan Bayan across the Danube where they repulsed the Slavs and freed thousands of Byzantine prisoners. However, their next move was against the empire: they besieged Sirmium, a Byzantine stronghold, which fell in 582 after a two-year siege. While the Byzantines were occupied with the siege, and a war on the Persian front, Slavs poured into the Balkans, raiding the environs of Constantinople where, according to John of Ephesus, they drove off 'all the king's herds of horses, many thousands in number'. This state of affairs lasted four years; during that time the Slavs grew rich 'in gold and silver and herds of horses and arms' and 'learned to fight better than the Romans'. Thereafter Avars and Slavs continued raiding Byzantium. In the Emperor Maurice's reign the Byzantines slowly gained the upper hand, and in 600 a treaty was concluded between the emperor and the Avars, fixing the Byzantine border on the Danube. An annual tribute was paid to the Avars to keep them out.

During the reign of Phocas (602–10) and the first few years under Heraclius (610–40) Avars and Slavs again raided and occupied the Balkans, and in 626, while Heraclius was absent planning an offensive against Persia, they mounted their biggest offensive against Constantinople. Under Bayan's 80,000 troops – Avars, Slavs, Bulgars and Gepids – comprising all three arms of cavalry, infantry and seamen, they attacked. The Avar cavalry breached the Blachernae district of the city, but the prepared Byzantine fleet destroyed the Slav ships, and the Byzantine general Bonus repelled the infantry. The Avars withdrew and returned to Pannonia, and thereafter ceased to be a major threat to the empire.[115] They had caused havoc, along with the subordinate Slavs, for over sixty years and, as we have seen, had prompted the Emperor Maurice to adopt many Avar military practices.

Though couched in terms showing a great distaste for the Avars' habits and faults, Maurice's *Strategikon* shows them to have used anything but the rash tactics normally associated with tribal warfare.

The Avars and Turks owed allegiance to their Khagan or Khan and not to the strongest war leader.[116] As aggressors they planned their moves, not staking all on a show of force.[117] Their battle array was drawn up in units of varying strength and depth deployed rapidly at need,[118] although later the text says these units were grouped closely together to give the appearance of one battle line, with a unit held in reserve to use as required.[119] Other tactics included night-time attacks, as at Heracleia in 592,[120] surprise attacks and cutting supply routes.[121] Both horses and riders wore protective gear. The horses of their 'illustrious men' had coverings of iron or felt in front;[122] we are told that these shielded breast and neck. The text does not mention chamfron, but that too could be included in a front covering, although the actual advice to Byzantine cavalrymen on armour for their horses stipulates that 'the horses, especially those of the officers and the other special troops, should have protective pieces of iron armour about their heads and breastplates of iron or felt, or else breast and neck coverings such as the Avars use'.[123] The front covering which shielded neck, chest and shoulders would have given protection to the all-important jugular vein in the neck and the vital area in front of the withers. Unshielded and subject to injury this could have rendered the horse very lame in the shoulder from a severe blow, or totally incapacitated if the vertebrae were damaged where there is little heavy muscle to protect them. The sensitive poll area would also have been protected.

The 'illustrious men' whose horses were protected in this way were heavy, front-rank cavalry rather than just individual leaders. The men rode mail-clad and carried swords, bows and lances.[124] The lance had a leather thong midway along the shaft, so that it could be recovered more easily if used as a spear in close combat, and a pennon at the base of the blade, which prevented too deep an entry into a wound and facilitated retraction. Most Avars used both bow and lance,[126] and presumably swords too. An illustration of an Avar horseman on a rock-carving from Suljek in Siberia shows the bow, bowcase, arrows, lance (with pennon but no thong) and horned saddle. The rider wears a conical helmet with ear flaps and a long mail coat. The horse has a blanket Appaloosa marking on the hindquarters, which are branded on the right flank, hinting at another steppe practice.[127] In the Mongol period, a decree of Kublai Khan's dated 1260 and issued to the Hsuan-fu-szu, in the Yuan-shi 91, states that all compulsorily purchased horses were registered and branded.[128]

A vast herd of male and female horses followed the Avar cavalry to be used as remounts and food, and to achieve an apparent amplification of army size when seen from a distance.[129] Most male horses were gelded, a common steppe practice in order to prevent indiscriminate breeding and to maintain a relatively peaceful herd free from damaging fights with stallion versus stallion, or stallion versus non-oestrus mare. The treatise comments on the Avar habit of spreading their horses out to graze until battle was decided upon, then selecting those required, hobbling them next to their tents, and forming battle lines under cover of darkness. To avoid their being surprised, sentries were posted at intervals.[130] Once engaged, spare horses were kept close by in the rear of the main line, sometimes tied together as a form of protection.[131] This could mean either as a continuous line to intercept any enemy charging through the lines once the battles met, ensnaring them and leaving them easy to pick off in the resulting confusion, or as a grouping together to contain them. The former seems the more likely.

Although the Avars could operate at close range with lance and sword, their preferred method was long-range archery, retreats and sudden returns to fire again. An enemy who fled was harried until completely destroyed.[132]

Even though infantry is recorded in the host which attacked Constantinople, the Avars fought almost exclusively on horseback and were at a distinct disadvantage on foot, preferring to remain mounted when faced by close-packed infantry. Therefore they were always susceptible to a shortage of grazing as the herds travelled with them.[133] The *Strategikon* advised pushing campaigns against nomads in February and March when their horses were at their leanest.[134] By February grazing, even if available, would have been extremely poor, and although grass starts to shoot in March, its nutritional value is still low and its bulk minimal.

As with other steppe nomads from Inner Asia, the Avars started with their Turkic/Mongolian stock. These were augmented with better-bred animals raised in Asia Minor and with horses plundered from Byzantine herds. During their long stay in Pannonia their own herds and those of any indigenous stock, notably from the Älfold, would have interbred, but without new blood coming in the size would have reverted close to that of the steppe pony.

The Avars frequently buried the horse with its warrior owner. Evidence from a sampling of 107 Avar graves in the Bóly cemetery in Hungary shows that Avar horses of the migration period averaged 13.2 hh, with some individuals reaching 14.2 hh. It appears Avar horses were Roman-nosed with broad foreheads, and had an eastern origin.[135] This is what we would expect as regards size, but the Roman nose is not a characteristic of 'eastern' horses, which means specifically horses of oriental blood, such as hot-blooded Arabians, Turkmenes, etc. When denoting Mongolian ponies, which do have coarse heads, or other steppe pony breeds it is clearer to state pony or oriental horse. The same study showed that forty-nine horses were stallions and fifty-eight could not be sexed. Does this show that under more sedentary and controlled conditions gelding was not used so much? Also interred with the equine finds were Avar stirrups.

WARHORSE MANAGEMENT IN THE FIELD

The instructions for warhorse maintenance in the Byzantine lines, allied to comments made on the methods employed by Persians who prevented their horses grazing freely but gathered forage, and the nomads who allowed animals to graze at will, only those needed for immediate fighting being secured close by,[136] gives a picture of horse-management.

The Byzantines used whichever method suited particular circumstances. Before getting near the enemy, cavalry was to stay outside camp entrenchments. This was partly to impress spies with the size of the mounted forces who spread out, while still staying close to camp.[137] This allowed better grazing for horses, and prevented a systematic head count to assess true numbers. Once near the enemy, especially when penetrating their territory, horses were kept inside the camp, and detachments, protected by armed guards, sent to forage. Grazing under strong guard was permitted if the enemy was some distance away.[138]

Care was to be exercised over allowing horses to eat any stored grain found locally for fear of its being poisoned. An example is given of Byzantine horses dying from barley poisoned by the Persians.[139] There was reputed to be such an incident ordered by Chosroes II in 591.[140] Ergotism occurs when grain is poisoned by a fungus, and a graphic description of horses' reaction to what must surely have been such a case is given in Chapter Five. Maurice's advice to conduct campaigns when gain was ripe[141] implies that gathered grass or hay was the staple feed, and that horses were fed grain either because grass failed, or because grain was readily available. Grain is necessary to maintain condition in hard-working horses, although subsistence can be achieved on grass alone. There are several references throughout the treatise advising the use of horses in better condition, which gives the impression that stock maintenance was very much a feast or famine system when on campaign.[142] To curtail loss of condition, fodder was stockpiled at a camp 30 to 50 miles (50 to 80 km) away from the scene of operations,[143] and at intermediate camps a day's supply was stored so that, whatever the result, troops were assured their mounts got sufficient food to keep them going, management realizing hungry horses were a liability.[144] Even on the day of battle, if prior provision had been impossible, servants under guard were detailed to gather subsistence fodder to the rear of the battle or near the camp.[145]

Watering was the other major concern, and in the hot conditions of a summer campaign far more crucial than fodder. In camps care was taken to ensure adequate supplies by either taking horses downriver if the site was beside or near a river, or by watering from buckets if supplies were limited, as from a small stream. Attention was paid to guarding water supplies if a lengthy stay in one area was maintained.[146] Watering prior to battle was important, a warning given about the horses being unable to keep up in battle if this was neglected.[147] Caution was to be exercised, neither men nor horses being allowed to drink excessive amounts of water prior to engagements.[148] Too little water causes dehydration and total malfunction; an excess followed by hard work can cause severe colic, fatal in some cases.

Cavalrymen's horses were cared for by their servants who also looked after the reserve horses left in camp. This avoided confusion at the battle site, although for small raiding or scouting parties spare horses were to be available. Formation plans show reserve horses drawn up in two batches behind the supporting or second line and protected on their flanks by the rearguard.[149] All reserve horses were to be kept in good condition and healthy,[150] which meant suitable exercise and adequate feeding. Physical maintenance was important, for scouts' horses had to be fast.[151] This highlights different types of animals, the faster horses naturally being of leaner, more athletic build than those used by armoured cavalrymen, although even these were not of any great size, standing about 14.3 hh to 15.1 or 15.2 hh if one takes the permitted space allocation of 8 ft wide by 8 ft long (2.4 by 2.4 m) as a guide.[152] Standing four square, as would a horse in battle formation, horses of this size were accommodated in the space, although the width meant stirrup-to-stirrup riding was practised.

No doubt injured horses were cared for by camp servants. There is no mention of a veterinary surgeon, which is strange in such a detailed work. A large number of Byzantines were of pure Greek blood and Greece was famous for its equine practitioners. The earlier Roman army had a veterinary corps and this must surely have been continued in the Byzantine armies.[153] Equine injuries would include severe wounds to the body from missiles and swords, and to the hooves from caltrops and from 'horsebreakers' – sharpened stakes inserted into small, deep, round pits.[154] These were a common device with a long history, and must have been employed not only by Byzantines but also against them. Broken legs from the pits, and punctured soles and internal bone damage to the hoof from caltrops, would have cost hundreds of horse lives in a massed charge; horses also suffered tetanus from puncture wounds and sepsis from infection.

Some horses, which must have been specially selected, brought the injured soldiers into camp, supported and assisted by unarmed medical corpsmen. Doubly burdened these horses returned to camp and then were ridden back to the battlefield to collect booty, including loose horses – both those of injured soldiers and fallen enemies.[155] A steady weight-carrier with a reasonable turn of foot would have been most suited to this task as much booty would have been very heavy, and a badly injured armoured soldier a deadweight behind the medical corpsman, or even carried across the saddle-bow if unconscious. Some horses are flighty when asked to carry double and fractious about the heaving up of additional weight on to their backs.[156]

HUNTING

Horses and men were kept fit both physically and mentally by hunting. The men learned military tactics and stalking techniques which were useful when they were sent on scouting patrols,[157] and at the same time enjoyed a day's exciting sport, although in the context of the *Strategikon* hunting was a means of teaching manoeuvres and supplying meat to the camps. The Byzantine military hunt was a major undertaking, with 800–1,000 men per mile spread in a line across the country to be driven for game. Using the whole army, drawn up in similar fashion to a battle line with centre, right and left, and according to total numbers from one to four horsemen deep, game was trapped in a gradually closing circle, the right and left divisions eventually meeting, passing each other and tightening the circle till the centre was filled with animals ready for slaughter.

If infantry were present they came into the circle stationing themselves in front of the inner circle of horsemen, using their shields to prevent small animals escaping through the horses' legs. If no infantry were available the rear line of horsemen dismounted and lined up before the front line. Only then was permission given to designated officers to despatch quarry, the circle being large enough for safe shooting and the trajectory from mounted archers directed downwards.[158]

Apart from exercise and food shot, soldiers learned to negotiate any type of country while maintaining position in ranks. Powers of observation and physical responses were also honed. The horses had their tendons, bones and muscles toughened and their minds and responses sharpened at the same time, getting enjoyment from the chase with minimal chance of being injured.

THE BENEFITS OF *THE STRATEGIKON*

Study of the medieval warhorse is difficult because the subject never received adequate attention in the Christianized West. This makes the *Strategikon* useful. Its basic content remained relevant for the following centuries as Byzantium maintained its empire, albeit a much reduced one in the face of a succession of foreign aggressors. When in the tenth century Leo VI wrote his own *Tactica* it was broadly based on that of his predecessor, although some of Byzantium's enemies had been replaced by new opponents, most significantly the Arabs, Magyars and Pechenegs among the equestrian cultures.[159]

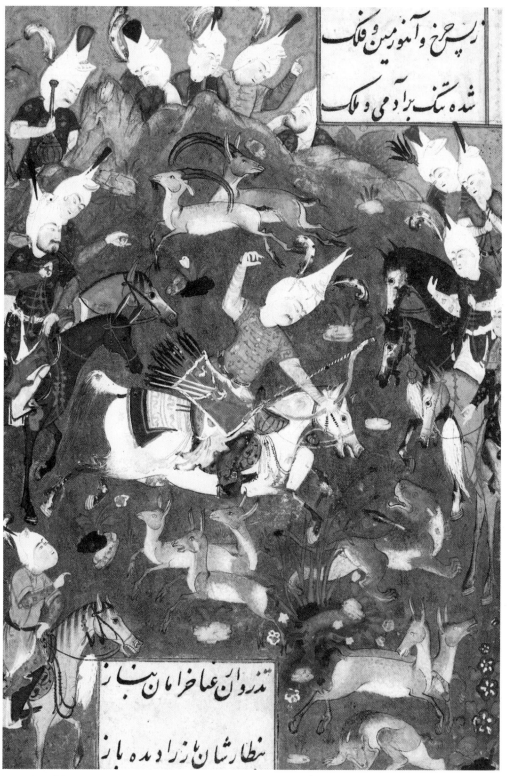

A medieval hunting scene. Note the elegance, in this and other Persian works, of the horse, compared with crude occidental depictions. (British Library, Add. MS 7784 f. 85a)

SUPPLY AND DEMAND OF HORSES AND MEN

One major change occurred in the composition of the forces which in Justinian's day, and to a lesser extent in Maurice's, had largely been made up of foreign mercenaries. From the seventh century onwards there was a reduction in foreign and an increase in home recruitment. The Byzantine Empire was gradually organized into administrative and military districts known as themes.[160] The first was the Armenian theme raised from the forces of Armenia who had fought successfully in Heraclius' Persian wars in Armenia from 623 to 625, and thereafter were permanently stationed in Armenia under an Armenian general.[161] Armenians had a long history of armoured cavalry, and Armenia itself was famed for producing excellent warhorses as far back as the days of the great Assyrian kingdom, maintaining that distinction throughout the succeeding centuries. Armenian horses are noted by Xenophon, Strabo and Plutarch.[162] By 687 the number of themes had risen to seven,[163] and by 950 to twenty.[164] Greater Armenia, the final theme, was created in 1045.[165] Each theme took its name from the army which was initially stationed in its territory, such as Optimates, who were the surviving *foederati*, Opsikion and Buccellarion, the native and foreign parts of the imperial guard. Later themes carried their geographical title.[166] A *strategos* wielded civil and military authority and the army was primarily internal. Although aid to neighbouring themes under attack was given, the bulk of the infantry remained at base garrisons, only the best cavalry being mobilized.[167] The number of cavalry raised in each theme differed according to its size. Themes changed borders as more were created, some from acquired territory, others from the division of older themes. According to Leo VI the total force of each theme was 8,000–12,000 men, of which 4,000–6,000 picked cavalry could be released for fighting outside the theme's frontiers, weak and untrained horses being left behind. The frontier themes no doubt had larger armies than those of the interior.[168]

A tenth-century Armenian archer, carved on the Church of Akdamar Island on Lake Van, Turkey

Any family owning land owed military service. The soldier was obliged to present himself fully equipped and mounted. The requirement for 'landed' soldiers to supply their own horses had been in force since the reign of Heraclius owing to the heavy drain on imperial finances caused by his Persian and Arab wars.[169] For those unable to meet the cost of equipping themselves the money was raised from surrounding villages.[170] However, common sense dictates that a considerable number of horses were issued to needy cavalrymen, even if paid for by fiscal levies. Horses killed or rendered useless in battle or service had to be replaced. Front-line troops could not fairly be expected to pay for replacements if casualties were recurrent. Horses were levied for the army, and were accepted as a form of 'scutage' for districts unwilling or unable to furnish manpower.

The *De Administrando Imperio* of Constantine Porphyrogenitus (905–59), a work written towards the middle of the tenth century and covering territorial organization, gives a résumé of horses levied from the province of Peloponnessus in the time of Romanus I Lecapenus, father-in-law of and joint emperor with Constantine VII. Instead of service in a campaign in Lombardy the populace paid in horses and specie. The clergy were capped heavily:

the metropolitan of both Corinth and Patras	4 horses each
the *protospatharii*	3 horses each
all bishops	2 horses each
the *Spatharocandidates*	2 horses each
spatharii, strators	1 horse each
the archiepiscopal, metropolitan and episcopal monasteries	2 horses each
monasteries without means	1 horse between two

A capitation of five nomismata from the district's military personnel was levied, and for those too poor to pay this the five nomismata was raised from each two persons. Up to 100 pounds of specie resulted. As each horse had to be fully tacked up with saddle and bridle, a considerable expense was added to the cost of levying 1,000 horses.[171]

Although this is an isolated illustration, there must have been other instances under similar conditions, and no doubt clergy were regularly taxed. It reflects the system outlined in the Theodosian Code where horses and money were raised, different scales of taxation being levied from different provinces.[172]

Another means of raising horses was through a controlled breeding programme. Constantine Porphyrogenitus' *Book of Ceremonies* gives valuable information on the army's back-up services, one of the most important being the cavalry remount department. The imperial estates in Cappadocia and Phrygia raised huge numbers of horses and baggage animals. In overall charge of this was the *Logothete* of the Herds whose official department administered the studs, military farms and inspectorate. From studs horses were sent to the main army remount depot and to the imperial stables, both situated at Malagina, located approximately 20 miles (32 km) east of Nicaea on the imperial military road to Dorylaeum. The former was under the direction of the Count of the Stable. The emperor's horses, some of which were sent to Constantinople, were under the office of the *Protostrator*, chief of the grooms, who had his own staff.[173]

THE BYZANTINE POST

Malagina was also the main depot for the Imperial Post,[174] which although not directly under the army, was linked to it as a means of rapidly disseminating news. Procopius outlines the postal system and criticizes Justinian for running the service down, substituting donkeys for horses on eastern routes, and making couriers use slow maritime travel between Chalcedon and Dacivicza. Only the road to Persia continued to have the normal horse post.[175] The journey of Haroun ibn Jahja shows the system's speed. Haroun, an Arab, was taken prisoner at Ascalon around 880 and travelled three days by ship to Attalia, capital of the coastal Cibyrrhaeot theme. From there by horse or mule it took eight days to arrive at Constantinople,[176] over 300 miles (480 km) away. In the service's heyday when the main stations, or *mansiones*, held forty head of picked horses, and staff capable of giving veterinary treatment, a courier on urgent business could cover 240 miles (385 km) in a single day, ten times faster than the normal daily stint of 24 miles (38.5 km).[177] Such a service clearly had military as well as civic value.

Until the eruption of the Seljuks into Asia Minor, and the disastrous battle of Manzikert in 1071, the service remained operative, particularly along the military route into Armenia and Mesopotamia, but subsequently it ceased functioning, urgent despatches being carried by state officers. In the time of Alexius Comnenus (1080–1118) a corps of couriers raised from among the Pechenegs carried urgent despatches.[178] Anna Comnena refers to a Scyth, the 'proverbial winged messenger' when she writes of the Norman invaders landing under Bohemund and their subsequent encampment on the Illyrian plain in 1107.[179]

HERACLIUS

Maurice achieved much. The Persian war was successfully completed in 591, and in 596 Belgrade was recaptured from the Avars. The Danube once more became a Byzantine frontier, the Avars bought off with a peace treaty laced with tribute in 600. However, the incessant campaigns, particularly when continued in winter and north of the Danube, provoked a mutiny led by Phocas who overthrew the emperor and was acclaimed in his stead in 602. The following decade was disastrous. Phocas, known for his brutality, quickly lost Maurice's hard-won gains. Avars and Slavs again overran the Balkans,[180] and Byzantium was once more at war with Chosroes II of Persia.

Heraclius, son of the Armenian-born Exarch of North Africa, succeeded Phocas in 610 and inherited a beleaguered empire. Avaro-Slav invasions continued, and the Persians advanced inexorably, occupying Egypt, Syria and Palestine in 615. The situation was so fraught that Heraclius contemplated moving the capital to Carthage but was dissuaded by the Patriarch Sergius who offered financial aid from the immensely rich and powerful Church. Thus encouraged, Heraclius started building his military strength, but it was not until the spring of 622 that the series of campaigns against the Persians began.[181]

In the spring of 622 Byzantine forces landed at Pylae in the Bay of Nicomedia, thence proceeding to Galatia and Cappadocia, gathering garrison troops and enlisting new recruits who were drilled and tried out in practice combats.

Using picked horsemen, skirmishing parties captured many small bands of pillaging Persians. Choosing guile over retribution Heraclius set their leaders free thus encouraging defections from the Persian ranks. From Cappadocia the army marched north into the province of Pontus where, summer now over, Heraclius found the passes blocked and the road east denied him. Sarbar, the Persian commander-in-chief, intended to isolate Heraclius and besiege his winter quarters in Pontus.

Using diversionary tactics Heraclius made a frontal assault as if he intended storming the passes, thus drawing the Persians out, at which he fled. Profiting from this his main army went first north then east, gaining possession of the hills. Meanwhile the Persians, knowing the Byzantine tactic of feigned flight, cut short their pursuit of Heraclius and returned to their position to be ready for a renewed Byzantine attack. When this did not materialize the

Persians relaxed their guard, allowing Heraclius to join his main force. Too late the Persians realized the Byzantines were in their rear and starvation faced them as the Byzantines controlled provisions along their route back into Persian territory.

The Persian commander first tried to force Heraclius to a confrontation, then to draw him off from Pontus, but failed. Realizing the passes into Armenia were unguarded he made a forced march through Cappadocia to the Upper Halys and was forced to fight on the open plain – ideal cavalry country which Heraclius used to advantage in numerous successful skirmishes over a fifteen-day period, driving Sarbar to array his troops in three divisions, with another Persian force set in ambush on the flank. Heraclius countered, arraying his troops similarly, a further body being sent to draw off the Persians waiting in ambush by feigning flight. Tricked, these charged the 'fugitives' and found Heraclius' whole army drawn up, Heraclius himself leading a charge of picked cavalry. The Persians broke and fled and by the time Sarbar ordered the general advance, panic had set in and a rout ensued. Heraclius won a resounding victory and much booty from his first Persian campaign, which was subsequently recorded by an eye-witness, George of Pisidia, the Byzantine chronicler.[182]

In this campaign can be seen much of *The Strategikon*'s strategy, especially the diversionary tactics, simulated flights and intensive use of top cavalry in constant skirmishes designed to wear down an enemy's vigilance without committing a whole army until circumstances were favourable, as in the final stages when Heraclius sent in his three divisions.

In 623 Heraclius campaigned in Azerbaijan crushing city after city and destroying the Persian Zoroastrian temples.[183] In July 626 an Avar coalition force attacked Constantinople. Across the Bosphorus the Persians mustered, waiting to be ferried across by the Slavs, but Byzantine military intelligence pre-empted their joining forces with the Avars by sending in a fleet of seventy Byzantine dromons which destroyed the enemy ships on 7 August. The Avars slowly dispersed and the Persians withdrew into Persia by the spring of 627.[184]

The final and decisive blow was inflicted on the Persians by Heraclius in 627 between Nineveh and Gaugemela, and in 628 the Persians sued for peace.[185] In this campaign Heraclius was aided by a military agreement with the Khazars, a Turkic tribe whose territory was north of the Caucasus. In all they supplied Heraclius with 40,000 troops.[186] Favourable links between Byzantium and the Khazars were to endure until the tenth century with only minor clashes in the Crimea.[187] Typical nomads, by the tenth century they had become more settled but still relied on mounted power.

Abu' Ali Ahmad ibn 'Omar ibn Rusta, an Arab historian of the early tenth century, describes the retinue of the Khazar King Aysha. His personal guard consisted of 10,000 mailed horsemen drawn partly from professional soldiers, partly from fief-holders rendering military service with men equipped and mounted at their overlord's expense.

A slightly later chronicle of the mid-tenth century written by the Persian Abu' Sai'id 'Ab Al-Hajj b. ad. Dahnak. b. Mahmud Gardezi confirms the description but quotes only 2,000 in the king's immediate retinue. Both chroniclers agree on the 10,000 horsemen the neighbouring subordinate Burta tribe rendered as tribute to the Khazars, but Gardezi adds that only the wealthy and the herdsmen possessed horses.[188] This tribute was a real drain on the wealthy classes. The animals produced by both Burtas and Khazars must have been a mix of coarse steppe ponies ridden by the men-at-arms, and the rich landowners' more refined horses from Ferghana and Bactria.

There had long been a trade route carrying silk from China to Europe, crossing Chinese Turkestan, Kasgar, Bactria and Ecbatana, then across the Euphrates to Antioch and onwards to Byzantium.[189] Along this route would also have come valuable horses, particularly those of Bactria who are known to have been of the Turanian/Turcoman breed.[190] This silk route into Europe was known to the Chinese as the 'horse road' and they used it to import Ferghana horses for improving their cavalry mounts.[191] The Khazars also aided Byzantium in its attempt to prevent Arab incursions into Armenia in 642,[192] but by then the empire had already felt the whirlwind force of the newest and most violent of her enemies.

THE ARABS AND THEIR INFLUENCE ON EQUESTRIANISM

The Arabs were to strip Byzantium of many territories, lodge themselves permanently in Asia Minor, sweep across what is now modern Iraq and Iran, spill into India, and implant their armies and culture in Europe, too, in Spain, Italy and Sicily. In this they were aided by the horse.

At the start of their exodus from Arabia the Arabs possessed few horses, being for the most part camel riders and infantry, but even at Islam's beginning the Meccans were always able to field a cavalry unit.[193]

This book is primarily concerned with the military role of the horse in the Middle Ages. It is, therefore, relevant, when touching on the Arab nation, to explain something about the Arabian horse, but to do this adequately requires approaching the subject on a broader front than the purely military. There are many Arabic equestrian works in which Arabian horses are the most highly esteemed. Most date from the high Middle Ages, but many give information from the early Islamic period. Some, especially those of poets, contain information from pre-Islamic works. Lady Wentworth's classic work *The Authentic Arabian Horse* refers to many of these. Two valuable works on breeding, raising, training for war, racing, tournaments, warlike games and veterinary care are the *Naceri* of Abou Bekr ibn Bedr, written for the Mamlūk sultan of Egypt, El Melik el Nacer Mohammed ibn Kalouan (1290–1340), and the work of Aly ben Abderrahman ben Hodeil el Andalusy, written at the order of Sultan Mohammed VI (1392–1408) of the ibn el Ahmar dynasty of Granada, which traced its history back to Deilem el Ancary el Kazrajy, a companion of the Prophet Mohammed. Ibn Hodeil's work was written to encourage preparation for the jihad.[194]

Mystery surrounds the origin of the Arabian horse. Many theories have been pronounced, from the purely desert origins put forward by Lady Wentworth, who claims he sprang from Arabia in the exquisite form we know today, to the Ridgeway theory, which gives him Libyan ancestry.[195]

The oriental type called variously African, Libyan, or Numidian had already appeared on the Roman racetracks of Rome, Spain, Byzantium, Alexandria, Antioch, etc. For much of the era, Roman North Africa supplied the most successful racehorses. It is certain that African stock raced in Spain, which had a strong nucleus of oriental horses from very early on, as shown by Celtiberian cave paintings. At the time of Hannibal, Spain received Numidian (African) mounts, many of which were akin to the horse we now know as the Barb. A Libyan skull found at the Roman fort at Newstead in Scotland during the excavations conducted by James Curle in 1908 was measured against the skull of a purebred Arabian in the British Museum and found to be almost identical in size. It would therefore appear that Roman North Africa had both breeds. The name 'Arabian' was not then in use unless we follow the theme in the poet Oppian's *Cynegetica*, written in the late second century of our era. He refers to the Erembian horse mentioned by Aristarchus, and in a different section of the same work discusses the Erembian lion of Arabia Felix![196] However, this does not solve the question of prior location of the Arabian, and at this late date it is not likely to be irrefutably solved. We have many references to movements of horses in and close to the breed's heartland, the Arabian Peninsula. What can be stated is that the Arabian was perfected by the bedouin tribes from the Islamic period onward and became a breed with

The author's purebred Arabian stallion, Nizzolan

world-wide recognition for excellence.[197] From biblical times Egypt, Koa in Cilicia and Syria were suppliers of horses to the armies of Solomon.[198] All three areas continued as important exporters of horses. The Arabs have an extensive range of legends and verbal records concerning the origins and usage of the purebred Arabian, which their books call the Faras or Atik. Many of these records are from the *Hadith*, or sayings of the Prophet Mohammed. They illustrate movements of and trade in horses among the bedouin tribes, as well as noting spoils gained from war.

Very briefly, there are two main Arab traditions: first, that a delegation from the Beni Azd tribe of Oman visited the court of Solomon and one of the diplomatic gifts they received was a stallion named Zad el Rakeb;[199] and, second, that when the Marib dam in Yemen burst in 542 BC five mares escaped, which were captured and from which came the five families or principal strains of Arabian blood.[200] Each tradition has a factual core: Solomon did trade with Arabia,[201] and the Marib dam did burst.[202] Horses have always been used as diplomatic gifts, and still are.[203] Before the dam burst the surrounding area in Yemen was extremely fertile, capable of raising horses on a larger scale than elsewhere in Arabia which lacked adequate grazing except in oases. Yemen was also an importer of horses, receiving a 200-strong shipment of Cappadocian horses in the fifth century.[204] In the very early days of Islam Yemen was still under Persian authority against which the Beni Bekr had been engaged in guerrilla warfare.[205] The tribes of Arabia were notorious for their looting forays, and Persian horses must have offered tantalizing booty.

Even before Mohammed's time many Arabian tribes bred quality horses, though total numbers were few. Here we are on more certain ground with specifics of known animals mentioned. Hojr, father of the poet Imrul Qeis, presided over his tribe's migration from the Hadramaut to Syria in the fifth century AD, and relocated beside the Beni Hilal who were settled in North Hejaz adjacent to Nejd. From that time the territory of North Hejaz, reaching to the Syrian desert, was noted for horses of the line of A'waj. His descendants went with the Beni Riah into the Yamama region of central Arabia, the most noted being the stallion Dul'Oqqal, and in the sixth century the tribes of 'Abs and Fazara, subtribes of the Beni Azd which roamed from Medina to the Euphrates, successively owned the stallion Dahis. Both these stallions were known to the poet Nabira Dobyany. From the sixth century onwards the Beni Ratafan camped part of the year in the Hejaz near Mecca; they also bred an esteemed line of horses. Other horse-breeding nuclei were located in the Nejd, Yemen, Bahrein, central Iraq and Syria – wherever the tribes travelled on their annual peregrinations.[206]

From the *Naceri* we read of specific animals owned by the Prophet himself:

Daris, a stallion, renamed Sakb, bought at Medina from the Beni Fazara
Sabhah, a mare, bought from the Beni Djoheinah
Mourtediez, a stallion, bought from Sawad of Beni Mahazin
El Lizaz, a stallion, a present from the Governor of Egypt
El Zarib, a stallion, a gift from the Beni Djouzamides
El Lahif, a stallion, a gift from Rabiah
El Ward, a stallion, a gift from Beni el Dar
El Mouraweh, a stallion, a gift of Beni Mazhidj from Yemen.[207]

Others are cited but these show a wide tribal spread.

The Arabs divided their horses into many categories, reserving the name Faras for their own pure Arabians. The Islamic armies quickly gained possession of enough horses to mount considerable numbers of troops. Details of remount stations and mass appropriations are available, but most early mass acquisitions were by way of booty. The speed of Islam's conquests meant it was imperative to acquire foreign horses rapidly, and when they returned

*A fragment of a tenth-century papyrus
depicting an Arabic horseman*

to Arabia, as they did in the early days, some booty horses introduced new strains. It is impossible to believe that the Arabian was kept totally unsullied by outside blood from the start of the Islamic drive for power. Maybe a few very rich Meccans kept a select few isolated genetically, but this is not a healthy way of preserving a breed which needs a broad-based foundation. Later when horses became plentiful, and therefore of diverse origins via conquests no doubt, the preservation of the Arabian prepotent characteristics were of prime concern to the bedouin. In the *Naceri* we have clear-cut divisions of the types and breeds of horses available and for which task they were suited. By the time of Abou Bekr, the Arab himself had largely ceased to be solely the Arab of Arabia.

Eventually Arabia became a large-scale exporter of horses, as well as provisioning the Islamic armies of the crusading era. Marco Polo gives a résumé of many equestrian practices in his *Travels*, in particular noting different breeds of horses and their countries of origin. Some Arabian exports were on such a large scale that the breeding and dealing process must have been of very long standing. Several Arabian ports were used – Aden, Dhofar and Shihr, as well as Hormuz – and from these 'provinces with every breed of horse' huge numbers were exported annually to India.[208] Valuable Arabian horses are specifically noted as being shipped out of Dhofar and Aden.[209] In 1187 when Saladin attacked Acre his army was bolstered with a massive contingent of cavalry and camels sent by the Sultan of Aden. Marco Polo says there were 30,000 horsemen and 40,000 camels,[210] numbers which are probably inflated, but meant to indicate a very large number. The camels' main task would have been to carry baggage and water. In 1821 the Pasha of Tripoli sent a military expedition of 2,000 cavalry and 500 infantry across the Sahara to Bornu. Their transport allowance was one camel to two infantrymen, and two camels to one cavalryman and his horse.[211] The Arabian deserts would have posed similar water problems.

Marco Polo makes a clear distinction between horses and Arabian horses.[212] The *Naceri* makes the same distinction between Faras and Atik, Hedjin, the half-bred Arab, and Berzaun or Berdhun, the cold-blooded horse with no Arab in its breeding.[213]

THE EARLY ARABS AGAINST BYZANTIUM AND PERSIA

The history of the empires of Byzantium and Persia is closely interwoven, particularly towards the end of Heraclius' life when the Arab explosion took place.

Mohammed of the Beni Quraish was born in Mecca around 570, but it was not until 610 that he began preaching his new doctrine of Islam. Fanatical in his zeal, he made many converts. As his adherents multiplied, the rich, pagan merchant class of Mecca felt its supremacy threatened and Mohammed was driven out in 622. He went north to Yathrib, later renamed Medina, where converts flocked to him.[214]

In January 624 the military aspect of Islam began with the battle of Bedr: 300 Muslims raided the caravan of Abu Sofian, which was guarded by 750 camel riders and 100 mail-clad horsemen. In the wild mêlée forty-nine Quraish were killed and a similar number taken prisoner. Mohammed's band had only seventy camels and two horses as transport,[215] but horses were among the booty taken from the defeated Meccans.[216] Thereafter the Muslims used booty from successful skirmishes to purchase horses, and on one occasion at least exacted them as tribute in return for a peace treaty, thirty being demanded from Najran in time of war.[217] A year later in 625 the battle of Mount Uhud resulted in victory for the Meccans who had despatched a large force of 3,000 to Medina to avenge their Bedr defeat. Among them were 700 armoured men and 200 cavalry. The Muslim opposition fielded 1,000 of which 300 decamped before the battle led by Abdulla ibn Obey, leaving 700 combatants; none were cavalry. Khalid ibn al-Wālid led Meccan cavalry in an ineffectual flanking manoeuvre against the Muslims, but the undisciplined Muslim archers dispersed prematurely to plunder. Then with room to manoeuvre the Meccan horse moved in and cut the Muslims down.[218]

By 627 the Quraish decided to make an end of Mohammed and Medina and set out with an army of 10,000, to find that the Medinites had dug a ditch around the town. Though an impediment to cavalry this ditch could have been neither very wide nor very deep as four Quraishi cavalry recklessly charged and cleared the ditch, landing among the defenders; one was killed in single combat, the other three retreated, jumping back to safety. Medina was laid under siege but after twenty days the situation became untenable. Horses and camels were dying for lack of grazing.[219] Then a storm broke, followed by heavy rain, and the departure of Abu Sofian started the general abandonment of the siege.[220]

In March 631 Mohammed delivered an ultimatum. The tribes of Arabia were ordered to convert or prepare for war,[221] but he was not yet powerful enough to implement his threat and accepted token conversion and a small tribute; most of the tribes were left almost as independent as before, with the exception of Hejaz and Nejd, which were in the immediate sphere of Mohammed's influence. On his death in 632 the tribes stopped paying tax, some killing the tax collectors, some driving them out. Abou Bekr succeeded Mohammed as the first caliph and deputed a now converted Khalid ibn al-Wālid to send out punitive mounted raiders to chastise rebellious tribes and plunder their property. When the Medinites protested the Beni Yerboa were taken prisoner and massacred.[222] By 634 Abou Bekr had suppressed internal strife sufficiently for the Arabs to launch offensives against Byzantium and Persia who were exhausted by their continual wars. Plunder from early raiding had swelled the numbers of horses available to the Arabs, but the way was now opened for them to become even more effective. The camel was still extensively used, but there can be no doubt that as the acquisition of horses enriched their armies, fighting became more efficient. The horse's conformation offered a better position and a lower stature from which to wield weapons, particularly against infantry; the gait was more comfortable; and the mount was infinitely more manoeuvrable and faster than a camel in tight situations. In pursuit the horse is definitely the more efficient mount.

The battle of Ajnadain fought in July 634 between Ramla and Beit Jabrin, 20 miles (32 km) east of Jerusalem, was a resounding defeat for the Byzantine army faced with very mobile bedouin under Khalid ibn al-Wālid. In August of the same year the Persians were targeted at Babylon on the Euphrates; Hira fell and the Arabs under Muthanna now controlled a 400 mile (645 km) stretch of the river as far as the Persian Gulf. One-fifth of the booty was sent back to Medina. From the proceeds needy Muslims were cared for, and horses, weapons and armour were purchased,[223] to add to the superior equipment and mounts seized from battlefield loot.

Initially the Arab horseman was ill-equipped. The chronicler Al Jahiz (died 868) relates how Shu'ubiyah, a Persian of his day, held Arab horsemen in contempt, saying of their early riders: 'You were accustomed to ride your horses in battle bareback, and whenever a horse did have a saddle on its back it was made of leather but had no stirrups. But stirrups are among the best trappings of war for both the lancer who wields his spear and he who brandishes his sword, since they may stand in them or use them as support.' Al Jahiz replied: 'As to stirrups it is agreed that they are very old, but iron stirrups were not used by the Arabs before the days of the Azraqites.' Al Mubarrad (died 898) said: 'Stirrups were first made of wood and therefore broke very easily, with the result that whenever [the warrior] wished to brandish his sword, or the lancer to strike with his spear, he had no support. Consequently Al Muhallab ordered them to be made of iron. He thus became the first to have stirrups made of iron.' Al Muhallab was an Arab general campaigning against the Azraqites in central Persia in 694.[224] Whether the Arabs were using stirrups prior to 694 is not definite, but the text suggests they did use wooden ones. This indicates that Persian and Byzantine tack influenced future Arab manufacture. A fresco from Qasr-al-Hair-al-Gharbi in Syria shows an Arab huntsman with a recurved bow at full stretch aboard a galloping horse. Tack illustrated is a curb bit, high pommel and cantle on the saddle, and long stirrups.

The Persians probably adopted the stirrup at approximately the same time as the Byzantines as they were in such regular conflict that they had ample opportunity to assess its usefulness. As Arab mercenaries fought in Byzantine and Persian armies[225] the stirrup would have been known to them and knowledge filtered back to the desert tribes. The Beni Ghassan fought for Heraclius as cavalry under their Prince Jabala ibn al-Aihan,[226] and as a client tribe or state would possibly have used superior Byzantine saddlery, weapons and armour.

Once settled in their new territories, the Arabs had access to Persian armourers who had a centuries-long reputation for excellence.[227] The earliest reference to armoured Arab horses comes from Mohammed's time when felt armours along Persian lines began to be made.[228] However, for the horse armours of the wealthy Persian cavalryman of the period we have the carving of Chosroes II (AD 620) at Tāq-i-Bōstān showing his heavy charger in lamellar armour covering the neck and complete forequarters as far as mid-cannon bones, with the head protected by a chamfron. There are no stirrups, but as the carving is much eroded the point cannot be proved either way.

The sudden raid was a part of Arab life in which horses were used effectively, with a quick strike and retreat to the desert. Even enriched by spoils from raids and early battles only a few warriors would have had armoured horses. Supplies increased as the scale of battles escalated and they took over the arms factories of conquered enemies. The armour worn by the luckier horses must have been a mix of whatever was available and therefore hardly of uniform construction.

The rich Meccans were more fortunate and constituted the first heavy Islamic cavalry. Of the Meccan wealth, gained largely by trade, we have no doubt. Othman, the third caliph (644–56), came from the aristocratic Umayya branch of the Quraish and during the early years of Mohammed's guerrilla activities was able to supply 960 camels and 50 horses from his own resources.[229]

Cavalry used lances and swords, the former being the Arabs' favourite weapon.[230] Archery was mainly used by infantry, as at Uhud. A Persian who fought at the battle of Qadisiya commented on the superiority of Muslim over Persian firepower. Muslim arrows had pierced Persian armour and cuirasses.[231] Other offensive weapons included javelins and slingshots.[232]

From a collection of pre- and early Islamic poets, writing in many cases of incidents known to them and of contemporary Arab customs, Lady Anne Blunt quotes:

Our pride was in stout lances and surpassingly fine mares and robbery by violence. (From El Qutami)

[Riding to the rescue of the distressed] Fierce on my steed the led one, a wolf roused and thirst-stricken. (From Tarafa, c. 538)

Khottyan lances are laid along on the withers of those warhorses – grimly set are they of countenance, scarred they are with wounds, wounds yet dripping with blood or already dried up! How the riders then throw themselves off when straitened in fight, the more swiftly to strike out at death. (From El Nabigha, c. 604)

[There were] riders who carried their lances in this way, and when a scout reported their approach said, 'Let them come', but when the scout next warned, 'I see riders looking like young boys with no lances at all', the reply was 'Beware then of death! for those are the Beni Yerboa with their lances between the ears of their horses, and from them is sudden death. (From an unnamed poet)

From El Wakidi we learn that Khalid ibn al-Wālid also used his lance this way; that considerable numbers of horses were mustered at Medina; that Khaled had at Damascus a huge force stated to total 13,000 – Amr ibn al-Aasi had 9,000; Yezid 2,000; Sherhabil and Amru 2,000. Amru ibn Kulthum writes: 'Lo, the mares we bestride at the dawn of battle! . . . charge they mail-clad together.'[234]

These and many other quotes show aspects of Arab warfare: the way the horse was led alongside the camel until needed for fighting; the unprovoked raids for loot; the use of mares (in other passages stallions are also named); the different methods of wielding a lance; the readiness of horsemen to dismount and fight on foot if necessary; the use of mail armour on the (occasional) horse.

Lady Anne Blunt had the chance to read a folio copy of the manuscript of El Wakidi's history of the early Islamic raids and conquests and to compare it with a Boulac edition. In the manuscript copy Abou Bekr's son Abd el Rahman is described as 'riding a thin filly, swift as the wind'. The Boulac edition makes no mention of this.[235] I suspect cuts and alterations have frequently been made when other works were translated and edited by writers who had no interest in or understanding of the importance of equine material, and much of value concerning the horse's role in early Arab history has therefore been lost.

Byzantium and Persia suffered catastrophic reverses that left the Arabs in control of large tracts of Byzantine territory and virtually the whole of Persia.

Ajnadain was followed by a succession of Arab attacks on Byzantine Syria. At Deera Gap on the Yarmouk, the Arabs forced their way through in August 634. A year later Damascus fell to Amr ibn al-Aasi. He then returned to Palestine and unsuccessfully laid siege to Jerusalem. Beisan and Tiberias surrendered to Sharahbil ibn Hasama; Baalbek, Homs and Hama to Abu Ubaid; and Khalid then established himself at Homs, which had been Heraclius' headquarters. Moab, the Shera Mountains and Edom surrendered to Yezeed ibn Abu Sofian, and all that was left to Heraclius, who had withdrawn to Antioch, were Jerusalem and Caesarea and the coastal cities of Tyre, Sidon, Beirut and Tripoli.[236]

Heraclius now raised a huge army to oust the Arabs, two-thirds of which was from the Christian Beni Ghassan and Armenians. The Muslim Arabs then withdrew and concentrated south of the Yarmouk. For four months the position was deadlocked. Morale fell in the Byzantine camp. Meanwhile the Muslims obtained reinforcements and on 20 August 636 the decisive battle of the Yarmouk was fought on a day when the wind blew so strongly that it contributed to the Byzantine defeat.[237] Facing the Byzantines across the river chasm the Muslims prevented their using the heavy cavalry effectively,[238] as well as blocking the possibility of a Byzantine retreat by capturing the bridge behind the enemy's position. The Byzantines were annihilated. According to Sayf ibn 'Omar the Arab cavalry were divided into several *karadis* or troops,[239] although at this stage their size would have been small. Jerusalem surrendered in the winter of 637/8 and Caesarea in 640. Thereafter all Syria and Palestine came under Arab rule.[240]

With the control of Byzantine resources Arab cavalry soon became the main arm of the Arab forces. However, Persia was still to be overrun, and shortly after Yarmouk the Persians suffered a huge defeat in Iraq at Qadisiya in the spring of 637. The Arabs fielded cavalry but it was not of sufficient quantity or power to make a major contribution and was apparently the first to attack, repeating the charge thirty times[241] – which implies a lack of cohesion and massed strength. The Arab horses refused to face the Persian elephants. According to Tabari, in four days of fighting 8,500 Arabs were killed, out of a reputed total of 36,000. The Persians suffered even more heavily; thirty regiments were annihilated and the majority took to flight.[242]

Many horses were taken from Qadisiya and at the siege of Medain later in the year the Arabs fielded 600 cavalry.[243] By the end of 638 the valley of the lower Tigris and Euphrates became an Arab province.[244] By 642 all Egypt had been taken from the Byzantines.[245]

The Arabs now had large military bases at Fustat in Egypt; Kufa and Basra in Iraq; and Jabiya in Syria. Under Omar, the second caliph (634–44), remount stations were set up, especially at Kufa, which had 4,000 head. A large area was set aside in North Syria for Muslim mounts. Omar granted a fief to Nafi' ibn al-Hārith at Basra so that he could raise horses.[246] No doubt this was not an isolated grant of land for the purpose of running studs. Malagina, the district where the Byzantine military horse herds were kept, was pillaged in 789.[247]

By 750 Islam included North Africa and the Maghreb, and across the Straits of Gibraltar almost all of Spain. To Syria, Iraq and Persia were added Afghanistan, Baluchistan, Turkestan, Khorasan and Uzbekistan. In this massive spread the Arabs, with their capital now at Damascus, had access to many of the breeds that were to serve the Islamic army: from North Africa the Barb horse; from Spain horses noted for their superiority since Carthaginian and Roman days;[248] from the homelands of the Turkish tribes the Turkmene/Turcoman/Turanian horse with its many strains, including the Akhal Teke and Iomud. As the Arab race blended with peoples of conquered nations, preservation of their own Faras became important to bedouin tribes in Arabia's heartland. Ibn Hodeil and Abou Bekr ibn Bedr clearly demonstrate the continuity of the purebred Arabian horse.

ATTACKED ON ALL SIDES

As Islam spread, religious fanaticism fuelled warlike tendencies of the Turks who were the major equestrian enemy of eleventh-century Byzantium, but other steppe incursions also show how fiercely Byzantium was assailed, often on more than one front. She had frequent recourse to diplomatic and military strategy to preserve her empire. Although it emerged shrunken after the first wave of Arab incursions, and the rise of the Bulgarians who annexed much of her territory, it yet retained its core of Asia Minor intact. Byzantium emerged under the Macedonian dynasty (867–1056) as a strong military power.[249]

HORSE SUPPLY AND ENDEMIC DISEASES

One underlying reason for nomad incursions was pressure from other tribes competing for grasslands for their livestock. Ally this to aggressive and acquisitive tendencies and the lure of rich pickings from tangible wealth and a settled agrarian economy, and land that was a passageway to further territories, and it is a wonder Byzantium survived at all.

Behind the parade of battles was the huge logistical problem of supplies: men and animals and the means to maintain both. Even though Byzantium preferred bribing nomads to fighting them, the cost was still enormous as armies were constantly kept ready. On the equestrian side this meant the little recorded stud management, keeping imperial herds and those of the ruling classes at peak production. There is documentary evidence from Charlemagne's era for the breeding and raising of horses and their resulting incorporation into the military. The Byzantine system would have functioned on broadly similar lines, multiplied many times over as cavalry formed the main arm of Byzantine forces. There was considerably more risk raising horses in eastern and Anatolian territories owing to the many fatal endemic diseases. Before the First World War when many countries still had appreciable cavalry forces contagious diseases abounded. Among them were Equine Infectious Anaemia, Glanders, Farcy, Epizootic Lymphangitis and Ulcerative Lymphangitis, to name a few, all of which had a high mortality rate. Surra, an intermittent fever due to a trypanosome, a parasite in the blood, is usually fatal, and is transmitted by fly bites. Dourine, or equine VD, is a disease difficult to diagnose in its early stages. It has high mortality in mares, and almost total fatality in stallions.[250]

These diseases were found within the Byzantine Empire and adjacent countries. The density and mobility of cavalry afforded ideal avenues for diseases to travel, as did insect bites.

Add to the above the losses from fatal or incapacitating injuries and captures by the enemy – either remounts run off from stud farms, as happened at Malagina in 789,[251] or horses captured on the battlefield or from the army's main camp. Keeping the cavalry supplied was a major task on a scale that western Europe never approached in the medieval era.

THE BULGARS

The early Bulgars, known as Kutrigurs, came from the Russian steppes west of the Don river. Early in our period they launched plundering raids into the Balkans, often grouped with the Slavs. In 540 they ravaged as far as Constantinople and thereafter their eruptions occurred almost annually till a major invasion was repulsed by Belisarius in 559.[252] In 680 the Onogur Bulgars, a Turkic tribe from the Eurasian steppe, invaded in strength, and in 681 took up permanent residence under their leader Asparuch, annexing Byzantine territory on the lower Danube, and settling in southern Bessarabia, part of the Wallachian Plain, the

Dobrudja and lower Moesia, which later became Bulgaria proper with its capital at Pliska. Emperor Constantine IV (668–85) paid Asparuch annual tribute to keep the peace, but in spite of this and subsequent treaties under his successors the Bulgars continued their depredations. From 756 to 775 Constantine V (741–75) was at war with the Bulgars, conducting nine campaigns, most of which were successful. Though exhausted, the Bulgar nation still maintained its presence and resurged under its Khagan Krum in the early part of the ninth century. He kept the pressure on Byzantium until his death in 814. The Bulgars annexed territories vacated by the Avars in Hungary after their defeat by Charlemagne, and in 811 inflicted a crushing defeat on a Byzantine army in the Balkans. Emperor Nicephorus I (802–11) was killed in this battle, his skull being made into a drinking goblet by Krum.

Krum's successor Omurtag concluded a peace treaty with Byzantium in 816.[253] But throughout the ninth century the Bulgars were to be an intermittent threat to Byzantium. They had concluded a peace treaty with the Franks in 845, and were on the verge of adopting Roman Christianity in 864 when their khan, Basil I, was faced with a Byzantine army on his borders; he quickly entered into Orthodox Christianity, relinquishing his Frankish treaty, only to revert to the Roman system two years later after sending Pope Nicholas a lengthy letter seeking approval for many of the Bulgarian aspects of social and military life, in which the horse largely figured. The letter shows that the Bulgar military organization was of a high order, and discipline harsh when they rode under the horsetail banner of their leader. A border guard faced death if he let insurgents slip past his watchpost, as did a cavalryman who presented either horse or weapons in a substandard state at a pre-battle inspection.[254] After four years of Roman Christianity Basil again reverted to the Orthodox system in 870.[255]

Basil's successor Symeon (893–927) spent the whole of his reign in conflict with Byzantium. This was initially sparked off by a trade war with Constantinople in 894 when heavy import duties were imposed on the agricultural exports which were the mainstay of the Bulgarian economy. Symeon invaded Thrace, defeated a Byzantine army and marched towards Constantinople. In 896 in retaliation the Emperor Leo VI (886–912) called on and bribed the Magyars for aid. They responded, inflicting several defeats on the Bulgarians in their Dobrudja territory, and forcing Symeon to conclude a temporary peace with the Emperor.[256]

THE *DE ADMINISTRANDO IMPERIO*

The *De Administrando Imperio* is a document which clearly shows how Byzantine politicians set one nomad race against the other to leave Byzantium free from their military inroads.

In the opening admonishment Constantine Porphyrogenitus, the author, advises his government always to keep peace with the Pechenegs by concluding treaties with them, backed by a yearly envoy and strengthened by presents, and in return to extract from them sureties, a diplomatic agent and hostages. As neighbours of Cherson, 'if this is not done they [the Pechenegs] make excursions and plundering against Cherson'.[257]

The following chapters continue on the warlike proclivities of the Pechenegs, saying they are neighbours of the Russians who are also careful to keep peace with them so their trade is uninterrupted as the Russians rely on being able to buy horses, cattle and sheep from the Pechenegs.[258] The Magyars also fear the Pechenegs, having often been defeated by them.[259] Therefore as long as Byzantium remains at peace with the Pechenegs she cannot be raided by either the Russians or the Magyars, or expect to pay them for such peace.[260] The Bulgarians, on whose borders the Pechenegs lived and who had often made successful war on them, also fell into this framework of bribery.[261] Clearly Byzantine policy was to keep peace by a mixture of military force and bribery; however, force was not to be used if danger could be averted by bribing the Pechenegs to serve as mercenaries *en bloc*. In Chapter 13 the *De Administrando Imperio* returns to the Magyars, noting they had totally devastated the country of southern Great Moravia and subsequently occupied it, and to stop further inroads the neighbouring Pechenegs could be used against them.[262]

THE MAGYARS

The Magyars left the most indelible imprint on equestrianism in Europe, as the Hungarian was held in high repute as warrior and horseman from the time of the first Magyar settlement in Hungary in 895–6.

The Magyars were of Finno-Ugrian origin mixed with Turkic stock and they came swiftly into the Byzantine orbit as a result of nomadic pressure movements. Their migration is noted by Abbot Regino (died 915), a chronicler writing of their emergence from the Russian steppes in 889 having been driven out by the Pechenegs.[263] The Russian Chronicle for 890 reports Magyars passing by Kiev and camping on the banks of the Dnieper. In 892 and 894 the *Annales Fuldenses* and *Annales Sangalienses Majores* note that they had entered into the Hungarian Plain, taking part in the fighting between Moravia and the empire, and ravaging the country, and were regarded by their victims as a new pest.[264]

The Hungarian tradition states that the Magyars gave Prince Sviatopolk of Moravia a gorgeously caparisoned white charger in exchange for a token bundle of grass and a jug of water. The Magyars interpreted this as the right to graze their herds freely over the Danubian Plain. Later the same method was used against the Bulgars, the Magyars asking for water from the Tisza and grass from Alpar.[265] Successive battles were then waged to extract new grasslands in perpetuity. Unlike the Mongols, whose visitation of Hungary had been temporary, the Magyars settled there and practised herding and an agrarian economy in succeeding centuries.

Abbot Regino informs us of the Magyars 'who live like wild beasts rather than like human beings' and who 'have killed but few with their swords but thousands with their arrows'.[266]

For Byzantium the Magyars filled much the same place as had the Avars three centuries before. Bribed to work for the empire, they frequently fought against it. Leo VI's *Tactica* describes them in terms almost identical to the Avars. The Byzantines called them Turks because of their fashion of fighting and their nomadic lifestyle. Leo notes their ambushing tactics; their care in sending out scouts and posting watches; and the skirmishing tactics used in battle.[267] In common with the Avars they also used their spare horses roped together in the rear.[268]

Leo advised his cavalry to engage the Turks (Magyars)[269] without exchanging preliminary arrow fire; the Byzantine heavy cavalry could break them, and so could the Byzantine infantry with their more powerful bows which shot further, enabling them to shoot down the Magyar horses before the Magyars closed.[270]

The Magyar horses were mostly small; leaders and chieftians rode larger, better-bred stock. The Hungarian archives contain a wealth of information concerning Hungarian horse culture. From these it is clear that later Magyar horsemanship differed little from the earlier days of their nomadic life. Even in the fifteenth century their style of riding remained far closer to the oriental methods, the western European rigid leg and high school airs not finding favour with the Hungarian King Matthias (1458–90) who summed up the centuries-long preference of Hungarian horsemen: 'We have no desire for horses that hop about with bent hocks in the Spanish fashion, we do not want them even as a pastime, still less for serious business. What we want are horses that stride out and stand firm when required.'[271]

Skeletal evidence of early Hungarian horses is much on a par with that of the Pazyryk horse burials, noted earlier. Archaeological research done by the Russians and reported in 1966 by V.I. Calkin in his work on the animal husbandry of Central Asia in the Scythian period shows that the tall horse, corresponding to today's Akhal Teke, was the mount of the ruling classes, and the stockier 13–14 hh pony the mount of the masses.[272] These findings largely agree with work by Bokonyi quoted above.

Seeing the effectiveness of Byzantine diplomatic bribery, the Bulgars under Symeon in turn bribed the Pechenegs to hit the Magyars in the rear. This second Pecheneg attack drove the Magyars from their new Bessarabian territory along their migratory path into Hungary.[273] However, though they settled in Hungary they continued their depredations on two fronts: the western European and the Balkan territories of the Byzantine Empire. In the latter, Thrace, Macedonia and Bulgaria were frequently plundered between 934 and 961, and the Magyars appeared in strength before Constantinople in 934 and 959, but their methods of extreme mobility on fast horses were not suited to siege warfare.[274]

In western Europe Magyars became feared during the first half of the tenth century and conducted many plundering raids until finally checked by Otto the Great in 955 at the battle of the Lech. Their Turkish tactics of attacking in loose order were at last countered by the 8,000-strong combined cavalry of Bavaria, Swabia, Franconia and Bohemia, plus the King of Saxony's personal guard. Otto's army was divided into eight divisions of equal strength mounted on the heavier animals produced in Europe and capable of carrying an armoured man.[275] This battle stands out, not only because it reversed the flow of nomadic incursions into Europe, but because it was one of the earliest examples, if not the first, of purely cavalry warfare in medieval western Europe. The shock of cohesive heavy cavalry won the day, routing the light, and by now very tired, mounts of the Magyars, who were well over 500 miles (800 km) from their Hungarian heartlands on the River Tisza.

Thereafter the Magyars ceased raiding and began to adapt to a European community,[276] while maintaining their own equestrian integrity. Later the Magyar nation became a bastion for Europe, herself suffering from successive oriental horse-borne invasions.

BYZANTIUM UNDER THREAT

After engineering the Magyars' expulsion, Symeon renewed Bulgarian attacks on Byzantium, invading Thrace and routing a Byzantine army in 896, after which peace was concluded in return for Byzantium paying Bulgaria annual tribute. War erupted again when the tribute was withheld in 913. The Bulgarian forces invested Constantinople, but the walls, as before, proved impregnable and negotiations followed, which were broken off in 914 when the Bulgars took Adrianople. In retaliation the Byzantines hired the Pechenegs to attack Bulgaria in Symeon's absence, but when Byzantium again tried to hire the Pechenegs to attack the Bulgars they refused and the Byzantine army was routed at Achelous in 917. In 924 a renewed assault was launched against Constantinople, but Symeon was again forced to negotiate.[277] His death in 927 brought relief from incessant Bulgar aggression until the reign of Nicephorus II Phocas (963–69) forty years later when hostilities were renewed. This time the Byzantines called on the Russians to attack the Bulgars who were severely beaten in 967, but then, as so often in the past, the hirelings turned on their paymasters. The Russian Prince Svyatoslav had his sights set on the riches of Little Preslav near the delta of the River Danube, which was an entrepôt for luxury goods, including horses, from Bohemia and Hungary. There was always a dearth of horses in Russia so any chance to acquire mounts must have been welcome and increased their mobility.

Thus threatened, Byzantium made temporary peace with the Bulgarians; the Pechenegs having attacked Kiev gave the empire a respite as Svyatoslav hastened to deal with the emergency only to return at the head of a huge army of Vikings, Slavs, Magyars and Pechenegs. Negotiations with the new emperor John I Tzimisces (969–76) got nowhere, the Russians attempting blackmail in return for peace. Breaking with previous policy Tzimisces went on the attack, rapidly deploying his mailed cavalry through the Balkan mountain passes before Svyatoslav could strengthen them. In the spring of 971 Preslav was stormed, the Bulgarian tsar captured, and the Byzantine cavalry put the Russian infantry to flight at Silistria on the Danube. Under Tzimisces' military leadership Byzantium recovered the territories the Bulgars had held for three centuries, but on his death in 976 the Bulgars revolted and a new round of wars raged across the Balkans. The Byzantines suffered several defeats, in one of which as they retreated from Serdica in 986 the whole of their cavalry was lost, together with the baggage train.[278]

In addition to the external wars the Emperor Basil II (976–1025) had to contend with several major armed rebellions within the empire, notably the two revolts of Sclerus and that of the imperial general Bardas Phocas. These were not finally resolved until 989–90. Thereafter Basil ruled his subjects harshly and the army was kept constantly ready. Care was taken over the smallest detail to ensure efficiency; personal bravado was discouraged; and impetuosity against orders was punished by dismissal from the ranks. Although there was grumbling[279] the well-equipped Byzantine army gradually ground the Bulgars down in a campaign that lasted five years, until the final battle on 29 July 1014 in Macedonia, in the Pass of Kleidion, where the Bulgarian power was broken for good. Great numbers of Bulgars were killed, and 14,000 prisoners were taken and blinded before being released, only one in every hundred being left with one eye so they could guide their compatriots back to the Bulgarian Tsar Samuel who had escaped from Kleidion. For this victory Basil was known to future generations as Basil Bulgaroctonos, 'Basil the Bulgar-Slayer'. By the end of his reign the entire Balkans had reverted to Byzantine control and the empire was again powerful.[280]

THE COMING OF THE SELJUKS

Fifty years later all was changed. Romanus Diogenes (1068–71) was emperor, a brave but rash man who spent nearly all his brief reign under arms. His generalship was poor, and he was badly served by his mercenaries and by treacherous compatriots.

The Seljuk Turks had first invaded the periphery of Byzantine territory in 1045, penetrating as far as Lake Van; thereafter they made repeated and deeper inroads into the empire. At first satisfied with plunder, by 1068 they had territorial ambitions.[281]

In 1068 and 1069 Romanus led unsuccessful campaigns against the Turks who inflicted heavy casualties on his army, their own losses being slight.[282] In 1071 the Turks invaded under Alp Arslan at the head of over 100,000 light horse archers. Manzikert and Akhlat on the eastern Byzantine borders had fallen to them and Romanus led his third campaign with 60,000 cavalry, mostly heavy horse with some light skirmishers, to recover them, retaking Manzikert and besieging Akhlat. Cavalry from the eastern themes was commanded by Alyattes, *strategos* of the Cappadocian theme and contingents from European themes were led by Nicephorus Bryennius. Mercenary cavalry, under Andronicus Ducas,[283] was composed of Germans, Normans and Slavs, plus Ghuzz, Cuman, Pechenegs and southern Russian Turkish tribesmen.[284]

On 19 August 1071 the Seljuks converged on Manzikert, sending out an advance detachment to reconnoitre Romanus' camp. From then on the Byzantines made a succession of errors. Basilacius, *strategos* of the Theodosiopolis theme, charged the detachment, which precipitately fled, drawing him and his men far out of contact with the main army and into an ambush where they were all either killed or captured. A support division arrived too late, found only corpses and had to fight its way back to the main army. Although Romanus then drew his army up in the accepted right, centre and left divisions with the rear line of mercenaries under Andronicus, he was unable to use the Byzantine concerted strength. The Turks skirmished from afar, refusing to close, and the Byzantine skirmishers, far fewer in number, suffered severe horse casualties. In the afternoon to force the issue Romanus ordered the whole army to advance, the divisions keeping their distance. The Turks retreated, staying out of range and suffering few casualties, until with dusk falling and concerned for his insufficiently guarded main camp Romanus ordered a general retreat. Inevitably the Turks harried the Byzantine rear so badly that Romanus ordered his troops to wheel about to fight them off. The right, centre and left turned to beat the Turks back, but Andronicus kept on retreating with such of the mercenaries[285] as were left; Turkish tribesmen had defected the previous night and the Franks refused to fight.[286] The Armenians in the army had also deserted.[287] With the rear guard gone Romanus' front line was exposed to Turks circling and attacking the flanks and rear; the right wing crumbled and fled, the left wing, separated from Romanus in the centre division, likewise gave way and was driven off the battlefield, and in the bitter fight that followed Romanus' horse was killed underneath him, he and many of his officers were captured, the rank and file slaughtered.[288]

Manzikert was a battle of heavy cavalry versus light horse. The Turkish mounts would have been mostly Turcoman strains with some other oriental hot-blooded animals. These breeds are light-framed and do not carry excessive flesh; the constant skirmishing would not have caused them the same fatigue as that suffered by the heavy armoured horses of Byzantine cataphracts.[289] The Byzantine heavy cavalry horses were not meant to make extended marches under full kit, as we have seen from the *Strategikon*. At Manzikert they were under arms from dawn to dusk and well into the night in the heat of August.

Manzikert was a savage blow to Byzantium. Thereafter the Seljuks expanded their territory in Asia Minor, and Byzantium was again left with a shrunken empire over parts of which Turks, Mamlūks, Mongols and crusaders marched in the wasteful years of successive jihads and crusading wars.

THREE

Western Europe in the Eighth and Ninth Centuries

In the early medieval period there was only the memory of the Roman *alae* that had drawn heavily on Lugdunensis, Belgica, Narbonnsensis, Tarraconsensis and Pannonia for a major portion of her cavalry. Western European warriors were now decidedly infantry. However, from the sixth century onwards Europe was to feel a relentless drive from a series of aggressors, all of whom relied on their mounted arm to carry their conquests into Europe.

We have seen how the East Roman cavalry took eighteen years to defeat the Goths in Italy. In the battle at Taginae a huge mounted contingent of Lombards aided the Byzantines.

In Spain, from pre-Roman times an equestrian nation, the Visigoths relied on the horse to maintain their military supremacy, until the Moors successfully invaded, and in the ensuing years implanted an advanced equestrian culture that had a significant effect on the studs of European feudal nobility.

The Avars took up residence in the Hungarian Älfold, and although their warlike tendencies were waning they still posed a threat to Charlemagne.

There is no doubt that this succession of horse-borne warriors resulted in a growing pressure for the Frankish people also to take to horseback and so fight on more equal terms.

THE LOMBARDS

The Lombards were a fierce tribe which had migrated through central Europe, as had other Germanic people. On first entering Pannonia in 165 they had been repulsed by the Romans, but had returned to the Hungarian Älfold.[1] In 547 Justinian shared out Dacia, Pannonia and Noricum among the equestrian tribes to maintain Byzantine security by land and cash inducements to potential enemies. The Gepids settled in Dacia in and around Singidumum (Belgrade), the Lombards in Noricum and Pannonia on the Ister (Danube). Not content with Dacia, the Gepids 'enslaved' the resident Romans; the Eruli plundered Illyria; the Lombards Illyria and Dalmatia.[2] When the Gepids impinged on Lombard territory Justinian, upholding the Lombard cause, sent them more than 10,000 horsemen under the Byzantine generals Bouzes, Aratius and John, nephew of Vitalian; John was ordered to enter Italy after dealing with the Gepids, having under his command 1,500 Eruli, the only ones who had not revolted from Byzantium; en route to join the Lombards he met and defeated the Gepids and the bulk of the Eruli. To avoid confrontation with such a large Byzantine force the Gepids settled peacefully with the Lombards, leaving the Byzantines in a quandary. They could neither fight, after their allies, the Lombards, had made peace with the Gepids, nor leave Illyria to the mercy of the combined Eruli and Gepid tribes.[3]

In the wars against the Goths, Lombards provided Germanus with 1,000 heavy cavalry in 550,[4] and later in 553 the brilliant Byzantine general Narses hired them to fight against Totila. Their King Audoin supplied 2,500 Lombard warriors, plus a further 3,000 fighting men as servants.[5] Other Lombards, not in Roman pay, had helped themselves to a great number of the imperial warhorses from a herd at Apri in Thrace.[6]

In the conflict against Totila Narses dismounted the Lombards, the Eruli and other barbarian mercenaries to ensure they stayed to fight,[7] and following a decisive victory had the Lombards escorted to the Roman boundaries after paying them off, as they had celebrated by a rampage of burning and raping.[8] The Lombards returned, breaking into Italy in 568, to stay for the next two centuries, bringing their quality mounts with them. In the Älfold they would have had access to horses, by then integrated with indigenous stock, introduced by the Sarmatians who had settled there. Sarmatians were among the most renowned equestrian warriors of the Roman era.[9] As shown in the Altaic Pazyryk burials their horses fell into two distinct categories: a large pony type and a taller, more refined animal. Both would have been capable of use in an armoured heavy cavalry division, the ponies due to the greater strength to size ratio of ponies in general, and the larger type because of its size and inherent toughness.[10] The Lombards acquired other mounts as spoils and by thieving, as Procopius noted. Italy already had the product of centuries of quality breeding with frequent recourse to foreign imports, as mounts of *alae*, from Libya, Numidia, Spain, Gaul, etc. As stockbreeders, they would have been sure to keep quality consistent. Indeed in the later Middle Ages the Lombard breed was much prized in foreign courts.

The Lombards' own law code shows how important the horse was to them. Paul the Deacon described a Lombard heavy cavalryman: each noble, astride his warhorse, armed with cuirass, greaves and helmet, and bearing heavy *contus* and *spatha*. The buying, selling, valuing and breeding of horses were strictly governed by law. A warhorse full accoutred was worth twice as much as a slave and two-thirds the value of a free Lombard of the lower social rank. The king bred a superior type of warhorse[12] (superior in this context meant substantial).

THE MOORS

The Moors in Spain who made frequent incursions into Frankish territory from the early eighth century onwards rode distinctive mounts. Contrary to popular opinion, few Moorish horses were Arabians; undoubtedly there were animals from two breeds well known to the Moors and the Spaniards, the Barb from North Africa, and the Andalusian and Lusitanian from the Iberian Peninsula, which stemmed from the same genetic strain; habitat and the specific lines used giving the slight differences. The Barb has much in common with the Andalusian but is of smaller proportions. Its background is controversial, but Spanish hippologists have argued that it received much of its genetic input from horses indigenous to Spain via prehistorical movements across the land-bridge that once joined Spain to Africa. The Sorrai, from the area watered by the River Sorrai in Portugal, had an early impact on the Barb and the Andalusian, being the prehistorical foundation stock from which both these breeds evolved.[13] At a later period the Barb and the Andalusian developed in their respective locales, the Barb entering Spain in the Berber invasion of 711, by which time it had become predominantly oriental in blood.

As the Berbers were under the dominance of the Damascus caliphate some Muslim warriors in the successive invasions of Spain were of Arab and Syrian nationality. Very early

An Andalusian horse. Campanero XIV – the British National Champion of the Andalusian Society, owned by Mrs Christine Neeson

in the conquest there had also been a very large contingent of Syrian horsemen who had entered, under their leader Balj, to aid the ruling Muslims against Andalusian Berbers who had revolted, angry at the Arabs getting better shares of spoils and better regions to settle in. Originally hired only to help put down the revolt, they stayed when the Muslim governor broke his contract. Eventually the Syrians were settled in the Guadalquivir valley and along the coast receiving *iqtas* (fiefs) in return for military duties.[14] This augmented the Arabian presence in Spain and indicates that breeds other than the Barb were included in the equine complement, although Barbs predominated.

The Moorish reconnaissance probe into Spain in 710 was instigated by the Arab Abu Abderahman Musa ibn Nosair who had subdued Tangier in 707. In July Musa's lieutenant, Tarif ibn Malik Abuzura, a Berber of the tribe of Naja, landed at Tarifa with 400 foot and 100 horse, pillaged the area, and returned to North Africa with a report guaranteed to excite his master. Less than a year later a force of 7,000 under Tarik ibn Ziyad, a Berber freedman of Musa's, landed in Spain. The contingent was mostly of Berber tribesmen, but the officers were Arabs, among them Abdel Melic, Alcama and Mugheith. To this force of 7,000 was added reinforcements of 5,000 Arabs and Berbers who defeated the Visigothic King Roderic in battle on the Rio Barbate in late July. Subsequently the Moors subdued several cities en route to Toledo and divided their forces into two columns, one to Malaga, the other to Cordova, which fell to an attack by 700 Moorish cavalry. Thereafter events moved rapidly and Musa himself landed at Algeciras in April 712 with a huge army of 18,000, of which

8,000 were cavalry. Prior to that date cavalry had been only a small part of the invading army, but thereafter there were constant reinforcements sent over and the course of Moorish occupation accelerated. Musa marched on Medina Sidonia, Carmona, Seville and Merida in 712, and the following year on Talavera and Toledo where he combined his forces with Tarik ibn Ziyad to continue to Saragossa. In 714 the Moorish forces split again, Tarik going to Leon and Astorga, and Musa towards Orviedo. In September that year Musa returned to Damascus to report to the caliph.[15]

As war was the main reason for breed movements and subsequent genetic crossing, this résumé of the rapid conquest of Spain shows there was an exceptionally heavy introduction of new equine blood into Spain. The three main elements introduced – Barb (see above), Turkmene and Arabian – were the warhorses of the era. The Turkmene was already widespread as a result of nomadic horsemen and the powers – Assyrian, Persian, Roman, Byzantine – who had successively used them as mercenaries. Syrian stock can largely be accounted for by their tradition of horse-breeding, the seasonal Arab tribal movements, and the Arab remount depots as discussed earlier.

Therefore in eighth-century Spain we find the indigenous breeds, already augmented from the Roman period, and the new waves of equines brought by the Moors. They in turn availed themselves of the wealth of Spanish horses. The contemporary Muslim chronicler Tarif ibn Taric said the Moors found the Spanish horses to be bigger than their own as well as more numerous, quickly requisitioned them and converted their own infantry to cavalry.[16]

Berber horses continued to be regularly imported into Spain, most notably by ibn al-Amir, the chamberlain to the Umayyad caliph, Hisham II (reigned 976–1002). Al-Amir became known to history as al-Mansur and in effect from 978 to 1002 he ruled in place of the weak caliph. In his long reign al-Mansur is said to have led fifty-seven victorious expeditions in Spain, and in his rise to power brought over to Spain his own Berber troops, and also employed Christian mercenaries.[17] Al-Mansur was also known to have organized stud farms in Spain located around the Cordova area, stocking them with Barbs from North Africa.[18]

Spain's wealth of superior equines made her the focal point for western Europe. Spanish horses became synonymous with equestrian excellence on the battlefield, in the tournament and in the noble and royal studs from Norman times onwards. More immediately, mounted Moorish divisions greatly impressed the Franks and urged them on to convert their army to a preponderance of effective cavalry.

THE CHANGE TO MOUNTED COMBAT AND THE NEED FOR A HEAVIER HORSE

From Carolingian times onward Europe's dependence on the warhorse increased. He became part of the fighting force, rather than mere transport. As his effectiveness was proved, his accoutrements and those of his rider affected social and economic life. Weaponry underwent changes. With the gradual spread of the stirrup, combined with the ever-deepening seat of the saddle, it was possible to use the lance more effectively as a shock weapon, incorporating the speed and weight of the horse to deliver more poundage to the thrust. The lance became heavier and was carried differently, couched under the armpit with more length before the rider's body than when held along the middle of the stock.[19] The type of horse changed, gradually becoming more substantial but not 'carty'. It was not only because the rider, and eventually the horse too, was wearing armour that conformation needed to become heavier; the impact of two heavy lances, one delivered by a knight on a horse travelling at, say, a moderate and controlled 20 miles (32 km) per hour, the other by his opponent travelling at a similar speed, created a powerful shock which a horse needed great strength to withstand.

The closest modern parallel, in which a horse receives a comparable jolt measured in poundage brought to an abrupt halt, is steer-roping. Outside rodeo competition and in a work context a steer may weigh 1,200 lb (545 kg). The art is in timing, accuracy, angle of roping, and using the roping horse's rapid stop and weight to bring the roped animal down, or to a standstill. [20] The analogy is in the impact of steer to roping horse, knight with lance to target. A modern roping horse weighs around 1,000–1,200 lb (455–545 kg) (some are heavier). A horse of less than 1,000 lb (455 kg) would not have the weight to do the job. Most stand around 15 hh high and are fast and well-bred.[21] With the earlier lighter lance or the heavier *contus*, used with the rider's weight to give maximum force, only a little of the horse's weight being employed, the rider thrust against the horned saddle on impact, and lighter horses were therefore suitable. I would suggest that a heavier horse was made imperative largely because of the shock poundage, not so much the weight he carried. A horse is able to carry a tremendous weight for a short period of time, and to deliver a rapid burst of speed under such weight. One result of breeding the heavier horse was to load him more heavily; the armour weight spiralled upwards till perfectly capable animals were overburdened by pushing the limits beyond common sense or good horsemanship, and even sturdier beasts were then needed: a vicious circle. Horses became unwieldy, as did their plate-encased riders.

According to archaeologists using bone deposits from Avar, Magyar and Germanic burials, it was among the Germanic and also some Avar peoples that selective breeding for heavier conformation began in the ninth and tenth centuries. Simultaneously horseshoes also began appearing in central Europe.[22] The shoeing lends force to the size augmentation. In a climate damper than that of their original steppelands horses' hooves would have become

A modern hunter: this type of horse, and not the carthorse, was the type used as a great horse in medieval times

softer; with an armoured man to carry, plus the requirements of use in war, the *combination* of damp, weight and pounding impact with the ground meant hooves had to be protected from splitting, cracking, laminae deterioration and sole bruising. The heavier body mass means that most hooves would have had a shallower and overall larger construction and the softer horn that goes with that. I have had experience of the adverse effect that climate and underfoot conditions cause. Two horses I owned in the USA and brought to Britain underwent significant hoof changes. One, a mare on which I had competed in 100-mile events without having her shod, and which had finished sound, needed constant shoeing in our damper climate. The other, a horse weighing 1,200 lb (545 kg) with weaker hoof laminae, needed constant shoeing in Britain.

THE FRANKS AND THEIR SUCCESSORS

It is inconceivable that the Franks did not learn a great deal from their mounted opponents whom they met repeatedly throughout the Merovingian and early Carolingian periods.

At the battle of Poitiers in 732 Charles Martel's foot put the invading Moorish horse to flight by maintaining a solid mass of infantry against which lightly armed Moors using traditional sting and retreat methods could do little.[23] That Martel forbade his troops to chase after the Moors showed common sense. The relatively few horses of the wealthier leaders were unsuited to the thorough harrying which can deter an enemy from regrouping and this must have accentuated the need for a higher concentration of mounted troops.

In 755 under Pepin I the traditional muster of troops was changed from March to May,[24] indicating that the army was now largely mounted. March grass, even if available, has little food-value. May and June are when grazing is thickest and most nutritious.[25] Three years later, after Pepin defeated the Saxons, he set their tribute at 300 horses per year.[26] By the end of the eighth century the Frankish army was composed mainly of cavalry, and successive monarchs were determined to ensure a steady flow of horses and men by enacting laws compelling all free men to undertake military service.[27] Other laws governed the use and production of horses.

Carolingian mounted soldiers depicted in the ninth-century Golden Psalter from St Gall

Liability for cavalry service depended on land tenure. It varied at different times and in different parts of the Carolingian Empire according to local custom, conditions and reiteration of laws with minor changes. Basically a man served if he had 4 *manses* of land. Each *manse* was between 25 and 37 acres (10 and 15 hectares) of land, it being considered that a man who had less than that could not afford to serve. In 808 Charlemagne altered this so that a man who held 3 *manses* was aided by a man who held 1, those who held 2 *manses* each must send one cavalryman, and a man who held 1 *manse* had the help of three others.[28] However, the cost of equipping a cavalryman with horse, armour and weapons, baggage horses, horse for squire and fodder for men and beasts for three months, meant that only those who had a minimum of 12 *manses* could afford the full outfit.[29]

Accounts of mounted conflicts appear frequently in the *Royal Frankish Annals*, but it is left to writers of the later *gestes* to describe the animal used, his breed, conformation and capabilities. These writers reflect the equestrian conditions of their own times, but, as noted above, breed changes usually occur extremely slowly and some of the references in Turoldus' *Roland* and in Wolfram von Eschenbach's *Parsival* and *Willehalm* are what one would expect for equine breeding for the area, in the case of the first and third of these tales, which show conflicts against the Moors.[30] I shall return to these *gestes* in due course.

We are luckier in having Notker's description of Frankish armour. At the meeting between Charlemagne and Desiderius, king of the Lombards. Charlemagne wore an iron helmet, iron gloves, iron cuirass, thigh guards and greaves, and was armed with spear, sword and shield – all iron. His close companions on each flank, in the van, and his rearguard were similarly equipped, lacking only thigh guards. There is a great play on words describing Charlemagne's spirited, dark grey horse, which 'gleamed iron-coloured and its very mettle was as if of iron'.[31]

In only one other passage do we get even a glimpse of another horse's physical description. Eishere, who was excessively tall, could not persuade his *great* horse to cross a river with him on its back, but was strong enough to pull it after him by the reins.[32] The use of the term *great* implies the horse was of superior size, and it is also probably the first time this particular expression is used in connection with a warhorse.

Notker is the only one to mention a specific breed of horse. Charlemagne received costly gifts from the Persian king, returning the compliment with a gift of Spanish horses and mules, a variety of Frisian cloaks, and some hunting dogs. Although Spanish horses were highly esteemed in Europe it was apparent that Harun al-Raschid thought little of them, showing interest only in the hounds.[33] This is hardly surprising as he had access to the finest oriental horses plus descendants of the highly prized Nesaean horses.

In virtually every year of his reign Charlemagne was at war expanding his domains. In Lombardy he was active from October 733 to June 734 when Pavia, the Lombard capital, fell, and again in suppressing a revolt in 775–6. Two years later he was in Spain but failed to take Saragossa.[34] The Saxon wars occupied him intermittently from 772 to 804, and the Avars strongly from 788 to 796; there were also other contacts and engagements. Even after their final subjugation Charlemagne continued to post troops in Pannonia to ensure no uprisings.[35]

Einhard gives us a very brief résumé of these wars but with scant detail as his concern was to show Charlemagne the man, not to give a military historian's account.[36] Almost the only pertinent detail of the Lombard campaign is that Charlemagne found crossing the Alps difficult owing to the lack of paths and the dangerous going, and a note on the siege of Pavia, and its victorious outcome, whereby Lombardy was added to Charlemagne's kingdom.[37] On the Saxons he expands enough to note Charlemagne's speed, thereby indicating the stress his cavalry mounts were subjected to. The only two Saxon engagements

*Archbishop Turpin and the Emperor Charlemagne (left) in a manuscript of Girard de Rousillon,
c. 1200 (British Library, Lansdowne MS 782, f. 27). Note that the horse equipment is of the thirteenth
century, not the eighth or ninth*

personally fought by Charlemagne were in 783 when the battles at Detmold and the River
Haase were fought, with only a few days between them.[38] Eventually border garrisons were
set up along the Saxon march,[39] freeing Charlemagne to take the war to Spain at the head of
a large force. He was returning through the Pyrenees, having failed to achieve the reduction
of Saragossa, when a Basque ambush annihilated the rear guard on 15 August 778. This is
the episode recounted in the *Song of Roland*, although for Basques we read Moors.[40] By this
time the Avars had already aided the Bavarians against Charlemagne.[41] The Avar wars were
waged far more aggressively than their Saxon, Bavarian, Spanish and Lombardic
counterparts.[42] To wind up his military reporting Einhard mentions the wars with the
Danes.[43] He records that Charlemagne 'spent much of his time on horseback and out
hunting, which came naturally to him'.[44] His death was either caused, or contributed to, by
his horse's sudden fall which pitched the emperor to the ground.[45]

As well as hunting, Charlemagne's court practised war games, showing that for the
nobility it was very much an equestrian life. The precursor to the later tournaments was held
at Worms in February 842 on the occasion of the Frankish king and the emperor meeting to
confirm a treaty. The games took the form of simulated charges, retreats and counter-
charges, lances swinging in so disciplined a way that no one got hurt.[46] Note that there is no
hint of the couched lance, although the stirrup would by then have been known, even if not
universally adopted. Quite clearly the '*en bloc*' charge had already become part of equestrian
military skills among the Franks.

In 782 Charlemagne led a campaign across the Rhine as soon as sufficient grazing was
available,[47] followed by an assembly at Lippspringe attended by most of the Saxons, and the

Norse and Avar emissaries. As soon as the assembly was finished, Charlemagne returned home and faced a Saxon rebellion. In the Süntal Mountains a fierce battle took place, the Franks ill-advisedly attacking the Saxons without waiting for the reinforcements under Count Theodoric. Clearly described, the engagement lacked all discipline, each Frank riding for himself 'as if he were chasing runaways and going after booty instead of facing an enemy lined up for battle, everybody dashed as fast as his horse would carry him'.[48] This foreshadowed many future episodes when Frankish (European) knights lacked discipline, fighting as individuals or small groups around their respective lord, rather than as ordered units. The Saxons cut them to pieces, only to be faced by a rapidly returning Charlemagne who had quickly gathered all the Franks he could and advanced to where the Aller flows into the Weser at Verden. There the combined Saxon host submitted to his authority turning over 4,500 rebels for execution.[49]

    This is one of the earliest passages where horses are specifically referred to in the *Royal Frankish Annals*, and their use in significant numbers is implied. In that year on three separate occasions a mounted force was raised: for the initial campaign; for the ill-fated defeat; and for the rapid raising of a retaliatory force. The fact that 4,500 Saxon rebels were turned over implies that Charlemagne's retaliatory force was of considerable size; clearly it impressed the Saxons sufficiently to bring them to terms without a fight. Even if the figure of 4,500 was grossly exaggerated, a large number were surrendered. As Charlemagne 'rushed to the place with all the Franks he could gather on short notice', his kingdom must have been well supplied with horses.

RUNNING A CAROLINGIAN STUD

The 'De Villis' capitulary, written at the end of the eighth century, has several regulations concerning stud management on the royal estates. There would have been similar set-ups on the estates of magnates, and small establishments with brood mares kept by all who owed mounted military service. Today 1 acre (0.4 hectare) per animal is needed on well-managed, fertile land to produce grass and hay for maintenance. Additional land is needed for cereals. As crop yields were lower in medieval times, stocking and amounts harvested would have considerably altered these requirements, so it can be seen that agriculture has a direct bearing on the ability of a landowner to produce not only the wealth to buy his helmet and mail coat, but also the means to breed and raise the horse to carry him to war, or alternatively turn his crops to cash to buy his charger.

    That horses filled an important role on royal demesnes is shown by the status of stablemen who were among the key officials working on these estates. They were given holdings of their own in return for which they owed their official services, plus a rent of pigs.[50] The stewards were in general charge of equine management. They decided on stable size, the number of horses occupying them, and how many grooms to allocate to their care.[51] This, combined with the order that stallions (in the plural) should not stay too long in the same pasture,[52] gives us more insight into stud operations, which were also in the stewards' province. Presumably they deputed underlings to do the actual work. Taken together these two orders show that although some horses would be stable-kept it was not the general practice to stable all stallions, or to segregate them from other stallions, as in later medieval times, except when each went to his respective mare band.[53] It also suggests stallions were rotated, not always staying with the same mare band in successive seasons. The stewards and their staffs had to have a good knowledge of breeding stock and its ailments, reporting to the king on any stallions who were unhealthy, too old, or likely to die prior to the breeding season, so they could be culled.[54] Pasture maintenance involved regular rotation to avoid paddocks becoming spoilt,[55] which means overloaded with parasites; overgrazed, with root damage; or exceedingly weedy due to quantities of dung souring the land.

Mare care was in the stewards' list of duties, and so was separating the colts,[56] presumably before they became a nuisance covering mares they should not, or fillies too young to carry a foal, and to allow the dam to recover condition in time for the next year's foal. If more fillies were dropped than needed for herd size maintenance new bands were to be formed,[57] and all foals were to be sent to the winter palace at the feast of St Martin.[58] As this feast day falls on 11 November, foals were apparently raised on much the same pattern as in modern times, being weaned at approximately six months of age. This indicates a yearly covering was likely for brood mares, thus increasing production levels.

Although the order regarding the foals to be sent to the winter palace does not specify colt foals, this is implied as all fillies were retained for future breeding stock. It also highlights the use of entires for military use. Increased production must have been a key factor in an era switching to mainly cavalry. Mare fertility is not that high, with an average success rate of about 60 to 70 per cent, though pasture-breeding increases the rate.[59] That pasture-breeding was used is shown by a comment about 'the season for sending them [the stallions] in among the mares'.[60]

Excess, unsaleable horses, presumably worn out and/or old animals were eaten as long as they were healthy and free of mange.[61]

These regulations governed military horses as no useful purpose was served by sending the colt foals on to the king if they were to be used for baggage beasts. Doubtless some later proved more suited to this task if found wanting as warhorses. The burden of providing baggage horses for royal emissaries and their retainers fell, in addition to the all-embracing 'other necessities', on the counts and other higher-ranking officials.

Stewards on royal estates also saw to other war provisions. A very long capitulary concerning income from a multitude of estate sources shows that all surplus goods were to be sold off for profit, including some that had a distinctly military application. These included production from shieldmakers, saddlers, smiths, forges, etc. Income from colts and fillies suggests the royal studs were in business as well as supplying military and hunting needs.[63] Smiths are noted under the same heading, and blacksmiths under heading 45. This could imply horseshoers, especially the latter though the correct term is farrier. Shoeing horses *en masse* was not yet customary, although the craft was well known. A law in the *Capitulare Aquisgranense* of 805 forbade selling arms outside the kingdom.[64] Stewards oversaw the construction of war carts and ensured they were sound, watertight, and provided with armaments of shield, lance, quiver and bow.[65]

Although 'De Villis' covers a host of agricultural aspects, nowhere is there a mention of horses being bred specifically for haulage purposes. At this period most traction was via oxen. Where speed was essential the use of pack horses was likely, and also more economical.

Other windows on stud management in the 'De Villis' are that a premium was put on healthy animals,[66] cleanliness,[67] keeping fences in good order, and emparking certain areas for animal containment.[68] Meadows and other land were to be kept in good order and a watch set on them at the appropriate time.[69] That this referred to livestock, particularly the horses which were not kept close to the farm during the covering season, is obvious from a later heading where it is ordered that wolves are to be caught, poisoned, or trapped with hooks, pits, or dogs.[70]

There must have been a considerable loss due to natural causes before horses reached maturity, not only from wolves savaging foals, but from injury and disease. The average life-span of a horse would have been much shorter than today when animals have the benefit of modern veterinary science and drugs.

Understanding the methods of Carolingian stud management makes it easier to understand the mechanics and difficulties behind recruiting the equine half of the cavalry.

STATISTICS AND MECHANICS

It has been estimated that between 800 and 840 the empire could produce approximately 35,000 cavalry using an average of twenty mounted men for every one of Charlemagne's direct vassals, of whom there were 1,800.[71] A sizeable remount pool would have been necessary or men-at-arms could find themselves involuntarily dismounted. In battle conditions horses get injured or killed, are seized as booty by enemies, or suffer sickness. To the horses present at the front must be added the reserves left at home, breeding stock, and youngstock. Therefore the number of 35,000 would need to be multiplied by at least eight for a rough idea of the actual and prospective warhorses kept within the empire, including the distaff side of the production line. To this number would have been added the numerous baggage animals, hunting and general riding horses, etc. It is worth noting that today there are an estimated two million horses in Great Britain, and except for certain racing centres – Newmarket, Lambourne, etc. – and moors where indigenous pony herds run, the horse population is very thin. In the Frankish kingdom the ratio of horse numbers to human head count would have been very high. This was of great significance in a farming culture whose land measurement was translated into cavalry service owed. It shows how well equipped the Franks were at that early date with saddle and pack horses. Populations were only a fraction of today's level, and the cost of raising a horse relatively much higher in terms of fodder and grain eaten to land productivity per acre, and manlabour hours to produce it.

It has been estimated that horses used in warfare in early medieval Europe would eat 22 lb (10 kg) of food a day, half grain and half long feed (hay/grass).[72] This gives us some idea of requirements although the figure is much too high. Animals were smaller, they needed less feed for basic maintenance, and in warfare a modicum would be carried in the war carts, rather than the maximum it was possible for a horse to eat. Nor does the figure take account of the available grazing utilized in the spring, summer and autumn months, hay only being used, and that largely appropriated *en route*, in winter. Horses lived off the land, as is shown by the summons to Abbot Fulrad (see below). A ration of 11 lb (5 kg) of grain is more suited to the later medieval great horse, although they too seem to have been grossly overfed, well over the amount we consider necessary or even safe.[73]

The *Royal Frankish Annals* set out the campaigns into Saxony during 793.[74] Charlemagne had celebrated Easter at Thionville on the Moselle about 20 miles (32 km) south of Trier, and then set out on a Saxon campaign. With place- and/or river-names given for each engagement, a rough idea of the mileage covered in the fighting months can be gained:

Thionville to Detmold	250 miles	(400 km)
Detmold to Paderborn (where the army assembled)	15 miles	(24 km)
Paderborn to the battlefield of River Haase	30+ miles	(48+ km)
River Haase to River Weser	30 miles	(48 km)
Weser to Elbe	120 miles	(190 km)
Total	445 miles	(710 km)

From the River Elbe he returned to 'Francia' and that year celebrated Christmas at Herstal which is on the River Meuse a few miles south-west of Aachen. The approximate figure of 750 miles (1,200 km) for the round trip could be roughly doubled to allow for valley and riverine meandering travel and the skirting of mountain ranges which intervened – the Vosges, Ardennes and Süntal.

The capitularies of Charlemagne give us what was expected of a nobleman or high-ranking ecclesiastic when summoned to war. In 806 Fulrad, Abbot of Altaich was summoned:

You shall come to Stasfurt on the Boda by 20 May with your 'men' prepared to go on warlike service to any part of our realm that we may point out; that is, you shall come with arms and gear and all warlike equipment of clothing and victuals. Every horseman shall have shield, lance, sword, dagger, a bow and a quiver. On your carts you shall have ready spades, axes, picks and iron-pointed stakes, and all other things needed for the host; the rations shall be for three months, the clothing must be able to hold out for six. On your way you shall do no damage to our subjects, and touch nothing but water, wood, and grass. Your men shall march along with the carts and the horses, and not leave them till you reach the muster-place, so that they may not scatter to do mischief . . .[75]

Charlemagne maintained supply depots during his Saxon wars in fortified garrisons at Herstelle, Eresburg, Buraburg, Fritzlar and Paderborn.[76] These are sited on rivers: the Lippe for Paderborn, the Weser for Herstelle, the Diemal for Eresburg, and the Eder for Buraburg and Fritzlar. Mileage between depots was approximately one day's reasonable ride, or two days if taking it easy or being slowed by Saxon harassment.

The Saxons proved obdurate, frequently rebelling until an intermission of peace in 785 enabled Charlemagne to journey to Italy in the following year to add the rest of that kingdom to his Lombardic possessions. This time he undertook a winter campaign.[77] Negotiations were conducted between Duke Tassilo of Bavaria, Charlemagne's renegade vassal, with the Pope acting as intermediary, but to no good purpose. Further campaigns were undertaken on three fronts, the Franks marching into Bavaria, East Franks, Thuringians and Saxons assembling on the Danube at Pförring, and an army from Italy surrounding Tassilo, who capitulated and swore homage.[78] The following year he reneged on his oath and allied with the Avars who attacked the borders of Friuli and Bavaria; repulsed with great losses, they returned to attack Bavaria again, and were again defeated. Thereafter the Bavarian boundaries were fortified against the Avars.[79] Thenceforward there were almost yearly engagements against the Avars, and in 791 Charlemagne took the war into Pannonia with an army of Franks, Frisians and Saxons. The Frisians had been known from Roman days as producers of some of the best warhorses.[80] The *Royal Frankish Annals* comment: 'This campaign was accomplished without any misfortune, except that in the army under the king's command such a pestilence broke out among the horses that of so many thousands of them hardly the tenth part is said to have survived.'[81] For an army strong in cavalry this must have been the understatement of the era, but what else would one expect from a cleric? For a later campaign into Pannonia against the Avars conducted in 796 Charlemagne is estimated to have raised between 15,000 and 20,000 horse.[82] From this we can get some idea of the numbers involved in his major offensives against these Avars. The epidemic is not named but to wipe out thousands of horses, even if the statement is too sweeping, meant a tremendous economic and military drawback. The most likely disease, which acts rapidly once its incubation period is over, is a streptococcus infection; without modern drugs it is deadly, is also extremely infectious, and travels through livestock when kept in herds, as in cavalry regiments.[83]

After the massive campaign of 796, led by Pepin, Charles' son, the Avars submitted to Charlemagne and were baptized. Thereafter they make rare appearances in the *Royal Frankish Annals*: in 805 they asked for new lands in Hungary between Szombathely and Petronell because the Slavs had driven them from their previous homeland; in 811 troops were despatched to Pannonia to settle disputes between Avars and Slavs, and an Avar prince was then ordered to report to the emperor.[84] The Avar strength had been broken and they had merged with the local population; their legacy was the horse and their equestrian culture, the remnants of which were to blend with that of the Magyars.

CHARLEMAGNE'S HEIRS

Although the external borders of the Frankish Empire stayed intact during the reign of
Charlemagne's son, Louis the Pious (814–40),[85] internally it was anything but peaceful. In
817 Louis divided his empire among his sons, giving Pepin Aquitaine and Louis Bavaria,
sharing his title of emperor with his son Lothair, and allotting to his youngest son, Charles,
born in 823, Alamannia by formal decree in 829.[87] This division engendered repeated armed
conflicts between Louis and his sons, and between the brothers themselves.

From the Loire and the Seine in the western part of the empire to the Rhine and the Saale
in the eastern zone engagements were fought between the factions in a period of unrest that
spanned the whole of his reign and left his eventual heir, Charles the Bald (843–77), a legacy
of internal unrest and dissent along with a disintegrating empire. Only the fact that the
armies were mostly mounted made it possible to keep up the scale of continual travel. The
period stretched the resources of the stud farms to the limit. The year 840 was filled with
activity, mostly by Lothair, eldest son of Louis the Pious, who, while professing friendship
for Charles, continually sought to subvert his subjects, at the same time waging war on
another of his brothers, Louis.[88] Meanwhile Charles dealt with his brother Pepin in
Aquitaine,[89] and in 841 at the head of a strong mounted force attempted to cross the Seine,
embarking his men, but being prevented from pursuing Lothair's adherents on the opposite
side as transporting the horses caused delays. Once across, horses were pushed to their limits
in an effort to reach the enemy, moving steadily night and day *en route* to Saint-Denis, Saint-
Germain and Sens, and travelling through the Forest of Othe, between Sens and Troyes,
before being forced to draw rein as horses and men were exhausted.[90] Lothair, meanwhile,
gathered an army and crossed the Rhine to confront and destroy Louis, who was forced to
return to Bavaria as his forces were disintegrating, some fleeing from Lothair, some
defecting to him.[91] Lothair next sent scouts out to locate Charles and demand a meeting at
Attigny.[92] Lothair's intrigues drove Louis and Charles into mutual assistance and together
they tried appeasing Lothair, who rejected their overtures,[93] in favour of a decisive battle. On
25 June 841 Louis and Charles met Lothair and Pepin in a bloody conflict at Fontenoy.
Louis' army was hampered by a severe lack of horses, but triumphed over Lothair who fled;
the troops facing Charles also fled, but in another quarter both sides fought bitterly, though
in the end Lothair's men also fled, thus giving the victory to Charles.[94] Even so Lothair
continued intriguing, but the empire faced a new and more devastating threat.

The Norsemen had been making probes into the mouths of the Rhine, Meuse, Scheldt,
Seine and Loire since 834.[95] In 840 they entered Aix,[96] and in 842 ravaged Quentovic
(Etaples, near Calais).[97] Thereafter they became a recurrent menace to the empire. In 845
they entered Paris, but were bought off by Charles. They returned in 852 and again in 856
when they ravaged the countryside between the Seine and the Loire on foot and on
horseback.[98] Towards 860 it became normal for the Norsemen to utilize horses continuously
for their invasions, appropriating them as means of rapid transport for their inland forays and
then fighting on horseback.[99]

By the early tenth century they had settled in the Caux region and the counties of Rouen,
Evreux and Lisieux.[100] Charles the Simple had ceded these territories to them in 911 in return
for peace.[101]

The era of the Normans had arrived and with it a marked emphasis on the warhorse,
whose exploits in war and the tournament are extolled.

FOUR

The Anglo-Saxon Period

Britain in the first millennium AD was far from being stocked only with the multitude of undersized ponies we have been led to think drew the Britons' chariots during Caesar's campaigns. Caesar does not refer specifically to ponies, but to chariotry and cavalry and their expertise.[1] Dio Cassius also says the Britons had chariotry and cavalry, which implies the latter had larger animals than those used to draw chariots.[2]

BRITISH STOCK AND ROMAN OCCUPATION

During the Roman occupation British stock received new equine bloodlines via the *alae* raised from countries known to have well-established equestrian cultures and to be possessed of superior horseflesh.[3]

The most important equines to land with the Roman *alae* came from Spain, Frisia, Thrace and Pannonia, as mounts for units originally raised in these Roman provinces. Over a lengthy period, recruiting into the *alae* became diversified so that not all members of an *ala* would have been from the country where it was originally raised.[4] An example is shown by one of the many Roman cavalry tombstones found in Britain, that of Sextus Valerius Genialis at Cirencester. Valerius was a Frisian tribesman enrolled as a trooper in *Ala* I Thracum. In AD 175 a huge Sarmatian contingent of 5,500 was sent to Britain to prevent recurrent rebellion after the Britons had surrendered to Marcus Aurelius. Initially Sarmatian tribal herds came from the steppe north of the Caucasus. They had settled in the Pannonian plains by AD 20, where their own horses interbred with indigenous Hungarian stock.[5] The best warhorses were considered to be the Frisian, Burgundian and Thuringian,[6] from areas under Roman rule. One thing prized in a Roman charger was size.[7] Roman imports would have improved British stock, adding height and bulk, and imparting hybrid vigour.

In the north Housesteads was base to the Cuneus Frisiorum;[8] Abballava (Burgh by Sands) also had a Cuneus Frisiorum.[9] Haltonchesters had the *Ala* I Pannoniorum Sabiniana;[10] Netherby the Coh. I. Aelia Hispanorum Milliaria Equitata;[11] Benwell the *Ala* I Asturum; Chester the *Ala* II Asturum; Ribchester the Cuneus Sarmatarum Bremetenraco.[12] There were many other *alae* and *cohortes equitatae* stationed throughout Britain in the north, but I have singled out the ones whose animals were considered superior in Roman times, as were their riders. These animals would have had a marked effect on future generations of horse-breeding. It is significant that the Fell and Dale, in particular, resembles today's modern Frisian, a breed valued in antiquity and highly sought after in medieval times. Horse bones from various Roman sites in Britain belonged to horses between 14 and 15 hh; Newstead in Scotland produced the remains of a 15 hh horse;[13] Colchester also a 15 hh horse;[14] Corbridge a 14.2 hh and a larger animal between 14.2 and 15 hh.[15] These indicate that the larger horse was by no means rare.

The reverse of the eighth-century Aberlemno churchyard cross, believed to depict the battle of Nechtansmere in 685 between the Picts and the Anglian warriors of Northumbria (wearing helmets). It shows fine equestrian detail

qui dictu eo quod qn qdregi iungebant equaba
tur paresq: forma & similes cursu copulabant.
Caballus a pede cauo dictus. propter quod gradi

The stallions of Powys. three medieval stallions, from a thirteenth-century bestiary (British Library, Harleian MS 4751, f. 27)

In Wales Brecon Gaer was the base for the Ala Hispanorum Vettonum in the second century AD.[16] Later, Wales, and in particular Powys, was famous for its studs of horses crossed with Spanish stallions imported by Robert de Belêsme [Bellême]. Giraldus Cambrensis tells us that this Spanish strain was highly prized and extremely handsome, and that 'nature reproduces in them the same majestic proportions and incomparable speed'.[17] The hybrid vigour had been retained from the late eleventh century, when the studs were inaugurated, to Giraldus' time nearly a century later. His phraseology implies a large but elegant horse. The comment about nature reproducing the same size and speed also tells us that the Spanish stallions were extremely prepotent, the offspring closely resembling the sire in all respects.

ANGLO-SAXON DEVELOPMENTS

As the Anglo-Saxon period opened, without the extensive resources that an occupying army could command (and commandeer), some degeneration set in. However, it was not all a downward slide. Equines were still needed. Britain has a wealth of strong, hardy native ponies, some of which are only around the 12 to 13 hh mark. The larger ponies were quite suitable as mounts to get the infantry rapidly from one place to another. The larger native breeds reach 14.2 hh.[18]

References to horses and riding run throughout the Anglo-Saxon Chronicle, and the Welsh laws of Hywel Dda (died 950) reflect the importance of the horse in Welsh society, a thread unbroken right up to the Norman importation of those prized Spanish stallions. The highly observant Giraldus (*c.* 1146–1223) comments that the Welsh people's interest in life 'consists of caring for their horses and keeping their weapons in good order'[19] and that their leaders ride into battle on swift mettlesome horses; most of the common people prefer to fight on foot; the horsemen will often dismount, as circumstance and occasion demand, ready to flee or attack,[20] and have gradually learned from the English and Normans how to manage their weapons and horses in battle.[21] Later we shall see that this use of the horse by the leaders was current in Hywel's day.

Although there is no full description of breeds or conformation, a hint of types can be garnered from scattered references in chronicles and legal codes of the Anglo-Saxons.

The Venerable Bede (died 735) comments on quality in an anecdote about Bishop Aidan giving a well-bred horse, a gift from King Oswine, to a beggar. Annoyed, the king exclaimed that a common horse, of which there were plenty, was more suitable for a beggar.[22] Bede also remarks on the love of racing among young clerics. Herebald, one of their number who rode

A mounted Anglo-Saxon warrior riding down the enemy. (From a fragment of a seventh-century helmet found at Sutton Hoo)

a 'splendid horse', begged and received permission for the group to test their horses' speed.[23]

There is scant early note of policies aimed at producing quality stock but this brief comment of Bede's implies such a policy was followed. This is strengthened by the laws of King Ine (688–726) which inform us that the *horse-wealh* stood in high regard and had charge of the king's stud. There was also the position of *horse-weard*, watcher of the king's horses. He appears in both Ine's laws and in Aethelberht's (860–6).[24] These references suggest that a self-contained stud was kept, under the *horse-wealh*, where controlled breeding was practised, and an open-range system, stallions running with selected bands of mares, under the *horse-weard* who was responsible for their protection, preventing straying, abstraction of mares by other stallions, and general care of the free-ranging stock. Studs were also maintained by wealthier magnates. Of the size of studs we have some indication from the Welsh laws, Anglo-Saxon wills, and a brief reference from the time of Athelstan (924–39). He had received a gift from Hugh, son of Robert of France, of 300 fine coursers and their trappings, besides other valuables.[25] Although not specifically referring to studs, this shows the king's wealth in horses, and that upgrading with new blood and breeds occurred much earlier than we had been led to believe; previously, it had been assumed to be a result of the Norman Conquest. This interchange is also shown in the Anglo-Saxon Chronicle when marauding Danes brought in French horses in 892. There must also have been unrecorded instances of interchange of horses between countries.

BEOWULF

Horses appear in the great Anglo-Saxon poem *Beowulf*. Written between 680 and 800, it recounts the hero's exploits as he aids the Danish king Hrothgar against the Swedes. Racing is to the fore as Danish warriors in holiday mood spur their bay horses, which are renowned for speed and stamina sustained in repeated friendly challenges.[26] Later, on a formal note, the warriors assemble in the king's great hall to watch as

> The guardian of thanes ordered
> that eight horses with gold-plated bridles
> be led into the courtyard; on to one was strapped
> a saddle, inlaid with jewels, skilfully made.
> That was the war seat of the great king,
> Healfdene's son, whenever he wanted to join in the swordplay.
> That famous man
> never lacked bravery at the front in battle,
> when men about him were cut down like corn.
> Then the King of the Danes, Ing's descendants,
> presented the horses and weapons to Beowulf,
> bade him use them well and enjoy them.
> Thus the renowned prince, the retainers' gold-warden,
> rewarded those fierce sallies in full measure,
> with horses and treasure . . .[27]

Hrothgar's horse was a stallion,[28] and down at the shore Beowulf's waiting ship was loaded with the armour and gifts of horses.[29] Not to be outdone in generosity Beowulf also matched Hrothgar's gift of warhorses by a gift of four matched bays to the king, and three graceful horses with brightly coloured saddles to the Lady Hyged.[30] These highlights hint at several customs:

Reconstruction (by Mary Storm) of tapestry fragments found in a Viking ship burial at Oseberg indicating the use of horses, both ridden and draught, in a military context

1. that warriors rode swift quality animals capable of sustained effort, totally unlike the later lumbering destriers whose energy had to be conserved for a short charge;
2. that fighting from horseback was by no means unknown among the Anglo-Saxons, even if restricted to the wealthy;
3. that import, export and consequently shipping for horses was conducted; ships needed to be either built or specially adapted for horse transport;
4. that horses were the currency of royal gifts;
5. that although the repetition of the colour bay and the attribute of speed need not be taken literally, a certain stamp of horse, commonly bay in colour, was known to the writer.

THE ANGLO-SAXON CHRONICLE

The Anglo-Saxon Chronicle frequently refers to horses used in a military context, by the Anglo-Saxons and by incursive Danes.

It used to be generally accepted that all Anglo-Saxon armies were infantry, using horses only for transport to battle. I have always found that a hard notion to swallow in its entirety because it seemed a complete waste of potential energy – and resources. I am not suggesting that whole armies were mounted on trained warhorses, but that common sense prevailed and the wealthier earldormen and thanes were capable of mounted fighting and would, as circumstances dictated, utilize the horse in offensive tactics. It is a very short step from harrying to fighting on horseback, especially when the harried on occasion turned to defend themselves. Nowhere in the Anglo-Saxon Chronicle does it specifically say fighting was never conducted from horseback, or that the 'army' or the 'force', i.e. the Anglo-Saxons and Danes respectively, always dismounted before an engagement.

In 1952 an extremely enlightening article, full of downright common sense, was written by Richard Glover. He showed by forceful arguments that the Anglo-Saxon army was capable of and did fight from horseback prior to the Conquest.[31] He argues cogently, and on the equestrian level has understood the capabilities of horses undertaking extensive, rapid travel.

The Danish incursions started in 789. Three Danish longships landed in Britain and the reeve rode out to intercept the warriors, capture them and bring them into custody, but he was killed: thus runs the first brief entry concerning what was evidently an initial probe by the Vikings to reconnoitre likely opposition. Four years later in 793 Lindisfarne was sacked, followed by an attack on Jarrow in 794. The Chronicle is silent on the incursions till 835 when Sheppey was ravaged. Thereafter, until 853, the coastal areas of the south and south-west were under almost constant threat, and in 855 'heathen men' overwintered in Sheppey, the first mention of a semi-permanent 'force'; a presence that was to be repeated in 865 on the Isle of Thanet.

In 866 the 'force' came to stay, putting down permanent roots in East Anglia. From there they conducted forays and major expeditions inland, terrorizing the natives and putting the country on a permanent war footing for the next half-century before a respite was possible for war-weary England, although the country was to suffer repeatedly from Scandinavian incursions until England and Denmark were temporarily united under Cnut (reigned in England 1016–35, in Denmark 1018–35). During that busy half-century the Chronicle gives us almost a year-by-year itinerary for the Danish forces. In 866, appropriating mounts from the East Anglian region, they were capable of moving rapidly throughout the island as their itinerary shows.

For the next twenty years the peripatetic 'force' rode throughout East Anglia, Mercia, Wessex and Northumbria, overwintering at Nottingham (868), York (869), Thetford (870) and Reading (871).[32]

As early as 870 we hear of an engagement between Danes and English under Algar in which, according to Ingulph's Chronicle of the Abbey of Croyland, the Danes charged on horseback.[33] In 871 King Aethelred and his brother Alfred spearheaded nine major battles south of the Thames. In addition there were numerous unrecorded minor engagements to which Alfred and his retinue rode – the first specific mention of the English army using horses at least as transport between battle sites, although it is to be expected that this means of locomotion was normal long before actually noted.[34]

Other Danish winter quarters were Torksey, Repton, Tyne, Cambridge and Wareham; from the latter at the turn of the year 876/7 the Danes slipped away to Exeter, their mounts staying just ahead of Alfred's pursuit enabling them to gain a fort's security. There Alfred besieged them, took hostages and forced them to a peace which was soon broken, as by 878 they were ravaging Wessex, having 'stolen in midwinter' to a new base at Chippenham. That year Alfred engaged the Danes repeatedly, taking hostages, and forced them to another place after routing them in a fight followed by a mounted pursuit. Surely this is one of many Viking versus Anglo-Saxon engagements where mounted warfare would have taken place as the Danes managed to flee rapidly enough to ensconce themselves in a fort. It seems highly improbable that the Danes, attacked on several occasions by Alfred's small and obviously mobile mounted force, would have had time to remount and flee rapidly enough to outdistance Alfred, or that Alfred would have had all his own band dismounted to fight, and from that position force flight on Danes who had the benefit of horses.

The Danes were also fighting on another front, and in this case at first definitely were on foot as the annals for 880–1 specifically state that the part of the 'force' stationed at Fulham ventured into Frankland, fought a battle there and were horsed after the battle. Thereafter the Chronicles give us accounts of Viking inroads across the water until in 891 King Earnulf is recorded as 'fighting with the mounted troops'.

The 'force's' next move was to re-infest England in 892, landing in Kent with 250 ships carrying the horses they had acquired in France. Shortly after, Haesten landed at the mouth of the Thames with eighty ships. From two newly constructed forts at Milton Royal and Appledore the Danes conducted new ravages in 893 with bands of mounted troops. Apart from two occasions the Danes did not appear in strength – once before Alfred's opposition was organized, and again when they crossed the Thames into Essex and were forced to retreat by Alfred's army, which had ridden ahead of them, defeated them at Farnham and drove them to flee over the river. Here horses were being used by both sides, the fighting quickly descending into flight and harrying.

The annals for 893 are particularly full and throughout that year Alfred went rapidly from one engagement to the next as the separate contingents of Danes struck. It is clear both forces used horses and ships for respective land and sea movements. At Benfleet in Essex Alfred successfully besieged the Danes, who retrenched to launch another offensive, travelling up the Thames till the Severn was reached where Alfred again besieged them at Buttingdon, starved them into a forced battle after they had been reduced to eating their horses, and in their weakened state defeated them, remnants which still possessed horses escaping by flight.

The tide was turning for Alfred. The Danes from East Anglia and Northumbria joined forces, secured their holdings, families and ships in East Anglia, and ahead of winter the Danish warriors moved *en masse* to the Wirral in a forced 24 hour march to Chester. Of the East Anglian strongholds mentioned by the Chronicle, the furthest west is Huntingdon. From there to Chester as the crow flies is approximately 140 miles (226 km). Even allowing for exaggeration of speed, this, along with other aspects shows the military side of equestrian usage, both by the Danes and by the English who, on several occasions, were unable to catch the enemy before they reached a temporary haven. Alfred's army laid siege to Chester, killed foragers caught outside, seized cattle, grazed their horses in the ripening corn and burned what was left. Starved out once more, the 'force' fled to Wales plundering as they went. Pushed ever onwards they sought safety once more in Northumbria and finally back in East Anglia out on the Island of Mersea. Other Danes from Exeter returned via ship to East Anglia ravaging around the south as they went, but not without severe losses.

The constant warfare conducted by horse and ship continued till 896 when the 'force' split into three, some remaining in their East Anglian stronghold, some returning to their Northumbrian retreat, and the landless sector reinvading the Frankish territories. Thereafter Alfred took more to the sea to repulse the Danes. The Chronicle notes the great losses in men and cattle suffered by the English and in the same year deaths of many noblemen and clerics. Alfred lost his horse-thane, Ecgulf, and soon after Ecgulf's replacement, Wulfric.[35]

Throughout these conflicts there was much wastage of horses, some killed, others taken as spoils. Outcross enhancement would eventually have resulted from survivors of the Danes' Frankish imports. A few good stallions can achieve this rapidly as a stallion's 'book'[36] can accommodate forty or more mares.

The endurance of English stock is illustrated by the decade after 866 which shows the 'force' to be constantly riding between bases and conducting seasonal forays. Distances were often over 100 miles. Anglo-Saxon countryside was heavily wooded; pathways, where they existed, were often rough and meandering, adding to mileage and effort. The Frankish imports which subsequently made that 24 hour dash to Chester were of sufficient calibre to carry a fully accoutred man while averaging over 6 miles (9.6 km) per hour. This is an exceptional feat.[37] It suggests the horses were shod as abrasion of horn and/or breakdown of laminae would have lamed all but the toughest hooves, especially over rough going. Horseshoes are recorded from Saxon burials.[38] The laws of Aethelbirht mention the *ambiht* or smith,[39] who was a person of consequence in the king's household. Horseshoes are known from ninth- and tenth-century sites, among them Thetford, York and London.[40]

Mounted warfare is shown in period sculpture and manuscripts. Sweden has a number of funerary stelae commemorating Viking warriors. A particularly fine one from the eighth century has a four-tier sculpture, the top depicting a galloping warrior in the act of launching

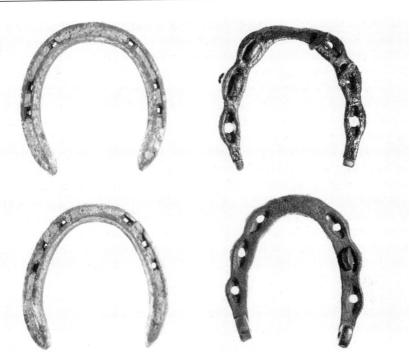

The two horseshoes on the right date from before 1150; they are set against two modern day shoes, used on a Arab mare of 15.1 hands

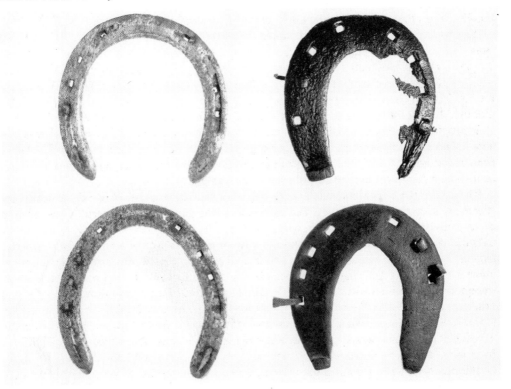

The two shoes on the left are from Granicus, 16.1 hh, 1,300 lb weight. Those on the right are dated to the mid-fourteenth century

his spear overarm.[41] The *Prudentius* manuscript, dating to the eleventh century, illustrates three groups of mounted warriors, many of whom carry spears. One group is headed by a nobleman at the charge with spear levelled.[42]

The Chronicle for the year 937 is an assessment of Aethelstan's triumph over the Scots in Northumbria.[43] The Croyland Chronicle is very clear on this campaign, stating that the chancellor Turketel took Singin, captain of the Wicci (Hwicci), and Singin unhorsed the Scottish king.[44] Whether the unhorsing was in confrontation or during the harrying is not stated.

Between 994 and 1015 heavy Danish inroads were again made, horses being demanded and seized, and in 1010 captured on the battlefield after the defeat of the English.[45] The tone of the Chronicle for these years is desperate, and even when they do not specify mounted raids the sheer range over which the depredations occurred implies horses were routinely seized after sea-borne landings. One other hint that horses were regularly used is the reference under 1003 to the Danes returning to their 'wave-coursers', an equestrian-oriented term for ships. Horses were vital, giving mobility and instilling fear into harried folk.[46]

ANGLO-SAXON WILLS AND THE MILITARY HORSE

The Croyland Chronicle lists basic heriots due from earls, barons and vavassours during the reign of William the Conqueror (1066–87), based on those due before the Conquest:

from an earl: eight horses, four of which shall be saddled and bridled, and four coats of mail, four helmets, four lances, four bucklers, four swords; the other four horses are to be palfrey and post horses with bridles and headstalls

from a baron: four horses, two saddled and bridled, one palfrey and one post horse (with comparable war gear)

from a vavassour to his liege lord: a horse such as was in possession of his father on the day of his death, plus his war gear. If he has not got this he is exempted on payment of 100 shillings.[47]

Some Anglo-Saxon wills go much further than the heriot demanded. The complement of arms and weapons places the horses in the warhorse category. The inclusion of palfreys and post horses after caparisoned horses indicates the higher esteem in which warhorses were held. Some wills indicate the size of the equestrian establishment and show that breeding-quality stock was an important part of estate management.

Under Cnut Danelaw inhabitants were liable for half the number of horses and military gear, and a lower sum of money. Frequently this was paid in gold armlets, cups, or gold decorations on scabbards, etc.

Horses nearly always feature first in the tally of possessions due to the Crown as heriot (and also form major bequests to heirs and friends). In some cases the heriot was paid to an immediate overlord, who in turn was responsible to the Crown for his own lands. Bishops were not exempt, as the will of Bishop Theodred (between 942 and 951) shows:

Heriot to the lord [the King]: 200 marks of red gold, two silver cups and four horses, the best that I have, and two swords, the best that I have, and four shields and four spears.

In addition there were three named estates. This heriot exceeded that required of an earl, although the number of horses was the same as for a king's thegn in Cnut's time.[48]

Other wills illustrate the point. The will of Alfgar (about 946/51) states:

First I grant to my lord two swords with sheaths, and two armlets, each of 50 mancuses of gold, and three stallions and three shields and three spears. Plus a very valuable sword.[49]

The will of Wynflaed (about 950) is as follows:

She grants to Aelfwold two buffalo horns and a horse, and her red tent . . . and she bequeaths to Cynelefu her share of the untamed horses which are with Edmaer's . . . and Eadwold and his sister are to have her tame horses in common.[50]

Wynflaed was obviously a very rich woman with much of her estate tied up in breeding stock. By tame horses is meant horses already broken to saddle, and by untamed horses those not yet broken, breeding stock, and animals still too young to be ridden. The will of Ealdorman Aethelmaer (dated 971–82/3) includes a straightforward heriot:

to my royal lord as my heriot four armlets of 300 mancuses of gold, and four swords and eight horses, four with trappings and four without, and four helmets and four coats of mail and eight spears and eight shields.[51]

The will of Aelfhelm (after 975) states:

to his lord 100 mancuses of gold and two swords and four shields and four spears and four horses two of them harnessed and two unharnessed.

This is almost the same as the heriot due to the king from the thegn nearest to him, as demanded by 11 Cnut 71.1. Aelfhelm pays double the money payment, but no helmets or coats of mail are noted. His other bequests include:

and I grant to my wife half the stud at Troston, and half to my companions who ride with me.[52]

The will of Wulfric (dated between 1002 and 1004) says:

Heriot to the lord. 200 mancuses of gold, two silver hilted swords and four horses, two saddled and two unsaddled, and the weapons which are due with them . . . and I grant to the monastery at Burton a hundred wild horses and sixteen tame geldings.[53]

The money payment is that of an earl, but the horses and their equipment those of a king's thegn.[54] However, the horses willed to the monastery make up a huge bequest and represent a very large stud.

Sometimes breeding stock was paid in lieu of sufficient military horses and weapons. The will of Wulfgeat (ascribed to 1006) shows a bequest to his lord of two horses and two swords and four shields and four spears and ten mares with ten colts.[55] The mares are valued at 20 Mercian shillings each. The *wilde weorf* which are valued in the same passage at 12 Mercian shillings must be the unbroken colts. The total comes to almost 43 mancuses of gold, a little short of the 50 mancuses normally required.[56]

The will of the Aethling Aethelstan (dated 1015) is comprehensive, bequeathing several estates and items to King Ethelred, plus

the horse which Thurbrand gave to me, and the white horse which Leofwine gave to me. [To Bishop Aelfsige] a gold crucifix . . . and a black stallion. [To his chaplain] a horse with the harness. [To the seneschal Aelfmaer] eight hides of land at Catherington and a pied stallion, plus military equipment.

There were many other bequests, but these show the prince to have had a considerable number of horses which he personally knew and valued.[57]

The last will to show any important equestrian element is that of Thurstan, dated no earlier than 1043 and no later than 1045.[58] It is unusual, showing the number of horses and the amount of military equipment to be that of the highest among the king's thegns in the Danelaw, although the gold paid is double that demanded by Cnut, raising the total value of his heriot to that of king's thegns outside the Danelaw. The king received two marks of gold and two horses with trappings and military equipment. Thurstan's servants received the wood at Ongar in Essex, except the deer enclosure and the stud. No mention is made of who is to inherit the stud, although his other lands are left to named heirs. Presumably his family kept it to provide future mounts for personal and military uses.

The evidence of heriots and their military dues shows that horses featured in the Anglo-Saxon army, known as the Fyrd. In 1016 the Fyrd, of 'all the English people', was summoned on no fewer than five occasions. It was divided into two categories: the Great Fyrd and the Select Fyrd.[59] The former was the people *en masse*, no doubt mostly on foot with some lucky enough to own a horse, or more likely a pony, particularly if they lived in an area noted for mountain and moorland breeds which have a very ancient history. The Select Fyrd was drawn from the class of thegns, landholders with sufficient acreage to give them status in society. For each 5 hide unit one warrior was obliged to serve in the Select Fyrd when called upon.[60] He went to war with his horses, weapons and armour consisting of mail shirt, helmet and shield. From this class the Anglo-Saxon mounted troops were drawn,

A group of eleventh-century Anglo-Saxon warriors

the horses being of a better stamp than mere transports as their value and importance in wills illustrate.

The pre-Conquest *Radcnights, Radchenistres* and *Radmanni* are all linked. The *Radmanni* were tenurial ancestors of the Anglo-Norman military serjeants, presumably with military obligations to fulfil. Anglo-Saxon *cnight* or *cniht* is translated in Latin sources as *miles*.[61] In France this denoted a mounted warrior.

The wills illustrate English horse production which enabled the heirs to pay their heriots and still have a sizeable equine establishment for military obligations. When the spread of studs is envisaged covering the country it shows that even before the days of heavy cavalry, England was already a nation of horse-breeders. It was normal procedure for thegns and earldormen to have their own studs. The gift of three stallions as the military heriot of Alfgar shows warhorses were entires. Other heriot horses are not specifically noted as stallions. Mares, other than those included in the collective term of stud, are always noted as such.

Indeed, far from Anglo-Saxon England being solely a nation of infantry, its warrior noblemen saw the horse as a prized possession. We need not be surprised at this. There was considerable traffic with other countries, notably France with royal marriage alliances, embassies and interchange of royal and ducal gifts, among them horses. The people of England would have had to be totally blinkered not to have noted Frankish military customs and, where suitable, adapted them to their own situations.

THE LAWS OF HYWEL DDA

The laws of Hywel Dda (died 950), originally drawn up during his reign, were amplified during the next three and a half centuries by changes in the life of the Welsh people.[62] Hywel was influenced by the traditions of Charlemagne and Alfred the Great, and by Asser, Alfred's mentor and biographer, who used to spend half the year at Alfred's court, the rest in Dyfed.[63] These influences suggest that the equestrian scene in England was comparable with that in Wales, even if not so heavily governed by laws.

The saddle horse added to medieval man's status. One of the earliest of Hywel's laws states that the king shall have a personal escort of thirty-six persons on horseback. These were his twenty-four chief officers and the twelve *Gwestais*, officials responsible for administering the *gwestva*, a twice-yearly tax on the freemen of each *trev* or district, amounting to £1 in money or its equivalent in victuals. In winter part of the amount had to be paid in provisions for horses.[64]

One of the largest sections in the code refers to the 'Chief Groom',[65] who also appears in many other laws. His perquisites and duties, both stated and implied, indicate that the chief groom was more a 'Master of Horse', but without the clearly defined military overtones of that office. No doubt any equestrian military use was in his brief, such as making sure horses were sufficiently trained for whatever purpose was necessary, including the yearly muster of the host to ride the boundaries of the king's territory, and the additional calls made on the host whenever he so desired.[66]

Among the twenty-four officials the chief groom stands seventh, behind the chief of the household, priest, steward, judge, falconer and huntsman. 'The King's Groom of the Rein' and 'the Queen's Groom of the Rein' are among the twenty-four select.[67] Every chief officer had a horse permanently supplied by the king,[68] and many of them were allowed two shares of provender for it. While on official duty the grooms received protection which made it an offence to injure or insult them, penalized by *sarhad* (a fine paid for an insult); should a groom by murdered another fine, *galanas*, was paid to the king.[69] The chief groom's *sarhad* and *galanas* were 50 per cent higher than officers of lower status.[70] He, and the other grooms, had lodgings in the house nearest the king's barn so they could be near their charges, the chief groom receiving individual accommodation.[71]

Among the chief groom's most valuable perquisites were all the old saddles and bridles of the king's steed, discarded spurs if they were gilded, silvered, or lacquered, and the king's old furred caps. His land was given to him free. He and the other grooms were given all the wild colts (i.e. unbroken) that were in the king's share of the spoil. Four pence was paid to him for each horse allocated to any official except those given to the priest, judge and jester. He had to provide a halter for every horse allocated, but as he received hides to make these they cost him nothing. He also had two shares of the money earned, presumably as tips, by the other grooms, and a third of the grooms' *dirwy*, a fine for fighting, theft or rape, and of *camlwrw*, fines for other offences. These fines went direct to the king. They could be exceptionally heavy – twelve kine for *dirwy*, and three kine for lesser offences. Sometimes the fines were doubled. No doubt this system served to keep law and order among stable staff, and if not the chief groom became a very rich man. He could also on occasion, though the circumstances were not specifically stipulated, claim a share of the perquisites of others.[72] Other posts such as falconer and huntsman had perquisites to do with their calling. The chief groom's post must have been eagerly sought as it is by far the richest in material rewards. This reflects the importance of an efficient equestrian establishment.

Horse values are set out in minute detail, going up every three months from a foal worth 6 pence to a two-year-old worth 48 pence. As a three-year-old the horse was worth 96 pence, with 20 pence added when caught up for breaking, and another 4 pence when bridled. A serving stallion which had been fattened for six weeks in a stall had its value doubled to £1.[73] There was another law which stated that a stallion's *teithi*, which meant his worth based on his ability to cover mares, exceeded his legal value because if he was lost the breed was lost.[74] The *teithi* was assessed as 'a horse which can cover with a mare before him and another behind him'.[75] This can only mean the horse had to be able to cope with two mares in close succession. If a stallion 'ran loose at grass' it lost its status;[76] this presumably means either if it escaped and therefore any breedings were unmonitored, or, alternatively, that an inferior stallion not considered to be of the best quality was therefore allowed to run with mares of a lower grade. These laws shed some light on stud practices and suggest all coverings of the king's mares were done in hand. There are several methods of standing a stallion at stud – the in-hand method, the travelling stallion, and the method noted in the Frankish capitulary 'De Villis' where stallions were turned in with a herd of mares at the appropriate time. No doubt all methods were used on Anglo-Saxon and Welsh estates, with the in-hand method being preferred for valuable stock. If a stallion savaged another animal during the covering season there was no legal redress. This also applied to bulls and boars.[77] Outside the stud season if he, or any other animal, bit someone the bitten person could claim the animal as *sarhad*, or injury money.[78]

Fifty mares constituted a legal herd.[79] This suggests that all horse-breeding with animals in private ownership was regulated by law, with horses valued for their potential military use, and that a strict system was needed to maintain quality. That horses were highly valued is shown by the status of the king's own stud which was considered the second of his three most valuable possessions, the first being his household. Any stray horses trespassing on his stud lands cost their owners a 4 pence fine.[80] In any military engagement the king had the choice of spoils for himself. Any studs on conquered territory were his.[81] Among his nobles studs were rated the most important of their possessions.[82]

Other laws governed sales. If an animal suffered from staggers within three days, glanders within three months, or farcy within a year of purchase, the seller was liable, but for an external blemish *caveat emptor*.[83] The seller was responsible for the horse being able to eat and drink and for its manners. If it proved 'restive', i.e. hard to control, the vendor had to take it back or reduce its price by a third.[84] Maiming a limb,[85] bruising or soring its back,[86] cutting mane hair,[87] cutting tail hair, docking a tail, injury of eye or ear: all have set values from 4 pence for a mane and 24 pence for tail hair, up to £1, the whole value of the animal, for docking its tail, maiming a leg, or injuring an eye or ear.[88] Stallion injuries were assessed far higher than those of other categories, so for the palfrey worth a mark, the rouncy 120 pence, and the workhorse 60 pence, the fines are much lower, in general reducing in the same ratio as the animal's total worth.[89] Cutting tail hair or injuring eye or ear of a stud mare valued at 120 pence attracted a smaller fine of six pence.[90] Presumably as she was not on show and these injuries did not affect her breeding value they were not penalized so heavily.

From the meticulous attention the legal code bestows on horses, and the later details Giraldus Cambrensis gives us, but which would have been practices of long usage, I would estimate Welsh military use for horses as transport and in battle as occasion offered, on a par with the Anglo-Saxon.

FIVE

Norman and Early Plantagenet Equestrianism

By the eleventh century the horse was vital to the European military on long-range campaigns. Mounted contingents from the duchy of Normandy affected warfare in England, Italy, Byzantium, Syria and France.

The initial Norman presence in Italy, according to an eleventh-century monk, Aimo of Salerno, was at the request of the inhabitants. In 1016 Salerno was besieged by Muslims; Norman pilgrims returning from Jerusalem were asked to help repel them, Salerno equipping the Normans with horses and weapons. Successful, they were invited to stay but declined and returned to Normandy laden with gifts. They were soon back again, initially to serve as mercenaries, and rapidly introduced Norman mounted warfare to southern Italy.[1]

In northern Italy too German cavalry regularly crossed the Alps assembling in the plain of Roncaglia to impress the Italians with the continued sovereignty of the German king who wore not only the crown of Lombardy but also the imperial crown of the Holy Roman Empire.[2]

Concurrently a stream of Frankish knights eager to fight entered Spain to join the Spaniards who were consolidating their efforts to repel the Muslims. As the Muslim emirates fragmented, Spain was able to present a more united front. In 1035 Castile was added to the Christian kingdoms of Leon and Navarre.[3]

THE HORSE AND FEUDALISM

Cavalry was now pre-eminent and inextricably bound up with the rise of feudalism. In its broadest sense feudalism meant the higher nobility held their lands from their respective 'heads of state', owing military service in return, the amount depending on the extent of their land-grants, and to some extent on individual arrangements with the overlord. Large landowners in turn awarded fiefs to their own vassals, thus ensuring emperor, king, or duke a well-equipped mounted army.

Land became the key to many aspects of service. The vassals who did not have much land, or even none, serving in the *familia* of a ruler, or in that of one of his tenants-in-chief, would look to their overlord to provide some or all of the accoutrements of war. This meant sufficient horses of an age suitable to be ridden, acquired either by breeding or purchase, or as spoils of war. Land provided the acreage to raise them on, or the cash from produce with which to purchase them. There had to be a considerable surplus of ridable animals, plus the breeding stock. Although Frankish stock-breeding methods have been outlined, we need to look further at provenance of the stock in the wider context, and in a narrower one where the Normans themselves were concerned; and to see how these animals were employed. This can best be illustrated from campaigns which show equine usage, its effects on the immediate action, and results on demand and supply, in that order. There must have been many occasions when demand outran remount availability.

In the period surrounding the Norman Conquest of England the horse was highly valued, often in connection with land tenure. Under William's rule the horse was placed first in the lists of effects due to the Crown before a member of the landed class took possession of his inheritance.[4]

Feudal tenures for Norman land-grants in the eleventh century were often settled by a mixture of payments. The grants were of several kinds, land sometimes being accompanied by military assets. The Church was a frequent recipient of benefices, monasteries and bishoprics, in particular, being handsomely endowed both by the duke and by the duke's own tenants-in-chief and their vassals. It was through subinfeudation that much military service operated, a tenant-in-chief rendering his quota to his overlord partly from his personal retinue and partly by calling on the duty owed him by his own vassals. This is illustrated by an early charter dated between 1043 and 1048 where Roger I of Montgomery, himself a vassal of the duke, confirmed a grant of an *alod* of land that one of his vassals, Geoffrey, held of him in the village of Fontaines 'for which he did service to me because that *alod* was within my sway'. Geoffrey in turn granted this to the abbot of the monastery of Jumièges, and in return the abbot and Geoffrey, who had become a monk, gave Roger a horse worth 30 livres and a hauberk worth 7 livres.[5] Clearly Geoffrey was making the gift to the abbot on entering religious life, but both he and the abbot paid for the privilege of so doing. Presumably Roger relinquished his rights in the land for such a payment. The horse's value was high when measured against that of the hauberk. The price and the link with armour implies it was a warhorse.

Another outright gift was made by Robert Bertram to the monastery of St Ouen of 'forty acres of land and two peasants and the tithe of his mares and two knights – namely Goscelin and Osbern'.[6] One foal out of ten dropped, peasants to work the land and care for the stock, and two knights who could act both as protection in time of unrest, and as part of the monastery's military rendering to the duke, made this gift one with a harvest well beyond that from the 40 acres.

NORMAN STUDS, ABBATIAL HORSE-DEALERS AND METHODS OF ACQUISITION

We are indebted to monks for most of what we know of the dealings with horses because monastic chroniclers often record the far more important lay happenings, and none more interesting than the bargains and deals made. These indicate that monks were practised horse-copers dealing in so much high-priced stock that breeding herds must have formed a priority in the running of their estates.

Orderic Vitalis[7] tells the story of two brothers, Baudry, one of Duke William's archers, and Viger, who held land in the fee of Boquencé which in 1026 was held by Giroie from William of Bellême, and in 1050 by his grandson Arnold of Echauffour, who gave this land to the new abbey of St Evroul. The brothers refused to accept the monks as their overlords. In 1059 the newly elected abbot, Robert of Grandmesnil, handed the land back to Arnold, who exacted so many services from the brothers that they begged to be taken back by the monks. In return they gave Arnold a magnificent warhorse they had just received from Engenulf of Laigle, and thereafter did their military service to the abbot. The monastery was in a marcher region where unrest and local wars were endemic. The abbey had a fully equipped band of knights who found employment not only in the duke's service but also as an armed guard should the abbot venture abroad. He also provided such escort to his own overlord when twelve abbey knights acted as guard for blind William of Giroie on his visit to Italy.[8]

One neat transaction by the abbey of St Evroul was to give Ansold of Maule 'as a free gift' a horse worth 100 shillings in return for confirmation of some land and tithes. The horse had previously belonged to a Grimoald of Saulx-Marchais.[9] On his death in 1107 Ansold bequeathed his best palfrey to the monks who promptly gave it back to Ansold's son in return for land at Montmarcien.[10] A well-bred palfrey cost as much as a warhorse, sometimes considerably more. Price evidence for the period is scarce, but there is ample record from Plantagenet times, and the ratio values would have changed very little.[11]

The abbeys of Jumièges and Fécamp also dealt in horses. Between 1020 and 1030 Jumièges sold a 'horse of great price' to Hugh, Bishop of Bayeux, in return for land and privileges at Rouvray; in 1030 it paid Drogo, Count of Amiens and the Vexin, six horses 'of very great price' for land at Genainville. Other instances abound. Fécamp's priory of St Gabriel near Caen was established between 1059 and 1066, and its lands were paid for in part by horses, in part by a cash sum of £312 2s. The seven horses were valued at a total of £39 4s 6d. Two more were loaned to Turstin, lord of one of the benefactors.

Tithes of mares were frequent. In 1050 William FitzOsbern donated to the abbey of Lyre half the tithe from his stud at Glos-la-Ferrière, near St Evroul. Raoul Tancarville gave the tithe of his mares at Roumare to St Georges-de-Boscherville, on the Seine below Rouen, and in 1067 a knight named Gerold gave the tithe of his mares in Roumare to the nuns of St Amand in Rouen. Hugh, Earl of Chester from 1077 to 1101, gave the tithes of all his stock, including mares, to the abbey of St Sever in Lower Normandy.[12]

The above indicates both that much income was derived by religious houses from horse-trading and that horse-breeding must have been a major occupation among the laity. To be liable to pay an annual tithe meant a man owned possession of a substantial herd, something that was an essential part of being able to fulfil military requirements. Each vassal needed a few horses – brood mares preferably – and would have used a travelling stallion, or one owned by his own lord, to prevent inbreeding. The tenants-in-chief and the wealthier landowners would have run larger studs on Carolingian lines. When a heavier horse was needed as the burden of armour increased, care would have been paid to breeding up to augment size. Horse-dealing, allied to other means of acquisition, brought new blood into herds. The references to horses of 'great' or 'very great' price indicated superior stock was not rare.

These details argue that in Normandy such activities were widespread. Several eleventh-century locations are close to modern horse-breeding areas. St Evroul near Merlerault is close to Haras du Pin, one of the French national studs; the district of La Perche is home to the Percheron. It is only in the last two hundred years that the Percheron has been raised as a pure breed.[13] Much oriental blood was introduced into the breed around the time of the crusades. In the mid-eighteenth century the massive draught element was emphasized with outcrosses to Danish, Belgian and English stock. Subsequently recorded infusions of Arabian blood were used.[14] Normandy continues to be a major horse-breeding area, its soil producing quality grazing, and other foodstuffs that encourage horses to reach maximum growth potential with sound limbs and substantial conformation.

Just over 25 miles (40 km) south-east of Haras du Pin is Bellême in the La Perche district, and home in the eleventh century to the Norman family of Bellême. Roger of Montgomery, one of William the Conqueror's leading magnates, whose service was rewarded by grants of many English estates after Hastings, was made Earl of Shrewsbury, a title to which his son

Robert, by his first wife Mabel, succeeded in 1098. It is this son that Giraldus Cambrensis refers to when noting the Spanish stock imported by Robert.[15] Such evidence of specific breeding is rare in the Norman period and indicates the provenance of some Norman horses as there were other equestrian links with Spain.

William is known to have ridden at least one excellent Spanish horse at Hastings which had been brought out of Spain for him by Walter Giffard, noted by Wace in the Roman de Rou.[16] Other leads to horses available to Norman cavalry can be gained by studying the movements of contemporaries in Italy. The main military elements the Normans brought with them were ruthless native aggression and the ability to capitalize on any advantage and to use existing elements of successful established military practices. This adaptability had already converted an infantry force of Northmen into the best heavy cavalry of the period.

Transferring their combined talents to southern Italy, the Northmen quickly seized their opportunities to become masters. Apulia and Calabria were under Byzantine rule, and in Campania the small duchies of Amalfi, Sorrento, Naples and Gaeta acknowledged the Byzantines, while the remnants of Lombard power ran in the Campanian principalities of Benevento, Salerno and Capua. Sicily was under Muslim rule.[17]

The most notable Norman adventurers were five sons of Tancred de Hauteville who held a small fief at Hauteville la Guichard a few miles from Coutances. Three sons held the title of Count of Apulia in quick succession: William in 1042; Drogo in 1048; Humphrey in 1051.[18] The most famous, Robert, rose to be a duke. By 1071 he had taken Bari ousting the Byzantines,[19] and his younger brother Roger was pursuing the lengthy conquest of Sicily, which began in 1060.[20] It is from Anna Comnena that we best get to know the Guiscards: Robert, his son Bohemond and his nephew Tancred. She was both fascinated and repelled by Robert. While condemning many of his actions, and those of his compatriots, she recognized their military prowess, especially the devastating charge of Norman heavy cavalry.[21]

When Guiscard first left Normandy for Lombardy his troop consisted of himself plus five knights and thirty foot. He boosted his 'arsenal' by 'piracy' thus equipping himself with extra arms and horses.[22] This shows that the Norman mounts in Italy consisted of a variety of animals, for Guiscard was not alone in his banditry, the Normans quickly gaining a name for rapacity. Lombardy had been famed for its heavy cavalry in an earlier period. Apulia, Calabria and especially Sicily were noted areas of horse-breeding from Roman times.[23] Procopius relates that the Byzantines had shipped considerable stock to Italy.[24]

TYPE AND CONFORMATION

Byzantine chargers were up to weight and of considerable size, reaching 15 hh.[25] In Muslim Sicily, to add to indigenous stock, some had oriental blood from Hannibalic times onwards, and the Muslims had their own Barb, Arabian and other oriental breeds. As the Byzantines already had centuries of cavalry history, and horse-breeding was an art, especially among Arab countries, there was a wealth of established breeds suitable as warhorses on which to draw. The countries already mentioned were able to select warhorses suited to the different types of cavalry warfare, including the heavier horse able to carry an armed and armoured man, plus a certain amount of self-armour, and the lighter, speedier mounts used by the Muslim archer. The Normans in Sicily drafted Muslim archers into their own armies, under their own Muslim officers (*Kaids*). Muslims' loyalty to their Norman paymasters was assured because papal interference in military affairs, always a force to be reckoned with in medieval times, made no impression on them.[26]

The European warhorse had not yet developed into the increasingly heavy destrier of the later medieval era. An extremely rough guide to the European type is shown on the Bayeux

Tapestry – a medium-sized animal of approximately 14.2–15 hh, with no particular distinguishing features, other than hinting it was fairly stocky. Evidence for the size I have given above comes from a multitude of Norman horseshoes. I measured a representative batch of these at the Museum of London, and compared the results with various sets of horseshoes I have at home from animals of similar height. In particular I measured those I used on an Arabian mare of 15.1 hh. One set of Norman shoes measured *exactly* the same as the mare's set, and many others were very similar. The size of the Norman shoes indicates the horses were not of any very great weight, as hooves of this size – rear shoes 4½ in wide by 4¾ in long (112.8 by 119 mm); front shoes 4½ in wide by 5 in long (112.8 by 127 mm) – would not be up to the burden of a heavy horse, but are more closely akin to an animal in the region of 800 to 1,000 lb (360 to 455 kg). Such an animal is able to carry considerable weight.[27]

We are more enlightened when seeking to discern breed characteristics of Asiatic and oriental horses. Illustrations from specific periods can be measured and similarities with modern live specimens sought; such exercises show that basic breed characteristics have remained constant, allowing for improvements resulting from rigid control. As there are so few references to breed provenance, with the exception of Spanish, in European literature, it suggests that Europeans were only just beginning to breed for distinct type. The wealth of good horses from Byzantine and Moorish sources must have been a revelation to the Normans.

The horse was better esteemed in oriental cultures which had a history of equestrian expertise, whereas the Europeans were backward in every aspect of equestrian knowledge. The switch to predominantly cavalry in the theatre of war hastened the process of appreciation and furthered equine development in Europe. Although there is a significant lack of western European literature from the early medieval period, a Persian work, the *Qabus Nama* of Kai Ka'us ibn Iskander, was written in 1082 by the Prince of Gurgan, of the Ziyanid dynasty of the South Caspian provinces of Tabaristan and Jurgan, for his son. Literacy was far more common in oriental cultures, which would explain the lack of comparable western European texts. The *Qabus Nama* outlines his education, which paralleled that of his European contemporaries from royal and noble houses who would also have received instruction in the warlike arts during their time as squires.

Heading the list was instruction 'in the arts of wielding arms and of horsemanship'. These included 'riding, javelin-throwing, archery, and wielding the spear. They [the instructors] further taught me how to play polo and bowls and how to throw a lasso.'[28] Instruction was also given in hunting, hawking and falconry.[29] Caution in riding was emphasized, and a large horse recommended in order to give a good impression.[30] Orientals played polo and hunted as part of their military training.

The *Qabus Nama* outlined what would be acceptable in either a refined oriental horse, or a heavier animal rather lacking in 'quality' but with basic good conformation. All warhorses needed good conformation to function efficiently; certain factors enhance an animal's usefulness, others limit it. The Prince of Gurgan's recommendations on buying a horse are applicable to both eastern and western cultures.[31] I have taken the liberty of putting some of his descriptions into more readily understandable English equestrian parlance: e.g. 'the part between flank and belly short' means short-coupled strong loins.

A suitable horse should have a good head, attention being paid to the dentition, special reference being made to avoidance of parrot mouth.[32] The facial plane should be straight, the forehead broad, ears long, fine and erect.[33] The neck should be long with an open gullet,[34] and it should be set on well into the shoulder without coarseness. The barrel should also be fine[35] with a long underline. The chest should be broad, the loins short-coupled. Limbs should be substantial.[36] Hooves should be black and long, the sole round.[37] The tail should be long with a short dock, and there should be absence of hair on the lower limbs.[38]

Other advice is that the shins should be smooth, which means the horse should have good clean bone free of splints, curbs, etc. The well-suspended quarters and wide crupper gave a broad, strong hindquarter, not a weak sloping croup. Colours preferred were bay, dun, or ash grey with black points, followed by cream or chestnut. Piebalds were disliked. Today it is recognized that dark bay and dun horses are frequently tougher than other animals, and their black hooves are exceptionally hard, especially those of dun horses.

MILITARY USE

The monastic chroniclers give a skeletal description of battles, sometimes with numbers of cavalry employed, albeit usually exaggerated. Our best chance of understanding the parts played by the horse in European military events is to read a selection of the *Gestes* that became popular from Norman times onward. Although these lengthy poems were often fanciful, embroidering a minor event on the field of tournament or war, the equestrian element is very revealing and far more trust can be put in it than in the human incidents. Writers drew on common knowledge about the way horses were used, where they came from and how they were equipped, and even on occasion gave good descriptions of conformation and action. Above all, the good writers put life and character into their horses, so that the thin chronicles are fleshed out, and we can see the warhorse for what he was, a valued partner on whose skill much of a knight's safety and success depended.

The tournament was where the medieval warrior practised his skills. Orderic Vitalis comments that when William FitzOsbern, the regent of Normandy for William the Conqueror, went to join William's overlord, Philip of France, in his 1071 war against Robert the Frisian, he was accompanied by 'ten knights as if he were going to a tournament'.[39] A much larger tournament contingent, 200-strong, was put into the fray by Charles the Good, Count of Flanders, who kept his knights fit for war by tourneying in Normandy and France.[40] Such honing of military skills was common with English knights and princes too, many

A manuscript of the romance of Lancelot showing a tournament in progress. (The Pierpont Morgan Library, New York, M.806, f. 262)

crossing to the Continent to take part in tournaments, though most records for these come from the end of the period covered by this chapter and even later. In 1252 William de Clare was badly beaten at a tournament in France, and to retrieve family honour his brother Richard, Earl of Gloucester, went overseas and won back his brother's horses and armour gaining much acclaim at home, according to the Tewkesbury chronicler;[41] and in 1260 and 1262 Prince Edward (later King Edward I) toured the French tournament circuit, none too successfully.[42] Without doubt the most successful of the tourneyers was William Marshall, a vassal of William of Tancarville in Normandy. He turned a knightly pursuit into a serious but risky business venture, and his skills brought him great financial rewards. At his first outing in 1167, and riding a borrowed horse, he won four and a half horses for himself and a like number for his esquires, together with their equipment. He then teamed up with another knight and they followed the tournament circuit for two years; in one ten-month period they captured 103 knights with their horses, harness and equipment.[43] Considering that a good horse could cost a knight the equivalent of a year's income or more, the partnership was well in funds. The tournament became increasingly popular as time went on, earning fulminations from the Church which eventually banned it, to no good effect because the ban was repeatedly flouted. The last time the Church interfered was in the papal prohibition of 1312, its concern being partly religious, partly economic, as not only did tournaments endanger men's souls, but they cost potential crusading forces men and money and not least horses of which the crusaders were in great need.[44]

The kings of England and France frequently banned and/or limited tournaments. Their security and authority could be threatened by large numbers of heavily armed knights gathering together, as is only too evident from the troubled reigns of Stephen and Henry III of England.

The competitive element must have been a spur to producing superior animals. There is a world of difference between a horse working in a large cavalry group where herd instinct to gallop together is an asset, and one used solo and needing individual courage to face an intimidating enemy. From the horse's point of view a tourneying knight and a military enemy were the same. Although tournaments as such are not the concern of this book, they show that frequent participation in them of knights not at war had many results in the equestrian field, apart from allowing knights to keep their eye in with weapon practice. In the heyday of tournaments the horse used became a specialized beast and far too valuable to risk in war, but back at the studs the majority of male animals would have ended up as quality destriers for the warring knight. Eventually preference for certain types and/or breeds became evident from results gained on the field. From the thirteenth century onwards royal accounts and documents give specific details, but for the earlier periods the *Gestes* show that the horses being used were not the lumbering destriers modern conception has envisaged for the armoured knight.

LITERARY SOURCES

The best-known work is the *Song of Roland*, the much enlarged account of the ambush and massacre by Basques of Charlemagne's rearguard in the pass of Roncevalles as he returned from war against the Moors in Spain in 778.[45] Three centuries later the event had been transformed into a huge epic battle engaging vast armies, and the author, Turoldus, while setting it in the eighth century, gives us the horses, weapons and accoutrements of the late eleventh, and replaces Basques by Saracens. In the intervening centuries the Muslims had intensified their grip on most of Spain, but some areas were under Christian control as the *reconquista* advanced.

Just over a hundred years later Wolfram von Eschenbach composed his great works, his *Parsival* from the late 1190s to 1210,[46] and his *Willehalm*, which he completed by 1226.[47] Wolfram came from the minor aristocracy of northern Bavaria, and around 1200, at approximately thirty years of age, he entered the service of the Landgrave Herman I of Thuringia,[48] producing the *Willehalm* in the reign of Herman's son Ludwig IV. *Parsival* is concerned with the legend of the Holy Grail; *Willehalm* with two historical battles of Aliscans. The first occurred in 793 when the Muslims suddenly invaded the lands of Count William of Toulouse (the Willehalm of the poem) who met them *en route* to Carcassonne; he was beaten in a hard fight, but not without inflicting such serious damage on the Muslims that they withdrew to Spain. Recurrent raids from 796 onwards led Charlemagne to retaliate by conquering north-eastern Spain in 801–3. The second battle of Aliscans occurred in 803; as retold in *Willehalm*, it was an epic, but in truth it was an exploit by Count William leading a flying column against the relief contingent of Moors coming up from Cordova to Barcelona,[49] which had fallen to Charlemagne in 801 after a two-year siege.[50]

Taken out of the poems' romantic background the equestrian elements reflect the changing situation, particularly in equipment, in relation to horses over the years that span the writing, as well as outlining aspects of training, management, etc.

In the *Roland* several general points come across as the poem unfolds. Nowhere is infantry mentioned. The total forces of both Saracens and Christians were mounted. By the eleventh century cavalry was the important arm. Although foot were still used in strength, leaders felt battles were won by the heavy cavalry charge. Only once is a specific *en masse* charge referred to when 'the French all charge together'.[51] Individual engagements of spear and sword highlight warriors' prowess on both sides. No apparent utilitarian difference is shown between the types of weaponry, tactics, armour, or horses used by either side. The famed Saracen light-horsed archer is totally absent, and about the only difference in equipment is the proliferation of jewels on Saracen horses' gear. The horses are interchangeably referred to as destriers and coursers. All are swift-running and several times coursers are also described as light, referring to conformation not colour.[52]

A distinct impression is given that while apprised of the Saracens, Turoldus had never seen them in action, whereas his own countrymen's military attire and basic fighting techniques were well known to him.

Muslim and Christian armies, fighting for supremacy in Spain, were both noted for their horsemanship and as breeders of horses. It was inevitable that each would be influenced by the other. The Spanish horse was, and remained in later times, more agile and lighter-framed than that eventually produced from the heavier European breeds, but he was larger and heavier than the oriental breeds. He continued to be used as an improver throughout the medieval period.

In the *Roland* we find mention of the Barb, Veillantif, which was Roland's mount,[53] and of Barbemouche ('Barbary Fly'), the mount of the Saracen Climborin;[54] there is also reference to the wealth of horses and mules in Spain.[55] Unusually for European literature conformation is described. Good points were that the steed was swift and smooth-paced, and had flat knees, a hollow hoof, short thighs, ample croup, long flanks and a well set-up back, and small ears, which is a sign of good breeding. Colourwise the white tail, yellow plume (forelock) and tawny head suggest a palomino. The other points noted would be considered adequate today.[56] There are frequent references to horses charging, or running swiftly, and always with a loose rein, while the rider, usually a Christian, wields his lance, the impact of swiftly hurtling horse enabling the rider to lift his opponent clean out of the saddle. Nowhere is the lance said to be couched, but its stock is very thick.[57] To have the effect of numerous unhorsings by lifting on the point of a weapon it had to be couched. Turoldus seemed to

Highly disciplined ranks of troops charge in close formation. Note the couched lances. (The Pierpont Morgan Library, New York, M.736, f. 7v)

delight in these episodes and the injuries suffered by fallen foes.[58] On the couching of the lance, and on its dimensions, as well as on many other aspects of war, we have specific information, but from an Arab source (see below), although the instructions are valid for Christian and Muslim alike.

Throughout there are references to exaggerated swordplay, cleaving through the opponent's helmet, armour, body and saddle, down to the horse itself. The swords doing such grim work are frequently given names, marking them as more intimate weapons than the lance.

Complete armour for the rider is also described, but there is a total lack of horse armour as would be expected for the period, although that was to change within the next few decades in the Christian area. Orientals as we know had been using horse armour for centuries. The hauberk and byrny are described interchangeably and several types are noted: triple, double and single ring mail, banded steel, jazerant and double cordwain.[59] Much praised is Saracen armour manufactured in Spain: the hauberk, Saragossan helmets, Viana steel swords, Valencian spears.[60] Hauberks are also shown as extending to a mail skirt which gave protection to the thighs.[61] Head and throat protection is very detailed – steel cap, helm with nasal, coif plus ventail.[62] To make sure of recognition shields were painted with 'cognizances gay',[63] an early example of what was to develop into armorial quarterings that could be read by a trained herald able to put names and lands to the bearings. These were a vast improvement on the haphazard methods recorded many times by the early Norman chroniclers. At the siege of Gerberoi in 1079 Robert of Normandy wounded his father,

William, in the arm, unhorsed him, killed his horse, and recognized his opponent only by his voice, at which he offered his father his own charger, albeit earning a curse from William. William of Malmesbury[64] offers the bare facts of wounding and killing the horse; Florence of Worcester adds the location of the wound, the unhorsing and offer of Robert's own charger;[65] while Henry of Huntingdon is the only one to recall the king cursing his son, but adds that the king was thrown from his horse, not unhorsed by his son.[66] The king's younger son William Rufus also risked his life in an engagement on horseback, had his horse 'killed under him', and was thrown and dragged, being saved from injury only by his mail, and from being killed by crying out to the soldier who had unhorsed him.[67] Presumably the horse was in fact badly wounded and died later from his injuries, as he could hardly have dragged the king if he were dead.

Shipping horses in specially constructed transports was well known to the Normans in Italy who had plenty of experience of so doing, having learned much from the Byzantines. In the *Roland* it is the Byzantine *dromond* that is noted,[68] not the Arabic *'us'ārī* or Latin *uscerii*.[69] Anna Comnena tells us that the Guiscard shipped horses, and several times she numbers *dromon(d)s* among the list of ships gathered to transport military personnel and mounts.[70] In William the Conqueror's army at Hastings there were Norman mercenaries from Apulia and Sicily,[71] so it is quite possible that they advised William on building horse transports when he began to assemble his expedition for the conquest. The practice of unloading horses and immediately riding them to an engagement is met with.[72]

Warhorses travelling overland were led to the proximity of conflict, warriors riding palfreys or mules.[73] This custom applied to both Christian and Muslim. In the desert areas, as we shall see later, Arabs rode on camels leading their precious horses alongside to conserve their fire and energy. It was also customary to don armour just prior to engagement where feasible, and to warm one's horse up, executing preliminary exercises to sharpen it up for the

Horses being led from Norman ships prior to the battle of Hastings

coming fray.[74] Stirrups are also mentioned;[75] these were not universal at the time of the actual engagement, but by the time of the Normans were vital for retaining one's seat and putting extra emphasis into the thrust of a couched lance. The Bayeux Tapestry shows that Normans used both overhand throw and couched methods of weapon delivery.

Stripped of the narrative element the *Roland* illustrates eleventh-century mounted action. The *Parsival* and the *Willehalm* amplify certain aspects and show new elements in equestrian equipment. The horse is now being protected as well as his rider; whereas the equestrian content of the *Parsival* concerns the tournament, and the *Willehalm* focuses on warfare, the practicalities are applicable to both.

As a knight brought up to ride and handle weapons, no doubt getting his own share of tournament practice and skirmish experience in the endemic squabbles of medieval nobility, Wolfram von Eschenbach had a keen eye for a good horse. He drafted into his work the types that made a lasting good impression on him, and outlined several other equestrian practices. We meet a variety of horses, especially in the *Parsival*. Castilian horses appear several times,[76] also the Welsh,[77] Hungarian,[78] Danish,[79] and Arabian.[80] The descriptions linked to the horses are specific, rather than the more general 'good, beautiful, of great price', etc. This gives us a much better picture of what was available in Europe in the eleventh, twelfth and thirteenth centuries. Although Spain possessed the best horses, other horses were valued too. As Wolfram is so careful to state the origin of each special horse, he can be trusted when noting that the Spanish-bred Arabian was tall, and this can serve as a key to overall sizes of horses of the era. The purebred Arabian has maintained its typical height-range of 14–15 hh for centuries. However, there were exceptions in every breed, and Arabians in excess of 15 hh would have caused Wolfram to comment. *Parsival*'s Castilian horse with its long slim legs[81] was of elegant form, not coarsely built. This was in the era when Spanish horses were becoming the vogue in European courts. It was capable of great exertion, and did not sweat.[82] One comment that there was no need to tighten the girth even after two days of hard travel,[83] shows a horseman's observation – a fit horse fines down to a working weight, and a good shoulder helps keep the saddle in place. Wolfram was a contemporary of Giraldus Cambrensis who commented on the Welsh horses of Spanish descent,[84] so there could have been a practical reason for Wolfram's noting the prized Welsh horses.

Hungary had a reputation for good horses. The description in the *Parsival* of Hungarian horses as slit-nosed with branded sides is explained by the practice of slitting the nostrils of a horse touched in the wind, to facilitate its air intake, and by the constant brandings to cure ailments.[85] Firings on all parts of the equine anatomy were a crude method of (hopeful) cure. Some brandings may have been for identification. Evidence for this comes from 1270 in the village of Barcza,[86] and from a 1336 document of the Kállay family.[87]

Danish horses were not large but strong and beautiful. Scandinavia acquired much of its equestrian knowledge from Constantinople via the Varangian guard and from merchants travelling in Kievan Russia and in Hungary.[88] Such knowledge equipped the invading Northmen with equestrian skills, later pefected, as shown in the Frankish and Anglo-Saxon annals.

Several passages in *Parsival* recount iron coverings for horses, some armour even covering the lower legs; the horse's armour is described as being constructed of mail, and of 'close welded metal rings'.[89] There is evidence for arming a horse to the hooves, but it was thought to be a most unusual practice. Either Wolfram is highlighting it too much, or it was more common than is thought.[90] From the Roman period there is a passage in Heliodorus' *Aethiopica*[91] describing a cataphract's horse's armour, and this mentions *estivals* or greaves for the legs. When plate armour came into vogue it would have been possible to use such protection, provided there was sufficient padding on the inside and a secure fixing. It was not until a few decades after Wolfram's death that plate armour arrived; however, horsemen of all periods have tried out new practices before they became an accepted part of the equestrian scene. Could this have been what Wolfram was seeing? Some sort of lower leg strapping covered in mail or laminated armour? As his other equestrian observations are so accurate it is hard to feel he was totally inventive on this one score!

The comments on tournament procedure and use of equines show a knight was expected to know the rules and appreciate the finer points of horsemanship, training a mount who could spring quickly from a gallop to a full career;[92] just as readily answer the bit and come to hand;[93] obey the rein and wheel; or respond to leg pressure to accelerate.[94]

The *Willehalm* reiterates the preference for Castilian horses in use by both Saracens and Christians.[95] Most horses appear armoured, some to the 'very hooves'.[96] One other horse is especially noted by breed: Volatin, taken by Willehalm after he had killed his rider, and variously termed Arabian, Persian, Syrian, or Aragonese.[97] This is one of the few equestrian inconsistencies shown by Wolfram. Today we would say the horse was of oriental breeding. However, it could have been all of these, the Arabian then being found in all four countries. The trade in Spanish horses was significant throughout the medieval period, any knight of means aspiring to own one as implied by the phrase 'so many handsome Castilian steeds' which were well adapted to a relentless and violent charge.[98] Opposing the Christians the Muslims charged in the wedge formation, their leader mounted on a mare scarcely up to the weight of her own and her rider's armour. This also drew the comment 'here in this country we ride stallions to the charge'.[99] Muslim equestrian warfare showed a deal more sense than the Christian variety, using stallions, mares and geldings according to the task undertaken.[100] Wolfram obviously knew of these customs, as the name Brahane, given to a horse described in *Willehalm* as belonging to Terramer, a Muslim king, is noted in the glossary as implying the sense of gelding.[101]

Maybe the most succinct description of individual tactics/attacks is to be found in the passages which verify methods. In single combat two comments stand out: 'The Frenchman rode a horse swift and he gave it the spurs so hard that his spear in its thrust went through the Saracen's arm and sheild and right into his very chest'[102] and 'Then King Purrel rode a horse strong, bold, swift, and armed to the hooves which in clashes often performed his will as he desired'.[103] Combined, these show a high degree of equestrian skill, and that the horse was trained to be aggressive, a much easier task if it was an entire with a natural tendency to aggression, although some mares can be quite unpleasant, geldings less so.

Before leaving these illuminating epics there are several references to spotted horses that deserve comment: 'Tachëbrun', brown spots,[104] 'Puzzat', white spots,[105] and 'Passilivrier', a horse described as 'swift, dragon-hued, spotted all over as it were with fiery sparks'.[106] The translator says this is Wolfram's fanciful description, but I do not agree. It is a very accurate description of a chestnut snowflake Appaloosa: another link to Spain, as spotted horses frequently came from that country throughout equestrian history. They appear too often in the art of the medieval period in a military context to be ignored.[107]

Ibn Hodeil has much to say pertinent to the above, and to Spanish and European warfare conducted in Italy, southern France and Spain. It is hardly surprising to find similarities in weaponry and techniques. In résumé Ibn Hodeil's recommendations are to use a saddle with a large seat with pommel and cantle raised,[108] a thick felt pad, and a girth of sufficient tightness to prevent the saddle slewing to one side when the rider took up his weapons.[109] These would somewhat counterbalance each other, but the left side would be more burdened than the right with the weight of the shield.[110] The stirrups were to be longer rather than shorter to aid seat retention in a sudden stop.[111] The Moors in Spain and the Spanish themselves used a shorter-stirrup style of riding that allowed the knee to be bent so that the horseman rode much as in a modern balanced seat. This style was known as riding *à la*

*The four horsemen of the Apocalypse
as depicted in a twelfth-century Spanish
manuscript (British Library, Add. MS
11695, f. 102.)*

ginete, the French very long-stirrup style as *à la bride*. Other similar Moorish and Spanish customs were the spiked noseband of the Spaniards and the iron *hakama* of the Moors, which has a long history – being the *psalion* of Rome, the *Jaquima* of Spain and the hackamore of the USA.[112] Ibn Hodeil advises riders not to jerk the horse to a stop as an inexpert rider could be thrown out of the saddle.[113] This would not have occurred with a western European medieval saddle, but the rider's lower back could have received a very nasty blow from the high cantle.

The lance was flexible, strong, but not over thick or weighty in construction, nor was it excessively long, unlike the huge tournament lance. As the Muslim training and techniques were to be used with the couched lance the comments, mostly derived from ibn Hodeil, could be equally applicable to the European warrior, although it is to be doubted that the approach to cavalry training in the west was as systematic as that undertaken in the east. The quintain which knocked a man flat on his horse's croup if he misjudged his timing, must have been a far cruder method than the system used in Muslim training. Ibn Hodeil comments on Frankish swords, or, as he terms them, double-edged Frankish sabres,[114] and the safety precautions and methods of manipulation would have had much in common whether used by Saracen or Christian. He also gives useful advice applicable to all mounted warriors. When fending off a lance thrust the rider was warned not to use his full body weight behind his shield for fear of being unhorsed; not to hit his chin on the shield rim when mounting; and not to use an overly heavy shield which made its manipulation difficult.[115]

Finally the description of the mail coat is detailed. Three basic constructions were used: small riveted plates; double ring mail; and a broigne or leather coat covered with metal rings, as was the European byrnie. The hauberk was similarly constructed, but also had an aventail. The Arabs had a great variety of body armour from the full coat to the short plastron covering only the man's front.[116] One wonders if, in spite of various European laws requiring a man of means to possess a mail coat, the reality was just such a variety?

There was a lack of contemporary European works on warhorse training. This makes Wolfram von Eschenbach's work valuable for the insight it gives us. Methods must have been basically the same for training oriental and European animals. No doubt the cruder horsemanship of the Franks was better suited to the cruder horses they rode. It is indeed significant that the Spanish horse was in constant demand to improve western European breeds. From practical experience with many breeds, I believe the Arabian, and its crosses, is definitely more intelligent than others. Some colder-blooded horses are what is termed 'thick', being not nearly as responsive mentally or physically.

THE PERIPATETIC WARHORSE

The monastic chronicles of the Norman and early Plantagenet era concern themselves with two main themes. Of first importance to the ecclesiastic is the 'who's who and where' of abbots and bishops. Next come the royal histories from William I to Henry II; some chroniclers give a comprehensive royal diary, others are more sketchy.

It has been generally accepted that when Norman William invaded he introduced a type of warfare new to England but already well established in Europe. The battle of Hastings in 1066 was fought by English infantry, stiffened by dismounted huscarls, against Norman horse and foot. The Norman cavalry was in large measure the means by which William overcame the English on Senlac Hill.

That the English never fought on horseback is to be strongly doubted. However, in spite of Richard Glover's cogent reasoning, it is still accepted that the English did ride to battle and always dismounted to fight.[117] If so, why was so much emphasis put on the heriots of the ruling classes where warhorses had to be accompanied by the requisite saddle, byrnie, helmet and weapons?[118] These horses and their appurtenances were a sizeable addition to the king's stables and armouries, out of which he could augment the mounting and equipping of is personal retinue, the huscarls so vaunted in Harold's army. The Anglo-Saxon wills that stipulate bequests of valuable warhorses are also to be considered. If the huscarls and the select fyrd rode to battle and always dismounted, any sound pony would have sufficed, but would have been far too small to be used as a warhorse. That William the Conqueror continued levying the same heriot in his reign[119] when cavalry was *the arm* is indicative that pre-Norman equine usage among the wealthy was little different to that post-1066.

On the occasion of Harold's visit to Normandy the famous oath-swearing was followed by a military expedition undertaken by Harold and his retinue who were fitted out by William with 'weapons of war and mettlesome horses' to enable them to take part with the duke in his war in Brittany.[120] There is a vast difference between riding a linear route and being able to fight on horseback; the latter requires a degree of confidence in one's own riding ability so well founded that violent movements, either of aggression or defence, cause no loss of equilibrium, and the ability to dictate to a strange horse how he shall behave in a mêlée. If Harold and his retinue did not know how to fight from horseback there would have been no point in providing them with the means. Instead they would have been a liability.

The reason for Harold's lack of horse at Hastings has to be sought elsewhere. Hastings was fought on 14 October 1066, only twenty days after the battle of Stamford Bridge on

25 September 1066. The news of the Norman landing reached Harold, who was celebrating his victory over the Norwegian king at York, on the night of 1 October 1066. From Pevensey and Hastings to York is 250 miles (400 km) as the crow flies, and considerably more using any road. The messenger, using a relay of very swift horses, carrying the news to Harold had a journey of closer to 330 miles (530 km) to travel. Even though using the old Roman road north, along which the modern A1 is constructed, gave him the best access, the route is not arrow straight. The figure of 330 miles is not a random figure but arrived at by a series of checks.[121]

We do not know Harold's precise movements after he received the devastating news. In between 2 October, which is the earliest he could have left, and 14 October, Harold re-organized the forces he had with him, marched via London, augmenting his numbers as best he could, and camped at Senlac 7 miles (11 km) from Hastings by 13 October. If he spent a single day in London so that levies could be assembled, that leaves only eleven days to travel the total distance, raising troops *en route*. Those returning from York must have used horses.

That horses were involved in the battle of Stamford Bridge is shown by two occurrences. First the battle is described in detail in the Norwegian saga of Snorri Sturleson, the *Heimskringla*; it is true the chronicler wrote later, but many medieval chroniclers also wrote of events prior to their own times and are not discredited over the main issues.[122] Glover has shown the *Heimskringla* is accurate in salient points. The saga definitely states that the English had cavalry, not mounted infantry,[123] and that King Harold of England was described by King Harold Hardrada as 'but a little man, yet he sat firmly in his stirrups'.[124]

> The hard-fought battle was first loose and light, as long as the northmen kept their order of battle; for all the English rode hard against the northmen, they gave way immediately, as they could do nothing against them. . . . Now when the northmen thought they perceived that the enemy were making but weak assaults, they set after them, and would drive them into flight; but when they had broken their shield rampart the Englishmen rode up from all sides, and threw arrows and spears on them.[125]

The second point is the considerable number of small horseshoes found at the scene of the battle.[126] We also have the testimony of Florence of Worcester, a chronicler writing of his own time, in a style that was very concise and gave more detail of secular events than most of his brethren. He states that five months earlier Harold had assembled a large fleet and an army of cavalry.[127] This was to repel a landing by his brother Tosti, who departed for Lindesey rather than face Harold. Harold then spent the summer waiting for William, disposing his land forces, i.e. his cavalry, at suitable points along the sea coast, but when supplies ran out he disbanded his forces in early September, only to reassemble them and travel north where he met both Tosti and the Norwegian king in battle at Stamford Bridge. Florence also comments on several other engagements where English cavalry were used: 1054 against Macbeth, King of Scots; 1055 against the Welsh, although here he does state that the English, contrary to their custom, were ordered to fight on horseback; and 1063 when Harold took a small troop of horsemen to Rhuddlan to fight Griffin of Wales. The isolated English on the Welsh borders at Hereford in 1055 have been taken to mean *all the English* but it is hardly surprising that hilly border territory was unsuitable for cavalry warfare. However, as the Herefordshire English with the Frenchmen and Normans were pursued and cut down to the tune of four or five hundred dead as well as a great number injured, it would appear the Welsh were either mounted, or exceptional Olympic-style marathon runners.[128]

The disbanded cavalry of early September would still have had campaign-fit horses for the long, fast trek north. The quantities of shoes found at the battle site are to be expected.

Fast hard travel wears out shoes more quickly than the same distance done more slowly. Clenches loosen, so that shoes are liable to be pulled off easily, or may merely fall off. A horse used to shoes goes lame and is unserviceable if ridden barefoot for any great distance. The return trip to London and Hastings was obviously deficient in mounted men for several reasons: the horses had been exhausted by a summer's use on patrol on the south coast, followed by disbanding and being ridden home, then reassembled and pushed over 300 miles (480 km) to Stamford Bridge, fighting a battle there on 25 September and doing the return trip by 13 October. On top of that, horses were lost at Stamford Bridge. The *Heimskringla* makes it clear that weapons were aimed at the horses as much as at the riders.[129]

The depleted horse numbers that reached Hastings would have been unfit for battle. As Harold had taken a huge army north with him the stocks of readily available animals in the south must have been non-existent.

If we allow that horses, in whatever numbers (and we shall never know how many), were present in a combative role at Stamford Bridge, the period from 8 September, when Florence of Worcester informs us Harold disbanded his cavalry (originally raised at the beginning of May),[130] to 13 October when the remnants camped at Senlac Hill, must rank as one of the most intensive periods of equestrian action known. Most of a warhorse's energy was used in transporting its rider from home to muster, muster to conflict, and, if he was lucky, home again. The English ranks were very depleted, the incoming Normans restricted to what their fleet could accommodate. Even Duke William used force to obtain a remount; when his first was killed by Gyrth, Harold's brother, he resorted to 'upturning a knight of Maine'.[131]

Of the battle of Hastings itself much has already been written, and the Norman cavalry's role on the whole given due credit. A few points will suffice. Far more illustrative is the aftermath and the heavy use to which those same cavalry horses were put.

Although exceptionally biased in favour of William the Bastard, William of Poitiers gives a brief description of the equestrian element at Hastings: on landing at Pevensey a mounted reconnaisance party, of which Duke William was a member, explored the vicinity;[132] the district was swept clean by foragers;[133] and on the morning of 14 October the Norman assault opened with infantry to the fore followed by cavalry attacking head-on. They failed to break the English shield wall and turned to flight because they thought the duke had fallen.[134] Enraged and 'bellowing' at his troops the duke rallied them. They turned on their pursuers, encircling them and cutting them down.[135] The shield wall still held, though gaps were appearing. This induced the Normans to pretend flight, having already had their initial panic retreat turned to advantage when they rallied. For a second time it worked, English pursuers being massacred. By now the cohesion of the Norman cavalry had disintegrated into individual assaults.[136] William had three horses killed underneath him.[137]

The Bayeux Tapestry, from which information about equipment is drawn, shows three horses being violently overturned. One has an empty saddle as his rider pitches off; another no saddle at all; and the rider of the third has been thrown forward on to his horse's neck, obviously injured, while an Englishman wields a lance against him, and at the same time jerks the horse's girth loose. Yet another horse, still upright, has his skull cloven by an axe. In the border below two riderless horses gallop away from the conflict. Grouped together, this scene shows more of violence and its cost than the rest of the tapestry, indicates that horse losses were heavy, and illustrates the type of wounds suffered by the animals.

After his victory William spent the next few years in systematically subjugating England, investing towns, erecting castles and criss-crossing the country to put down rebellions. The numbers of horses involved cannot be estimated, as although the chronicles note garrisons were imposed on strategic strongpoints they do not break down the numbers into foot and horse.

Horses suffered during the battle of Hastings as this detail from the Bayeux Tapestry shows

After Hastings William granted estates to the major barons who had been instrumental in his victory, and made lesser land-grants to a host of the minor nobility. In return for their fiefs they owed the king mounted service. The number of knights owed from each estate was fixed on an individual basis, not according to the value of the land-grant.[138] The number raised from *servitia debitium* was around 5,000 but these were insufficient to cope with the extended military actions that spanned the whole reign. To augment these William engaged mercenaries, and to maintain them he extorted heavy taxes from his English subjects. The numbers demanded from his tenants-in-chief were far in excess of the service demanded from the same magnates for their lands in Normandy. There the burden was light, few rendering more than ten knights. In England before the end of the reign of William's son Henry I in 1135, no fewer than eleven lay lords owed sixty or more knights, at least twenty-seven owed twenty-five or over, and six bishoprics and three abbeys owed forty knights or more. If they could not raise this number the magnates also employed mercenaries.[139]

In Normandy many magnates owing a low number of knights to their duke enfeoffed considerably more, thus employing a sizeable private army which could threaten the overlord. In England William forbade private war, confiscating lands of any lords guilty of it.[140]

The first to feel the crushing order were the counties of Sussex, Kent, southern Hampshire, Surrey, Middlesex and Hertfordshire.[141] In 1067 William returned to Normandy leaving Bishop Odo of Bayeux and William FitzOsbern, newly created Earls of Kent and Hereford, to govern in his absence. In 1068 on his return to England William moved north, garrisoned and strengthened Nottingham Castle, then proceeded to York and did likewise with its two castles, leaving behind a 500-strong garrison.[142]

By the end of that year Exeter, Warwick, York, Lincoln, Huntingdon, Cambridge and others had been taken.[143] In 1069 the king was beset on all sides. The Danes invaded Yorkshire; the English rebelled in the north, Malcolm, King of Scotland, aiding the insurgents; Dorset rose; and the Welsh made inroads across the marcher lands. William responded, hurrying north, diverting westward to deal with the Welsh, leaving the Counts of

Mortain and Eu to keep Yorkshire subdued. Once the Welsh were suppressed, he hurried east to Lincolnshire, and on reaching Nottingham was apprised of renewed Danish inroads at York. His second reduction of York was accompanied by wholesale devastation of lands and massacre of male inhabitants in the surrounding territory.[144] The land was wasted for a distance of 60 miles (96 km) around,[145] famine forced people to eat horses, dogs and cats, and even cannibalism was practised.[146] From York William crossed the Pennines in the depths of a particularly severe winter, even his own Normans threatening to mutiny. He occupied Chester and Stafford leaving garrisons in newly erected castles and by Easter in 1070 was celebrating at Winchester. The constant campaigns, and Norman atrocities, which drew condemnation from his own countryman Orderic Vitalis,[147] ensured William dominance in the wasted territories, but still other uprisings had to be quashed. East Anglia rose under Hereward who was joined by Earl Morcar, but the rising collapsed when William marched on Ely. Morcar was captured but Hereward escaped.[148]

From the above it is clear that horses were in great demand on an ongoing basis. *Servitium debitium* meant sizeable contingents came from the greater magnates, and a system of regular procurement was necessary. Horses would have continued to come in from Normandy. Shipping horses across the Channel was relatively easy after the experience of transporting over 2,000 horses for the invasion. However, it would not have been feasible to import all their needs from Norman studs. This points to many suitable horses being produced by the appropriated Anglo-Saxon studs, which we have seen were already of considerable importance. Warhorse breeding would have been undertaken in a major way, but there would never have been a surplus; veterinary science was primitive, fatal diseases were frequent, and the drain on youngstock as soon as the mounts reached riding age must have depleted reserves. Added to that the incessant campaigning, often in atrocious weather as shown above, would have taken its toll from injuries and mortalities, from natural hazards, and even by starvation in periods of winter campaigning over wasted territory. In 1085 William is recorded as having brought in the largest contingent ever of Breton and Norman foot and horse to repel a Danish incursion. Billeting them on his magnates meant the cost was evenly distributed, even if unwelcome. When the rumoured invasion did not materialize he shipped half his force back.[149]

The frequent imports by William and his magnates must have contributed to changing the horse used for war in England. With cavalry the major arm a certain stamp of horse was needed and augmentation of size with strength traits eagerly sought, though the peregrinations followed by military engagements needed a horse that was also tough, sound, reasonably speedy and certainly not too coarse, the latter type usually being prone to breakdown under sustained fast work. Wales already had a heritage of horse-breeding and it would appear that East Anglia also had a similar reputation. A manuscript written by the Mass priest Leofric, a contemporary of Hereward's, shows that the Fenland hero acquired a very swift mare named Swallow and her beautiful colt called Lightfoot from a breed raised on an island in the Fen country. Later he used the mare to effect his escape.[150] It was an ancient custom to drive livestock into fen pasture where there was a superior heritage of natural ley, on which animals do particularly well.

STEPHEN, 1135–54

After the strong reign of Henry I (1100–35) wars flared due mostly to the disastrous struggles for the throne between Henry's nephew Stephen, Count of Mortain, and Henry's daughter Matilda, whose chief ally was her half-brother, Roger, Earl of Gloucester. In addition, in early 1138 England was invaded by Scotland's King David whose army devastated Northumberland. Stephen answered, rapidly marching north with a large force of horse and foot, causing the Scots to withdraw into Roxburghshire. Instead of pursuing them he retaliated by laying waste territory north of the River Tweed, but was forced to withdraw because many knights refused to stay under arms, and his supplies were running out. He returned to the south, and recurrent Scottish depredations carried into Yorkshire.[151] Unable to leave the south where the Earl of Gloucester's adherents were in arms against him,[152] Stephen sent Bernard de Baliol north with a troop of knights to raise the northern nobility, and on 22 August 1138 at Northallerton Scots and English fought the battle of the Standard. Most of the knights on both sides dismounted and the horses were held at a short distance, the English mounts being so treated 'lest they should take fright at the shouting and uproar of the Scots'. With these imparked horses was the reserve troop of English cavalry.[153]

The various accounts concur that the knights dismounted to fight. There is no mention of the reserve English cavalry being used. Henry of Huntingdon asserts that Prince Henry of Scotland and a body of English and Normans fighting for the Scots had retained their horses and attacked the English, but could make no headway 'against men sheathed in armour and had to retire with wounded horses and shattered lances'.[154] Florence of Worcester states the English knights dismounted to fight; he is vague about the Scots, but infers that some at least were mounted as after the first onslaught the Scots either fell or fled in terror, and it was the fact that the English were all dismounted and their horses too far off for effective pursuit which made the Scots' flight possible. Out of 200 Scots mailed warriors only 19 retained their armour for the rest had thrown theirs away, and much spoil in Scottish armour and horses was taken by the English.[155] It would seem horses were used by both sides, but in very small numbers, and more by the Scots than the English. English losses were light, the numbers not stated, but the Scots lost heavily, from 10,000 to 11,000 according to all three chronicles.

On 2 February 1141 Stephen and Gloucester faced each other at Lincoln. Stephen had laid siege to the castle which had been illegally seized by the Earl of Chester, Gloucester's son-in-law. Stephen's own household knights were dismounted, but his forces formed two lines of active cavalry, constituted by the earls and their retinues. The rebel earls fielded a cavalry force comparable to Stephen's, but their infantry body was smaller. At the first clash the column of Stephen's forces in which were Earl Alan, the Earl of Mellent, Hugh, Earl of Norfolk, Earl Symon and the Earl of Warenne, was routed. The other column commanded by the Earl of Albemarle and William of Ypres charged and scattered the Welsh, and in turn was routed by the Earl of Chester's assault. Stephen's dismounted knights and infantry were assailed by the rebel cavalry and took heavy losses, the king continuing to fight with axe and sword until both had broken, leaving him defenceless. Captured, he was incarcerated in Bristol Castle.[156]

In the autumn of the same year the Bishop of Winchester rallied the barons who had fled the Lincoln battle and in turn Gloucester was captured on 14 September after continuing skirmishes. Each side now having a bargaining counter, both prisoners were liberated on 1 November.[157]

Gloucester, ever loyal to his sister, continually tried to overturn Stephen.[158] He was much concerned with acquiring horses, bringing in consignments from Normandy,[159] as well as purchasing several valuable animals while he was held in free custody at Rochester, and was later to find them 'both serviceable and beneficial' after his release.[160]

HENRY II, 1154–89

During the reign of Henry II the horse was even more indispensable. Henry had vast lands; he inherited Anjou from his father, and England and Normandy through his mother and maternal grandfather; acquired Aquitaine through his wife Eleanor; and took Brittany and

Maine under his rule. In governing these lands he put great emphasis on personal representation. When rebellion flared he was a master of the swift strike, rapidly bringing recalcitrant vassals to heel.[161] He made great use of well-trained infantry mercenaries, and when they were needed he called on large cavalry contingents.[162]

An energetic horseman, Henry loved hunting and hawking, and in order to exercise more eschewed riding on an ambling horse, instead riding one which trotted.[163] From Henry's time onwards we get better specific descriptions of horses in Europe.

In 1128 at his father Geoffrey's knighting 'the horses were drawn up, the arms brought and distributed to each as was appropriate. To the Angevin, a Spanish horse was led, marvellously bedecked and reputed to outstrip many birds as it ran. . . . Armed thus, our young soldier . . . set forth on his horse, wonderfully fleet and poised, and graceful in his speed.'[164] Geoffrey's marriage to Matilda, daughter of Henry I, was celebrated with a tournament in which Bretons fought Normans, the groom fighting with the Bretons who had a long history of expert horsemanship.[165] Unsurprisingly the Bretons won.[166]

In 1155 William Fitzstephen vividly described the horses at London's regular Friday Smooth Field (Smithfield) horse sale. Elegant palfreys, fast hackneys, powerful sumpters, warhorses and farmhorses, plus well-bred, unbroken colts, came under the hammer. The Palfreys ambled, hackneys trotted, and costly warhorses, larger than the rest, high-necked and large-haunched, but withal fast animals fit for a race, either as a group or as a pair matched one to one, fretted to be off. The sumpters also showed spirit. Farmhorse 'mares fit for the plough, some big with foal, and others with brisk young colts closely following them' were in another part of the fair.[167]

No doubt the mares' colts were intended as warhorses, fillies being used for farm work and breeding. The London Fair was reproduced in other major towns throughout England, and on the Continent the great fairs of France, Germany, Italy, etc., served a similar function. International horse-trading had a very long history, and English kings had frequent recourse to horse-dealers. Horses formed part of the merchandise of Spanish traders at least as far back as the twelfth century and were commonly found in English and Gascon ports.[168]

Henry had need of horses from all sources – dealers, tribute, stud farms, gifts, spoils – and each avenue of acquisition was utilized, as scattered references in various chronicles attest. How this was done is outlined in the pages of Robert of Torigny (also known as Robert de Monte). The whole of Henry's adult life was spent personally policing his vast territories, on three occasions raising armies for major campaigns – against Toulouse in 1159, Wales in 1165 and Ireland in 1171.

Before his accession to the English throne Henry had already given proof of his abilities. When his rights to lordship of Normandy, Anjou and Aquitaine were threatened by King Louis of France, who was aided by Henry's own brother Geoffrey among others, Henry marched from Barfleur with a large body of horse and foot intending to relieve his marcher castle of Neuf Marché, which was treacherously surrendered. Changing course he wasted the Vexin between the Rivers Andelle and Epte, reducing several castles – Baskerville, Chitrai, Etrepagne and La Ferte. Crossing the Seine at Meulan Louis marched to meet Henry who hastened to intercept him at Verneuil, but changed course and headed for Pacy sur Eure (near Evreux) where Louis was headed. So rapid was his march that many horses died and others were disabled as a result. Intimidated, Louis retired, after which Henry burned further rebel castles: Brueroles, Bonmoulins, and one in the region of Dreux. At the end of August he crossed into Anjou and laid siege to Mount Sorel (Montsereau) taking his brother's adherents prisoner and forcing Geoffrey to a reconciliation,[169] after first securing the surrender of Chinon, Loudoun and Mirebeau.[170]

This blitzkreig would have been impossible without horse-power, and herein lies what I consider the warhorse's most important role, even though the Frankish charge was the most

The Great Seal of King Henry I

The Great Seal of King Henry II

The Great Seal of King Henry III, showing improved detail and equine depiction

spectacular. However, without mileage references the horse's achievements mean little. A very rough computation allows us to appreciate them. Henry left Barfleur on 16 July 1151, and by the end of August was at the furthest reach of Anjou. In just over six weeks he had covered well over 400 miles (645 km) of direct travel, not allowing for the reduction and subsequent burning of seven castles, the surrender of three more, and the siege of Montsereau, with all the concomitant route diversions this entailed, plus foraging to gather supplies and cattle to feed his army. Considering this campaign was conducted at the hottest time of the year it is hardly surprising that several animals died and others were injured. Dehydration, azoturia and lameness would have been the main hazards.[171]

In 1169 the first phase of the Norman invasion of Ireland started, sparked off by an appeal in 1167 by Dermot Macmurrough, King of Leinster, to King Henry for help against Rory

O'Connor, King of Connacht, who was seeking to dispossess him. The Normans came in a series of five landings, three in 1169, and two more in 1170, totalling around 2,000 men, to which was added Dermot's own band of 500. The Normans were led by members of an interrelated group of lords from the Welsh marches: Robert Fitzstephen, Maurice Fitzgerald, de Prendergast, de Cogan, Raymond Fitzgerald de Carew, and Richard Fitzgilbert de Clare, Earl of Pembroke, known as Strongbow.[172] Strongbow is said to have had 200 knights and over 1,000 *others* – men-at-arms, archers and foot soldiers.[173] He married Dermot's daughter and obtained the promise of Leinster as the price of his aid, and when Dermot died in 1171 Henry moved quickly to prevent the Normans in Ireland from carving out their own independent kingdom. He landed at Waterford on 17 October 1171, with 500 knights and 4,000 men-at-arms and archers, a vast amount of equipment, provisions, siege engines, horses, arms and armour. But there was no fighting, Strongbow taking the diplomatic way out, submitting and doing homage to Henry for having Leinster returned as a fief. With such a well-equipped army on their territory the Irish also submitted.[174]

The horses taken into Ireland, of which there must have been well over 1,000 in all from the several landings, were an innovation. The Irish had never seen horses in 'iron harness' before.[175] From this it appears that those of the wealthier magnates wore mail bards, others probably had head and chest defences.

Giraldus Cambrensis describes the Irish horsemen and warriors:

when they are riding they do not use saddles or leggings or spurs. They drive on and guide their horses by means of a stick with a crook at its upper end which they hold in their hand. They use reins to serve both the purpose of a bridle and bit. It does not prevent [as it usually does] the horse from feeding on the grass. Moreover they go naked and unarmed into battle. They regard weapons as a burden and they think it brave and honourable to fight unarmed. They use, however, three types of weapons: short spears, two darts, and big axes well and carefully forged.[176]

Clearly Irish horsemen were natural riders and from the way the passage is phrased it would appear they fought as javelineers from horseback. The horses appear to have worn bitless bridles or hackamores with nasal control. Against heavy Norman cavalry the Irish had no chance, as the Ossorians found in 1169. The Normans brought them into the open, pursued them and cut them down.[177]

To counterbalance Strongbow's power in Leinster Henry installed Hugh de Lacy as his representative, giving him Meath as a fief and appointing him justiciar.[178] De Lacy's policy was fair. He enfeoffed his Norman followers with lands in Ireland, only dispossessing Irish when forced by circumstances; and he encouraged the peasantry back to their land.[179] Once when his army was out in force in Meath, presumably foraging, his men stole some corn from churches and a mill and Hugh ordered that it be returned. Two soldiers held back a small quantity of oats for their horses. 'One went mad and died that night having broken his head in the stable, while the other whose rider was scoffing at the others who through superstition had returned the corn, fell dead the following morning.'[180] Ergot poisoning, which causes encephalitis, commonly known as 'the blind staggers', in which horses go blind and in panic beat their heads against a wall, is the more likely reason for the deaths.[181]

Henry's militancy was also tempered with diplomacy and William Fitzstephen, a cleric with a good eye for pageantry and horseflesh, described the embassy Henry's chancellor Thomas Becket led to Paris in 1158 in which there were 50 draught horses, as large as chargers; 28 pack horses; 200 mounted knights whose horses were ceremoniously led by their shield-bearing squires; plus the mounted multitude of barons' sons, clerks, stewards and lesser servants, followed by the chancellor and his intimate friends.[182] In the inconclusive war against Toulouse Becket raised a force of 700 knights at his own expense and personally led it.[183] Fitzstephen's comment that the draught horses were as large as chargers is very helpful as it shows the draught horse of the era was anything but massive.

Horses formed part of princely gifts, Henry receiving presents loaded on camels and horses from the Moorish King of Valencia and Murcia in 1162.[184] In 1173 Raymond V finally did homage for Toulouse to Henry and his son Richard, Duke of Aquitaine, paying as annual tribute forty very valuable horses, plus the promise of supplying 100 soldiers for forty days' annual service if needed.[185] 'Very valuable horses' were certainly destriers, and constituted a considerable drain on the count's resources, either from stud farms or as direct purchases from dealers. Such a sizeable draft into the king's stable would have helped offset losses due to heavy and continuing usage.

In June of the same year King Louis accompanied by a huge force of 7,000 horse and a 'multitude of foot' besieged Verneuil, but withdrew when he heard Henry had countered by a rapid march to Breteuil, a scant 7 miles (11 km) away, ready to oppose him. Later that same year Henry conducted another of his lightning moves, this time against rebellious Breton barons, especially Ralph of Fougères. He first sent in his Brabançon mercenaries to ravage Fougères' lands, himself following, causing Ralph to flee, Henry's men taking huge spoils in abandoned horses and cattle. Meanwhile Ralph reached and took the strongholds of Combourg and Dol, his horse and foot opposing another group of Henry's Brabançons who routed Ralph's army, the horse taking to their heels, most of the foot being killed. Sixty horsemen unable to escape crowded into a tower in Dol, including Ralph and the Earl of Chester. Henry rode from Rouen to Dol in just over a day and erected his siege engines; before a shot was loosed the garrison surrendered, the rebel knights being sent to various castle prisons, though some stayed in 'open confinement' giving a sure promise not to escape.[186] From Rouen to Dol is over 150 miles (240 km). Shifting an army so fast was an outstanding achievement, though it must in this instance have been just Henry's immediate entourage.

In 1173 Henry was faced with armed conflict both in his Continental lands and in England. His sons were rebelling, and the eldest of them, another Henry, called 'the Young King', was backed by many magnates in England, with the heart of the rebellion at Leicester. Aided by the northern rebels headed by Roger de Mowbray, William I 'the Lion' of Scotland ravaged England as far as Yorkshire. He was driven back by Richard de Lucy, the king's representative, only to erupt again at Easter 1174.[187]

Jordan Fantosme, an eye-witness, writes that the Scottish king, with a band of 500 knights, was waiting for the rest of his army at Alnwick Castle. An English spy reported to a detachment of English knights stationed in a copse; among the English were Ralph de Glanville, Odinel de Humfreville, Lords de Vesci and d'Estuteville, and Bernard de Baliol. King William armed rapidly, mounted 'a horse which was not slow', and fought boldly, knocking his first assailant to the ground. He and his knights fought hard till a sergeant galloped up and rammed his lance into the king's grey horse, bringing both down. The dead horse pinned the Scottish king to the ground and he was captured by Ralph de Glanville along with other unfortunate Scottish knights. Great carnage was wrought among the Flemish mercenaries, lances and arrows flying on both sides, and even after the Scottish king had been captured the stubborn fighting and killing of Flemings carried on, for the English felt betrayed because the Flemings had fought for the Scots. Many Scottish knights were knocked to the ground from their horses, but rebel English knights Roger de Mowbray and Adam de Porz fled, fearing capture and punishment by King Henry.[188]

Of the Scottish captives Fantosme singles out the greatest:

Alan de Lanceles, old and valliant, defending himself on a grey warhorse was held for ransom.[189]

William de Mortimer, raging like a boar, striking out and in turn being captured by Bernard de Baliol, who struck him so hard he brought both horse and rider down . . .[190]

Raoul de Rus fought hard but so many came at him he had no option but to surrender.[191]

Richard Maluvel, who rode a very good horse, dealt heavy blows from the saddle, but when the warhorse was killed underneath him he was forced to surrender.[192]

So notable was Maluvel's horse that Fantosme says what a great pity it was that it was killed, and how sorry Maluvel was.

Of Scottish lords held for ransom William de Vesci had close to a hundred and Bernard de Baliol, Walter de Bolebec and Odinel de Humfreville likewise had a great number. The Scots were said to have more than a thousand badly wounded.[193] Although numbers are certainly inflated as customary, it would appear that the awaited reinforcements had begun to come up by the battle's end. The individual feats can be regarded as accurate since Fantosme states 'with my own two eyes I saw it',[194] referring to William being pinned under his horse and to his subsequent capture. Fantosme evidently knew his horses, singling out the notable ones, and in so doing highlighting their behaviour under battle pressure where they did not flinch from repeated blows to their riders, some of which must have landed on them. It also shows how important the knight's horse was to his safety. Once the horse had been felled, either temporarily bowled over, injured, or killed, the unhorsed knight had small chance of surviving except by surrender.

SIX

Muslim Armies and the Horse

Within the areas dominated by the Islamic faith there are no clear divisions between cavalry practices of successive Muslim peoples. The earlier Muslim incursions were characterized by Arab razzias, which were intensified once they had acquired sufficient horses to be able to strike and evaporate back into their deserts.

Plundering forays were also the hallmark of the early nomadic Seljuk Turkish raiders, made possible by the Turcoman and steppe horses on which their economy was largely based.[1] As the Seljuks took up permanent residence in Asia Minor and Syria, founding their principalities and kingdoms, the equestrian military aspect changed. Each petty ruler had his own permanent mounted *Askar*.[2]

The breed situation changed from the quality Turkmene and the steppe-bred pony, which Ibn Battuta refers to as mixed breeds or *Akadish* horses, to include horses from Arabia, which had become a major supplier of military mounts for Syria and India.[3] In addition there were the homebred horses of Syria.

Although in the era of the Seljuk Turks and the crusades, and throughout the later Mamlūk period, the Arabian was paramount, most Muslim cavalry did not aspire to the Faras but rode Berzaun (Berdhun) horses, according to Kemal al-Din El Damiri.[4]

ISLAMIC LAW AND THE WARHORSE

Islamic tradition and law concerning war booty go back to the time of the Prophet. They show in what esteem a horse of good breeding was held, and that he was regarded primarily as a warhorse. As such he was entitled to share in the booty taken in a jihad, or holy war. Booty was subdivided, a fifth going to the sovereign, four-fifths remaining.[5] According to the ninth-century historian Amr b. Bahr b. Mahbub Abu Othman al-Jahiz (Jahiz of Basra), a cavalryman was entitled to a double portion, an infantryman to a single.[6] A later text of 'Umar ibn Ibrahim al-Awsī al-Ansarī gives variations on the shareout drawn from two authors of Islamic law books: Abu Hanīfah agrees with Jahiz of Basra, but al-Shafi'ī awards the cavalryman three portions to the footsoldier's one.[7] The *Naceri* goes into detail mentioning the division of spoils; the rationalization behind the subdivision; the extenuating circumstances in which a horse was to be awarded his rightful share; and which horse was to be denied a portion. The division reflected the warrior's input, a cavalryman having more at stake in financial terms than an infantryman. Although the shares are noted above it was not always as clear-cut.

According to El Damiri the horse received two shares, the rider one, making the cavalryman's portion three parts,[8] which accords with al-Shafi'ī. A slightly different apportioning gave purebreds more than Hedjin partbreds.[9] Abou Bekr shows that the law was open to personal interpretation.[10] When spoils were being distributed in the time of Omar, the second caliph, Atik or Faras got two shares, Hedjin one, and Berzaun, also called Kauden, none. The reasoning was that the Faras or Atiks were swifter and better suited to a higher degree of training for war.[11] This shows that from the early days of Islam official encouragement was given to breeding excellent cavalry horses.[12]

The intricacies of booty allocation appear to be at the root of cavalry organization. Although a trooper fought 'for Islam', it gave him an incentive to place at risk himself and his valuable Faras, or his less valuable Hedjin or Berzaun, and the latter was usually rewarded (see below) according to worth. Religious fervour could hardly have operated across the board. Indeed, financial augmentation preceded the urge to Islamicize conquered territories.

The additional ramifications of Islamic law detail equestrian monetary insurance; under what circumstances recompense was due; and what other perquisites the cavalryman was entitled to. By the time Maqrizi and El Damiri were writing, the law had undergone considerable clarification, and the section relating to the horse had been expanded. His rider was entitled to the personal armour and weapons of any assailant he had killed in war, plus his horse, or the spare horse that was held in readiness by a servant. Not allowed were any non-military effects such as precious metals and jewellery. The recipient had to be a free man, past puberty, sound in mind, and to have taken an active part in the fighting. If either the trooper or his horse died prior to engaging the enemy, even if they had entered enemy territory, no payout was allowed.[13] This made it hard on the family of the trooper who died in service, but not in battle, particularly as his *iqta*, or land-grant, was then due for re-allocation. If a trooper's horse died prior to an engagement, but also in service, the trooper and indirectly his family and his farmer peasants suffered financially by having to find a replacement.

Once an engagement was under way, however, the trooper and his horse were entitled to recompense, which was given to:

all horses who participated in battle and were wounded or lamed as a result;
sick horses, provided there was hope of recovery so they could be used in future battles;
young horses who were fit to charge and could be used in an orderly retreat;
horses and/or their riders who became ill after and as a result of a battle.

The wording about shares is imprecise. Entire horses and mares received two portions and their riders the same. The Berzaun and Hedjin were likewise accorded booty. As there were separate clauses for these categories it would appear that entires and mares received a heavier share, the amount not being stated for Berzaun and Hedjin. The shares allotted to horses which had been given to the army, or hired for battle, were assigned to the warrior, not the donor or owner. If a warrior lost his horse in a pre-battle raid, or it was taken as booty by the enemy, the warrior who last used it in battle claimed the horse's share.[14]

Several points become clear about resources. Pure stock was more highly valued than common horses, from which it was not encouraged to breed. The stipulation about entires and mares receiving double portions suggests Hedjin and Berzaun, if male, were gelded. To donate horses specifically for war was a commendable deed, and augmented supply. Gift horses were maintained by the public treasury. If such a horse could not be taken to an official location it was sold and the proceeds used to buy arms. If the horse became insane, old, or infirm, and unsuitable for war use, it was sold and the proceeds used to replace it; if funds from such a sale were insufficient the money was added to the fund allocated for purchase of warhorses.[15] 'Insane' here probably meant a horse so nervous that he became uncontrollable, more than likely as a result of battle trauma. The above reveals that some warhorses were supplied by the state, although the bulk were owned by the warriors who rode them, or by their overlord.

MUSLIM CAVALRY

Cavalry constituted the greater part of the Muslim military. There were considerable differences in the composition of these forces. The Arabs continued to operate on a tribal basis providing irregular cavalry when needed. With the Ummayyad caliphate at Damascus, and their supplanters the Abbasids at Baghdad, there was a need for considerable horsed contingents. These were drawn from four sources: mercenaries, Mamlūks, Turcoman tribesmen and, to a lesser extent, members of indigenous populations. Units from defeated enemies were enlisted, as well as Islamicized freedmen of the Muslim conquerors.[16]

The most notable Muslim cavalry were the Mamlūks who were purchased as slaves and after military training, and conversion, freed to serve in the Muslim army. Turkish tribesmen were preferred because of their innate skill in and love of fighting, allied to a natural ability as expert horsemen. The first recorded instance of Mamlūks in the Umayyad caliphate was that 'Abdallah b. al-Isbahani of Basra, the commander of the right wing of Mu'sab b. al Zubay's forces in his war against al-Mukhtar, had 400 Mamlūks.[17]

Iranians from Khorasan settled in the Arab military towns especially Basra and Kufa, and served the caliphate. Under al-Mansur (745–75) the Mamlūks became the main military power of the Abbasids. After Islam's conquest of Transoxania, recruitment escalated, followed by a massive flow of Turkish Mamlūks into Baghdad as the Muslims penetrated Turkish tribal lands. They were shortly to supplant the Khorasanian element.[18]

Jahiz of Basra comments on both the Khorasanis and Turks in Abbasid armies, and gives valuable insights into their value as cavalry, along with some of their training methods. As Jahiz (776–869) enjoyed a high position in Baghdad[19] under the early Abbasids he was well placed to judge, even though he is very biased towards the Turks.

THE KHORASANIS

Delivered as a Khorasani boast, we learn of assistance given the new Abbasid caliphs by Khorasani cavalry which considered itself far superior to the army of Syria.[20] Long-haul cavalry expeditions were Khorasanis' forte when mounted on their superb 'Shihry steeds'.[21] Khorasan was well placed for a direct influx of horses of Turkmene blood. Horse-trainers from Balkh were held in high esteem, although Abou Bekr claims they had learned their trade from the Arabs via the Muslim conquest of Khorasan.[22] Even with this proviso it is clear Khorasani horses must have been of high calibre to have merited a history of excellence in both training and breeding. They were 'vigorous, beautiful to look at, with solid hard hooves, but rather short in the forehand part'.[23] This can only mean deficient in having an upright rather than the ideal sloping shoulder. When Khorasan was part of the Persian and later Sassanian empires it also boasted the huge Nesaean breed, as well as horses of neighbouring Ferghana which were recorded as standing 16 hh high.[24] One of these massively built Nesaean chargers is shown on the Sassanian rock carvings at Tāq-i-Bōstān depicting King Chosroes II (c. AD 620). The horse, Shabdiz, has his head protected with a chamfron, and his neck and complete forehand down to mid-cannon bones covered in what appears to be a double-layered barding. The top layer is of lammellar armour.[25]

Although pictorial evidence of horse armours of the early Muslim period is lacking and literary evidence is scant till we have John of Plano Carpini's description of armour made in Persia under the Mongols in the thirteenth century, it appears Khorasan was arming its horses to a limited degree in the eighth and ninth centuries. Jahiz comments on stirrups, breastplates and felt armour possessed by Khorasani cavalry. Although this armour was not specifically stated as intended for the horse its link with the horse's equipment implies this. Cavalrymen's armour was described in an earlier section. They were clad in mail coats and armed with spear, sword, dagger, axe and battle-axe, though the last two were carried *en route* on pack animals.[26] Khorasan and Ispahan were noted as the main centres for armour manufacture in Persia. Timur is reputed to have moved all the steel workers from Damascus to Khorasan in 1401.[27] Persia, Parthia and Sassanian Persia had been foremost in arming horses and in the expert use of heavy cavalry, which suggests the practice continued unbroken, even if the degree of arming fluctuated. The use of stirrups at this early date implies Khorasani technological superiority and efficiency in mounted warfare at a time when they were still unusual.

Cavalry training outlined by Jahiz shows that many practices which were used by the much later Mamlūk sultanate armies of Egypt and Syria had already been instituted. Formalized training included practice in a charge of lancers and a return to the attack after (simulated) flight. Mounted wargames included Dūbbūq, which must equate with the later Mamlūk gourd game; leaping on horses, presumably from all angles and at speed in full military kit, as it is mentioned as being practised by the young; and later, when adult, participating in polo. 'Throwing at the bird at rest, and at targets and at the bird of prey on the wing' is a reference to mounted archery skills.[28]

THE TURKS

The greater part of Muslim armies were made up of Turks who were superlative horsemen. Crusaders used the appellation 'Turk' for all their Muslim enemies regardless of ethnic background.

The Ghuzz (Oghuz) federation of twenty-four tribes living on the borders of Afghanistan by the seventh century had migrated from the Altai mountain region. In the early eighth century, at the time of the Arab invasion, and when the Oghuz had gained control of Central Asia and reached Samarkand, they became known as Turks. The Seljuk Turks formed one of these tribes and were named after an ancestor, Seljuk.[29] Humayd b. 'Abdulhamid, a general of the Caliph Ma'mun (813–33), listed their military qualities; foremost among them, showing what importance the Abbasid generals placed on good cavalry, were their equestrian feats.

The Turk trained his horse to run straight, swerving aside only on command.[30] Above all he strove to instil confidence in his horse so it would co-operate in the thick of the fighting. The Turk was feared in a charge, being skilled above others as a lancer, but his forte was as a mounted archer. Humayd admired the Turks' ability to shoot accurately at the gallop. They performed equally well on the flat, uphill, or down a steep slope, either in an attack or a feigned retreat.[31] When one considers the great strength needed to draw a bow on horseback, the draw-weight of which could be well in excess of 60 lb (27 kg), and sometimes up to 100 lb (45 kg), and that such a bow frequently had to be braced on horseback,[32] a Turkish archer's expertise is highlighted.

A weapon common among nomadic tribes was the lasso, which the Turks wielded adroitly, snaring enemy rider, horse, or both in a single throw.[33] Unfortunately Humayd does not expand on lasso technique. As Turkish saddles lacked a horn for anchorage one is left

Turkish cavalry pursue fleeing civilians (British Library, Add. MS 18866, f. 122b)

wondering how the rope was secured. At colt and cattle roundups in the New Forest in Hampshire New Foresters attach the rope round their horses' necks and it is effective enough for any restraint needed.[34] Roping success, apart from accuracy, depends on the snatch technique that snares an enemy (or animal) catching him unawares, to prevent his bracing against it. A roping horse must be trained to stop rapidly.

The relationship between a Turk and his personal mount was very close. He raised and trained it from foalhood, so it came when called. He administered necessary veterinary treatment and was skilled in getting it fit for the long hours it was expected to endure under saddle. Humayd comments that in his lifetime a Turk spent more time in the saddle than on the ground. Both stallions and mares were used in war, and in hunting game for food. If his hunter was a mare her colt tagged along,[35] gaining vital practice in negotiating tricky going and exercising muscles, heart and lungs.[36] If the hunt failed the Turk either milked a lactating mare, or bled a horse for nourishment. Spare horses accompanied him so he could spell them and avoid overstressing any one animal. Long marches did not unduly fatigue him or his horse, although he would ride a horse to death if necessary. The horses best suited to such endurance were noted as 'Thoroughbreds', which were far superior to any other horse possessed by cavalry nations. The use of the word 'Thoroughbred' in the translation is unfortunate; it means the best breed, which would mostly have been Turkmene or Turanian horses. Turkish horses of the Abbasid period were especially enduring when faced with intense heat or cold.[37] All these qualities blended into a mount fit for a warriror to be feared, especially as the Turk did not have the 'soft spot' of sedentary peoples with a home to protect, and therefore needing to split forces into defensive and offensive sections. Plunder was the Turk's aim. If the odds were unfavourable Turks would retire as a body without wasteful fighting.[38] The Turkish cavalryman was self-sufficient, adept at crafting his own horse's tack and his archery equipment. On a raid he carried armour, tack and weapons, which included as many as three bows of different types with strings to match each, lances which were of the short, hollow, lighter and more deadly type than the longer weapons used by other units of cavalry, and lassos.[39]

Khorasani and Turkish cavalry were much in demand by the Abbasids as crack fighting forces even though at first most generals were Arabs.[40] Turkish cavalry held its high position beyond the medieval period as a succession of horsemen poured into Persia, Anatolia, Egypt, the Levant and eventually much of Europe with the three major Turkish explosions: the Seljuks, the Mamlūks and the Ottomans.

THE SELJUKS

The Seljuks were allies of the Saminids who held territory in Persia, Transoxiana and Afghanistan during the tenth and early eleventh centuries. Under Israil, elder son of Seljuk, they aided the Saminids in 1003 in their war with the Karakhanids and were rewarded with grazing rights in Khorasan. Once entrenched they began to exhibit territorial ambitions. Israil claimed he could raise 100,000 archers by sending an arrow, and double that number by sending a bow, among his people. Mahmud of Ghazna, neighbour of the Saminids, in response to a growing Seljukid threat invaded Israil's territory in 1025 but failed to take his counsellors' advice to amputate the thumbs of all male Seljuks.[41] In retaliation Israil crossed the Oxus and invaded Ghaznavid lands but was temporarily repulsed. When the Saminid shah withdrew the Seljuks' grazing concession in Khorasan the Seljuks were spurred into carving out their own empire. In a subsequent attack on Ghazna they were victorious. By 1034 they controlled Khorasan. Under Tüghrül Beg, nephew of Israil and first of the Great Seljuk Sultans, the Seljuks crushed the Ghaznavids at the battle of Dandarqan in 1040 and began their inroads into western territories. Dandarqan was the first of a series of victories that carried the Seljuks across Persia, Iraq, Syria and Asia Minor. By 1043 Tüghrül had moved his capital to Merv. His brother Cagri Beg and his half-brother Ibrahim also conquered territory for themselves east of the Tigris, Hamadan and the Jebel. Ibrahim consolidated his hold on north-west Persia and in 1045, with Oghuz allies, invaded Armenia and raided Byzantine territory. The Seljukid movement pressed westwards. Tüghrül moved his capital to Rayy (Teheran), and in 1055, accompanied by his nephew Alp Arslan, Cagri's son, he took Baghdad. Although Tüghrül nominally upheld the Abbasid caliphate in its religious aspect all temporal power was now in Seljuk hands.

Alp Arslan succeeded Tüghrül in 1063 and continued rapid Seljuk expansion, capturing Herat, conquering Djand, restoring order in Fars and Kirman, and taking Mecca, Medina and Aleppo. Turkish domination now ran from Afghanistan to Egypt.

Byzantine border territories continued to be at the mercy of Turkish horsemen whose plundering raids were highly organized with men mustering at a focal point, splitting into four equal sections, each facing one point of the compass, and advancing to designated points, where each division split three ways so that the whole army could then fan out and advance on a wide sweep, pillaging and destroying everything in its path. The retreat, laden with booty, was as orderly as the advance.

The years after Alp Arslan's accession were marked by almost annual incursions into Byzantine lands:

1064   Ani was attacked, Antioch and Edessa pillaged.
1065   Incursions were resumed into Asia Minor.
1067   Caesarea was stormed, Byzantine armies defeated at Levitane and Sebaste.
1068   Turkish efforts were concerted into breaking into the heart of Byzantium.
1069   Turks broke through and reached Iconium (Konya).
1070   Turkish forces reached the Aegean.
1071   The Turkish victory at the battle of Manzikert gave them access to the whole of Asia Minor.

After Manzikert a 50-year truce was concluded between Byzantium and the Seljuks. Byzantium paid a heavy ransom for Diogenes and was forced to guarantee Byzantine soldiers for Seljuk forces when demanded.[42]

Alp Arslan was succeeded by Malik Shah (1072–92) as Sultan of Persia. In the north-western sector of Seljuk territory Suleyman, a cousin once removed of Alp Arslan, made it clear to incoming Turcoman tribesmen that the Seljuks were their overlords.[43]

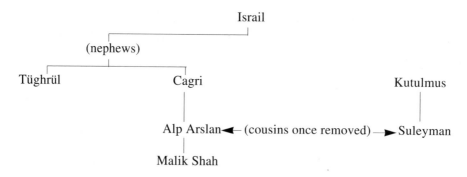

Michael VII Parapinaces (1071–8) succeeded to the Byzantine throne, and the empire was now beset by Turks and by Roussel of Bailleul, a Norman in Byzantine pay who reneged on his contract and with his independent mercenaries, and help from Suleyman, carved out a territory for himself in Anatolia in 1073.[44] Meanwhile Tutush, Malik Shah's brother who reigned as first of the Syrian Seljuks, entered Anatolia on a razzia but was bribed by Alexius Comnenus, then Byzantine commander-in-chief, to seize Roussel and hand him over.[45] The next decade was beset with Turkish raiding. The Turks gained control of land between the Black Sea and the Hellespont, and large tracts of the eastern provinces.[46] These raids continued into the early reign of Alexius I (1081–1118) who also had to contend with Robert Guiscard. Under Suleyman, who was camped near his capital, Nicaea, Turks raided as far as the Bosphorus until Alexius mobilized retaliatory forces. Eventually the two sides negotiated, the River Drakon being designated the border between Byzantines and Turks.[47] In his wars against Guiscard and his son Bohemond, Alexius now numbered Turkish mercenary horse archers among his troops.[48]

In 1086 Suleyman, taking advantage of Byzantium's weakness in which a rebel Armenian, Philaretos, had assumed power in Byzantine Antioch, took the city with the connivance of Philaretos' son.[49] This enraged Tutush who also coveted Antioch to add to Aleppo, Jerusalem and lands stretching as far as Mesopotamia and Baghdad. In the ensuing battle Suleyman was defeated and committed suicide. Another round of Turkish depredations started in the eastern sector of the empire as Abul Kasim, left in control by Suleyman, proclaimed himself sultan and raided Bithynia and as far as the Propontis. He was seized at the instigation of the Persian Sultan Barkiyaruk (1092–4) and strangled.[50]

Seljuk razzias had given them mastery over huge territories ruled by the Great Seljuks of Persia. Tüghrül, Alp Arslan and Malik Shah consolidated the Seljuk Empire. But even in Malik Shah's reign it started to fragment, and different branches ruled in Persia, Syria, Iraq and Rum.

On the eve of the crusades the Seljuks were warring among themselves. Tutush of Syria contested with Malik Shah's son Barkiyaruk for overall supremacy by marching into Khorasan. Meanwhile Aq Sunqur of Aleppo and several other Turkish generals conspired against Tutush in his absence, forcing him to return to Syria where in May 1094 he routed Aq Sunqur and the generals and executed them. He returned to Khorasan and was killed at Rayy fighting Barkiyaruk on 26 February 1095. In Syria Tutush's sons Duqaq and Ridwan fought for their father's territory.[51] In addition to the fragmenting of Tutush's Syrian possessions, Oghuz tribesmen made plundering inroads into Mesopotamia and Diyar Bakr. Many had formerly served in Tutush's forces, but now founded principalities of their own.[52] Ridwan held Aleppo; Duqaq Damascus and fiefs in Diyar Bakr and Mesopotamia; Yaghi Siyan Antioch; Il Ghazi succeeded his father Ortuq as governor of Jerusalem. In Rum the sultan was Kilij Arslan, Suleyman's son. Syria was in turmoil: internecine warfare, plots, counterplots and alliances made to be broken. Emirs appointed by rulers to govern towns frequently rebelled against their overlords.[53]

Had the Turks been united in purpose the First Crusade might well have been repulsed. Alexius had had some military and diplomatic successes against the Turks,[54] but the Franks delivered the first serious foreign setback to Turkish forces.

Nicaea, Kilij Arslan I's capital, was besieged by the Frankish armies in May 1097, and according to Anna Comnena they committed disgusting atrocities on the outlying population.[55] Throughout the *Alexiad* whenever Anna comments on the Franks it is usually with extreme distaste, and although she refers to Turks as barbarians she held the crude Europeans in still greater dislike.

In a letter reputedly sent by Kilij Arslan to Nicaea help was promised, the garrison told not to fear the Christians because 'due to the long journey and without horses to bear the weight of battle' the Franks 'cannot equal our strength with fresh forces'.[56]

In the event Kilij Arslan's forces were no match for the Franks. Turkish tactics needed room to manoeuvre and were not suited to close fighting on the limited field outside Nicaea, and the sultan withdrew. Losses had been heavy on both sides. Nicaea eventually surrendered on the night of 18 June, the day before an assault was to be launched.[57] A week later the Franks marched for Antioch, via Dorylaeum. The army had split, one section under Bohemond, the other 2 miles (3.2 km) away under Raymond of St Gilles.[58] The reason for the force's splitting is not clear. William of Tyre says it was possibly accidental,[59] but as the whole area had been devastated by constant Turkish raids forage was scarce and only to be had in widely separated pockets.[60] A huge amount of forage was needed, for warhorses, riding horses and pack animals, the latter group probably outnumbering the total of the first two. Even more important was the need for water and, not often considered, for salt, vital in hot climates where sweating causes heavy salt and trace element losses. The warhorses suffered more from the hot waterless conditions. When water and food, particularly the former, were found the horses gorged themselves and perished.[61] These statements show that the heavier-fleshed warhorses, probably overweight for the conditions they were expected to operate in, were more susceptible than tougher baggage stock. Deaths from gorging would have been due to colic, and possibly crippling laminitis. Bohemond's division had been lucky and camped in the Gorgon valley where there was running water and good pasture. On 1 July Kilij Arslan appeared, allegedly at the head of 200,000 horse. This wild exaggeration is partly to emphasize the success of Christian forces against overwhelming odds, and partly because Turkish tactics, which relied on constant mobility, prevented an accurate tally and numbers must have appeared greater than they were.[62]

Frankish horses and men fell in droves. The Franks made repeated charges with lances, and closed with swords, at which the Turks 'opened their ranks', deceiving the Franks who returned to their own lines, upon which Turkish arrow fire recommenced and continued till the Franks were weakened. Then the Turks closed in with swords, driving the Franks back to their own camp. What looked like a Turkish victory in the making was suddenly reversed: a messenger had got through to Raymond of St Gilles who arrived with a body of knights to the rescue. Kilij Arslan, apparently, was unaware of the splitting of the Christian forces. Bohemond returned, the combined forces putting the Turks to flight. They were harried for 3 or 4 miles (5 or 6.5 km) during which the Franks slaughtered many. The booty was huge, among it many pack animals, asses, camels and horses.[63]

THE EQUESTRIAN ELEMENTS

The Turks opening their ranks to let the Frankish horses pass through shows the essential difference in equestrian usage. Once committed to a charge the Frankish animal could not be turned easily, unlike Turkish horses. Abou Bekr has some deprecating remarks on the clumsy European warhorse. The equestrian methods were totally different. The European trooper was not used to tactics that needed a light-moving, nimble horse, hence he never trained his mount to manoeuvre quickly. It is safe to suggest his animal was lumbering along on the forehand, incapable of responding to a sudden change of course, or a rapid stop. Turkish tactics depended on light-moving horses working off their hocks and able to manoeuvre rapidly in any direction. A glimpse at the Arabs of the Nefud and their Arabian warhorses of the nineteenth century, in which they were used in lance warfare, much as their medieval counterparts were used, is useful:

> in fighting with the 15 to 20 foot [4.5 to 6 m] lance a rider's life depends on his [horse's] quickness. It must be able to gallop full tilt at a blank wall and stop dead in its stride. It must be able to spin around on its hocks and start away again like a rocket to a turn of the wrist, for the rider has no second hand to spare. An awkward change of leg may cost him his life. That the Arabian horse does not break down under this training is the greatest tribute to its soundness. The wonderful breaking of the horses in doubling and turning has been commented on with amazement by every traveller.[64]

Weight for weight the Frankish charge *en masse* with larger, heavier, but not massive, horses told over the Seljuks' lighter-moving Turkmene and Arab horses. For an example that can be readily applied to the crusading era modern weights are given below. Although certain breeds have increased in size due to good nutrition allowing an animal to reach its genetic potential, *basic* sizes of certain older breeds have not radically changed. The Arabian Purebred Registry admits *no outcross whatsoever*. The size has therefore remained constant within the breed, although different strains do have slightly different heights and builds, notably the Muniqidh for greater height.

A European horse of the crusading era would have ranged from 15 to 15.2 hh and been of medium to heavy build, weighing in the region of 1,200 to 1,300 lb (545 to 590 kg) with some considerably lighter. The Turkmene horses would have weighed 800 to 900 lb (360 to 400 kg) with a similar height range, tending to the lower height, and the Arabians would have been smaller, well under 15 hh, and weighing around 700 to 800 lb (315 to 360 kg). Of course some animals in all categories would have been smaller, some larger, but these weights are taken from the size of the respective well-fed types today. My 15 hh Arabian stallion Nizzolan weighed around 840 lb (380 kg) when in endurance condition. His coarser built stable companion Katchina at 14.3 hh weighs considerably more. My Granicus, a part-bred Arabian cross Standardbred, weighs 1,300 lb (590 kg), stands 16.1 hh and is much larger than sire or dam. Bearing in mind the preference for heavier-fleshed animals in the western sphere, and the lighter-framed and -fleshed Turkish/Arabian horses, and that this preference crosses the centuries as noted by Abou Bekr in the early fourteenth, Bertrandon de la Brocquière in the fifteenth, and Lady Anne Blunt in the late nineteenth centuries, suggests it applied to the era under discussion.[65] In the ensuing wars Turkish and European equestrian practices were constantly put to the test, although the European cavalry ceased to be mounted on purely European stock and became more and more dependent on Turkish, Syrian and Egyptian animals, either purchased, stolen, or won as spoils.

SELJUK LAND-GRANTS

Land-grants had equestrian connotations. Most were intended as a reward for service and as a means of maintaining the holder and his military following. In the Seljuk period *Iqtas* took the form of land or revenue and varied considerably. An *Iqta* could be a whole province, its revenues granted to the great Amir appointed as its governor, or a smaller grant from which the holder collected the taxes, sending a designated portion to the treasury and retaining the balance. Under the Seljuks the system was militarized, the holder administering the district, retaining the income, but owing service in the sultan's army when called on. The number of cavalrymen required depended on the size of his *Iqta*.[66]

TURKISH HORSE SUPPLY

The work of Abou Bekr describes the remounts available to the Mamlūk sultanate which had inherited a sound equestrian system from the Ayyubid era, even if under the Mamlūks it was to reach new heights of excellence. This information is therefore relevant to the period under discussion as equestrian changes occur slowly.

In addition to the Faras, Hedjin, Berdhun, Berber and Turkmene horses, other breeds are noted with their geographical distribution and physical attributes. Faras from the Hejaz were known for beauty, good feet and limbs; those of the Nejd for superior conformation – a long neck, large shoulders, full belly, strong thighs and fine limbs; those of the Yemen for a heavy body, thick legs, pointed shoulders, slender flanks and short neck, i.e. coarser bone but a rather angular frame. Horses from the Jezira had excellent hindquarters, large shoulders and forelimbs. Many horses from this area were either of pure, or heavily infused with, Arabian blood. The horses of Barqa were heavy-bodied, fleshy-chested, big-headed and thick-legged, and had huge feet. Egyptian horses which were plentiful, had a long neck, weak limbs, long pasterns, big feet and an ungraceful (i.e. weak) chest. The Berber or Maghrebin horse had a strong neck, thick legs, round knees and cannons (lower limbs). Most Berber horses exhibited a proud disposition but lacked wide, large nostrils.[67] The superior Berber resembled the Arabian due to heavy infusions of Arabian blood. The indigenous Berber mountain stock was known for its toughness, endurance and economy in keeping. It had a ram, or convex, head, and a sloping croup which assists balance in tricky going. It was shorter-coupled than the Arabian, which itself has fewer vertebrae than most breeds.[68] Yemen was a major supplier of horses. Unfortunately this supply was virtually, but temporarily, wiped out in AD 1327/8 (AH 728) by epizootic diseases.[69] The Chahri from Khorasan was a good warhorse. It was noted for toughness, not feeling wounds or severe bits. It also had such a vicious disposition that it behoved a fallen rider to be on guard against it. On the credit side it could be used to fight for its rider with hooves and teeth. According to Abou Bekr's warning the horse 'was very risky to approach'.[70]

Other points Abou Bekr made reflected purely superficial looks. Those I have drawn on indicate the types of conformation that would have an effect in general, and particularly in war. They indicate the Faras were superior; the Egyptian horse was a bit of a 'weed'; the Barqa was clumsy but up to weight, and the indigenous Berber was also stocky and proud, but lacked an efficient respiratory tract for sustained speed. The Barb has been noted as having a short burst of speed, but it can keep going indefinitely at a steady pace.

TRAINING OF HORSE AND RIDER

Surviving written instruction for cavalrymen comes from the fourteenth and fifteenth centuries, but the methods were of long standing, and indeed have stood the test of time as the recommendations for basic training are still relevant today. Ibn Hodeil gives clear instructions on riding techniques. He advises progression while riding bareback from walk to a slow trot, to a faster trot, then to a very slow canter, then a faster canter, and finally into a full gallop. He recommends the faster canter only when the rider has an independent seat and no need to assist seat retention by hooking the feet under the horse's elbow joint.[71] Once riding a saddled horse the rider was expected to maintain contact with the stirrup tread throughout all mounted exercises. Abou Bekr recommends placing a coin between tread and boot sole.[72] Any horse destined to be used for lance work was to be galloped only on short stretches.[73] No doubt this was to ensure the horse could erupt explosively to lend poundage to the thrust instead of dissipating speed in a long-drawn-out gallop.

Several points relevant to warhorse training are applicable to all cavalry in the pre-firearm era. Warhorse selection entailed choosing a well-trained animal devoid of natural vices and acquired performance faults. Of the latter, two to be assiduously avoided were, first, the horse who violently threw his head when under restraint, or indeed at any time while being ridden, as it posed an enormous threat to its rider especially in battle.[74] Mishaps included bloody noses and smashed front teeth. The second was the horse who 'places his lower jaw against the chest and pulls on the bridle', for 'there is no means of correcting this fault'.[75] Now we would describe this as grossly overbent, and such a horse, particularly if he has a strong neck, is almost unstoppable by normal means, and can be extremely dangerous to its rider. The warhorse must also be responsive enough instantly to answer the rider who found himself disadvantaged in battle or mock exercises by lance butts or sabre threats, so that the horse could help the rider regain his own bodily control.[76]

The charger had to be trained to move absolutely straight, and a rider was cautioned to take a central position in the saddle as this influenced the horse's movement; a crooked mover was impossible to direct in battle, and also impossible to cure once the habit was ingrained.[77] A vital requirement for a warhorse was that he was trained to wait while being mounted, and for the office to move off, and if the rider was thrown in battle the horse must wait to be remounted.[78] Lady Anne Blunt describes the age-old method used by the bedouin for teaching his mount to stand in battle. He tied the *reshmeh* (halter) rope to his hand and practised throwing himself off the horse again and again. At first the horse would drag him, but eventually it learned to stand and wait to be remounted.[79]

The pace that trainers of warhorses paid great attention to was the *bein el chiddein*, described by Abou Bekr as the strong gallop, between a racing gallop and slow canter, and the pace used in jousting charges, and what he terms *Naroud* between the battle fronts.[80] This is the hand gallop, a pace with much impetus but also with the horse well under control and able to manoeuvre at a touch from the rider. The *Naroud* was presumably the display sometimes resorted to by individuals, or small groups, to incite and/or impress the enemy.

A habit to be guarded against was the horse that in mid-gallop did a volte-face and ran back. Only a few would escape danger, and the likelihood was that they would land among weapon-wielding enemy,[81] presumably as the result of being harried.

Tact was needed in pushing a horse on and a cavalryman was warned not to rely solely on heels because when armoured the horse would not feel them, and if that was the only method of pushing him on he would refuse to budge.[82] Instead willing forward movement lay in the early training so that the horse linked being ridden with following the groom who led him in the early stages.[83] To accustom the colt to wearing armour he was introduced to a cloth cover before arming for war.[84] Some horses do panic a little when first blanketed. The noise of armour on a severely agitated horse could have resulted in an equine explosion and rendered the scared horse unfit for future armoured service. Other sensible advice was given about being careful not to scare a horse with a whip. If it was necessary to reprimand him, this was to be done lightly on the shoulder, otherwise he might react when a cavalryman used sword, lance, or bow, seeing it as a threat to himself.[85] If a whip is used on the shoulder, the horse need not see it coming; used on the flank, he will. The result could cause a charger to deviate from straight movement and the Mamlūk would miss his target.

It can be seen from the above that basic training for war was thorough. Abou Bekr commented that a rider could not achieve safety on an ill-trained mount and that if he did not personally train his charger he courted death.[86]

At the end of his lengthy instruction on training the Arabian horse for racing and war, Abou Bekr concludes with the Arab view of the European warhorse, its rider and its training, or lack of it. He praises the energy and courage of 'barbarians', by which he means Europeans, but deplores their lack of skill, noting that if they wish to move their horses they need a great space to do so, and that once moving can use the horse only in a shock charge lacking all skill and manoeuvrability. He notes that they ride without spurs or a goad because they do not know how to use them properly, and because of long stirrups they have a bad seat on a horse. He claims foreign horses (i.e. non-Arabian) needed harsher handling and a change of bridle, but eventually with schooling could be taught Arab skills.[87]

This is a very revealing passage and I must concur with much of what is said. It was not mere Muslim/oriental deprecation of occidental practices. Well-schooled Arabian horses are very nimble and courageous, and many, far too many alas, cold- or warm-blooded horses trained by certain insensitive riders are clumsy in the extreme and do need that large space to manoeuvre. At the root of the difference in war lay the contrast between the steppe and bedouin traditions and natural ability, and the European 'have a bash' system of riding. In the Levant during the crusades the Christians must have learned far more sophisticated techniques, as they would have found the more intelligent oriental horse either had them over a barrel or became unridable if they used punishingly crude methods and thereby provoked the horse into rebellious behaviour. This is implied by Abou Bekr when he says the 'barbarian' rides as above unless he is skilled at suppling a horse and has the energy (i.e. the brains) to ride Arabian horses.[88]

HORSE ARMOUR AND ORIENTAL HORSEMANSHIP

Several references to horse armour appear in this chapter, but most surviving evidence for the horse armour of the period is from the later years. Most oriental cavalry was of light horse divisions and did not caparison its horses. However, from the early days of the Parthians and Sassanian Persians orientals had been supplying their heavy horse with protective equipment. As has been mentioned elsewhere, Persia had the highest reputation for making armour of all types, and throughout the period most horse armours that were used were similar to each other whichever army they came from. This is not surprising because good armourers were in demand and produced their distinctive styles wherever they worked. The territories the Muslim armies fought over would have produced a steady supply of all types of armour, horse equipment included, as spoils of the battles that punctuated the periods of unrest.

Trainee cavalrymen were advised to gain a sound knowledge and practice of equitation; to ride in attack and retreat; and to gain control of a horse's head with the bridle, etc., until all aspects became second nature to him. The best method was to take instruction from masters in the art of lancing. From them also the cavalryman could learn sword- and mace-play.[89]

The key phrase in the above is 'to gain control of the horse's head'. This is not as easy as it sounds. Horses have many ways of avoiding such control, two of which have already been mentioned – head-tossing, and becoming overbent. Others include opening the mouth against the bit; for this the Arab horseman used a *hakamah*, which was made of iron and went over the nose and under the lower jaw.[90] This acted like a Roman psalion or a modern drop noseband, and helped keep the mouth shut. Some horses are one-sided in the mouth, drifting to one side, and keeping them straight is difficult. Most Arab bitting was harsh and basically of the curb variety; nevertheless it could and should have been used with tact, which Abou Bekr points out was the ideal attainment of the trainee cavalryman.[91]

Two Mamlūk horsemen whose lance-heads are between each other's shoulder-blades (British Library, Add. MS 18866, f. 97a)

Once the trainee had acquired this head control he could direct his horse and start learning the lance exercises. For this he needed a lance with a good, strong, flexible stock, thick enough for the hand to encircle it comfortably with the fingers meeting the palm. Its head was to be of iron with good penetrative qualities; its weight as light as possible as this improved the lancer's performance.[92]

To mount, the trainee held the lance in the right hand, resting the butt a little way to one side (of the horse), placed the foot in the stirrup and mounted using the lance to lean on. Once seated the rider was to turn the lance quickly over the horse's croup and grasp it in the right hand. Care was to be taken, once mounted, not to rest the lance butt on the ground because a fidgeting horse could step on it and damage or break the weapon.[93]

Ibn Hodeil advised couching the lance under the arm and holding it with sufficient of the stock behind the rider to make it easy to carry and use.[94] But there were many other ways to hold and use it, including using it like a javelin but without actually casting it; holding it above the head and looking from beneath it to strike a blow; resting it horizontally on the shoulder, the shaft braced against the cheek; holding it in the hand, leaning forward and using the horse's neck as protection; two-handed across the horse's neck, in the style of the Sarmatian *contus*; or two-handed with the lance along the right side of the horse's neck. Styles had been influenced by many countries with a history of horsemanship – Arabia with the bedouin two-handed method; Syria, Khorasan and even Europe with the couched lance.[95]

ARCHERY

Once his equitation was of a sufficiently high standard the horse archer still had much to learn about riding and shooting. Taybugha gives a detailed chapter on shooting from horseback.

The archer had extra aids to his horse's tack in the form of a martingale, or *sirifsar*.[96] This prevented the horse throwing his head and disrupting his rhythm which would have destroyed the archer's aim. The reins were shortened by means of a knot; they could then be slipped over the pommel. To the spare length a folded strap was attached, and a very thin thong tied to this, once the rider was mounted, was secured to a ring on the ring finger of the right hand to prevent the reins from leaving his hand while shooting.[97] These precautions enabled the rider to hold the horse in check by the reins without his using them. Once they feel the pressure on their mouths released, some horses tank off; securing the reins behind the pommel ensured there was a light tug at each canter stride because at this pace the horse's natural motion includes a slight reaching forward movement with the head at each canter stride, which is absent at trot. The thin thong would have broken easily in the event of the rider's being thrown, thus minimizing the threat of his being dragged by the reins.

The rider's seat was to be central, only leaning slightly forward as the horse went into canter or gallop.[98] This relieved weight from the hindquarters and allowed the horse to put more thrust into his movement. Stirrup length, and here is a very modern touch, was measured by the edge of the stirrup hitting the ankle bone as the rider's leg dangled freely alongside the horse's barrel. Once the foot was in the stirrup it was held level, although Taybugha remarks that there is something to be said for a heel slightly down. When the spur was used it was to a 'span or less away from the site of the girth'.[99] This meant the archer rode with a very still leg, needing only minimal movement to spur his horse, thus enabling him to maintain his upper body in a stable position for shooting.

Ibn Hodeil remarks on the rapid change of direction and change of leg,[100] and Abou Bekr and Ibn Hodeil both give instructions for schooling in the *Nawerd* (a Persian word meaning circle), explaining how to do it in a figure-of-eight pattern which would have entailed a lead change as the rein was changed.[101] Ibn Hodeil says this manoeuvrability is vital for a lancer. It would also have been vital for an archer who had to make many changes of direction. A well-trained, balanced horse will switch his leads as he changes direction. If he does not, the ride becomes jerky, which would have disrupted the aim. To aim well, be it with bow, javelin, lance, or sword, other than in a hand-to-hand mêlée, a horse needed a low-level topline with his head down. The movement is then much smoother and of greater help to weapon direction.

In action the archer had four movements to synchronize: kicking the horse into its charge, nocking the arrow, drawing the bow, and transferring the rein from left to right hand. He was to hold the bow steady at the draw till his stirrup was just a little ahead of the mark, then loose and follow through the thrust.[102] The heavy draw-weight of bows meant the archer needed a steady strong arm, and even stronger back muscles. There were ten primary and seven secondary shots,[103] with three basic divisions: shooting up, called gourd shooting; downwards at the slant; and horizontally.[104] The ten basic shots were:

1. to left flank, forward and downward parallel with the thigh (*qighaq*);
2. to left flank, forward and upward (*qabaq*);
3. in horizontal plane (target roughly level with left shoulder);
4. ahead with bow, upper limb to right, canted above horse's neck;
5. to right flank, forward and downward;
6. to left flank, rear, upward or downward, with bow canted over horse's croup;
7. to left flank, rear, upward or downward, with bow vertical;
8. *Jarmaki* of two kinds, each with four shots;[105]
9. beneath horse's neck from right to left;
10. beneath horse's neck from left to right.[106]

At all times the archer had to be careful not to hit the horse with the upper limb of the bow. This necessitated canting the bow out of the horse's way. When shooting under the horse's neck the rider dispensed with the martingale and leant over at an angle.[107] An archer had to be able to string a bow while the animal was manoeuvring at the gallop.[108] Taybugha's advice on shooting in battle was to sight the bow hand on the horse's forehead and shoot. If the arrow went high it would strike the rider; if low it pierced the horse's chest; if accurate it would hit the horse's forehead. A sideways shot was aimed at the rider's buttock and pierced his seat if accurate; if high it went into his body; if low into the horse's flank. A moving target was to be shot aiming a length ahead, or slightly more according to the target's speed.[109]

There was a variety of warheads including steel, the tips tempered and the heads sheared to pierce laminate armour. A bodkin head was the best for armour-piercing, but too fine a tip failed to penetrate and broke, the arrow falling to the ground with no harm done to the enemy. Accurate range was short, but a barrage by massed archers was effective up to 400 yards (365 m).[110] No wonder the crusaders had feared massed Turkish archery as their heavy charge would have been useless except in circumstances favourable to them and devoid of intensive enemy firepower.

SWORD TECHNIQUES ON HORSEBACK

Swords came in a considerable variety and from different locales in Arabia according to Ibn Hodeil who also says that those from India tended to snap in cold weather. Highly regarded were those called after their maker, El Junty, which were of the best iron.[111] Some Egyptian and Syrian swordmakers may well have learned their craft in Persia, which had the reputation of being the best country in which to learn the armourer's craft. Trained craftsmen then found their talent well rewarded in many countries.[112]

A Mamlūk horseman with a small shield round his neck and a sword in his hand which he brandishes to left and right (British Library, Add. MS 18866, f. 129b)

A Mamlūk horseman with a sword in his hand (British Library, Add. MS 18866, f. 122b)

Sword training was done on the ground and later on horseback, and with swords of different weights. For trial of strength a clay target was repeatedly struck until, over time, the swordsman built up muscle power and finesse.

On horseback the target was a reed stuck into the ground, the top of which reached the height of a horseman. This had to be demolished span after span by a charging horseman. Next a row of five reeds on the right-hand side were reduced in similar fashion, and finally five reeds on the left and five on the right were dealt alternate strokes. Only then was the horseman ready to be taught the use of the sword in battle tactics.[113]

Self-inflicted wounds were not uncommon, likewise wounds to the horse. The rider had to take care not to slice the horse's forearm or his own. His ears and foot were the most likely self-injuries. To avoid such mishaps trainees were advised to draw only when necessary, and to hold the sword as far as possible to the outside; also to have the enemy on the right, especially if a lancer.[114]

POLO

Polo[115] was a popular game with the Muslim cavalry and used as part of military training.[116] It taught teamwork to the riders and tested the horses in manoeuvrability, speed, wind,

Playing polo in the medieval Orient (British Library, Add. MS 7784, f. 85a)

tendons, ligaments, etc. Rapid turns, starts and stops were all part of the game, and the horse gained the excitement and courage needed to ride an opponent off, a valuable asset in a battle situation.

FORMIDABLE PARTNERS

Cavalry had given Middle Eastern, Anatolian and Persian leaders victories and had enabled Islam to spread rapidly. The crusading/jihad era continued with a succession of campaigns in which East met West. From the middle of the thirteenth century onwards the horse became an even more formidable partner in the equestrian cultures that had such an impact on the next centuries. The Mamlūk cavalry was to reign supreme from Egypt to the Euphrates; the Mongol steppe system underwent changes in the Persian Ilkhanate; the Ottoman cavalry became proficient with the new weapons as firearms became commonplace. Horsemanship and cavalry warfare reached new heights in the Orient. Instruction manuals offered the Muslim cavalryman expert advice, and horse production policies offered an even wider selection of war mounts.

SEVEN

The Horses of the Mongols

In 1162 Temuchin was born to Yesugai of the Borijigin clan, one of the many tribes in the fragmented Mongolian nation. His birth came a year after the Chin had once more gained the upper hand in the periodic wars between China and Mongolia.[1]

Temuchin's destiny was to unite the tribal confederation, consolidate his grip on Mongolia, arrest China's intermittent ascendancy over his people and start the territorial expansion into Asia Minor, Russia, Persia, Europe and India that his successors carried forward into a devastating avalanche of conquests. Most warring nations have some cause, irrespective of justification, for aggression. With the exception of the wars against China, Mongolia's aim was pure territorial acquisition.

The Mongols had two elements that gave them mastery over almost all their adversaries: absolute obedience to their overlord, and superlative organization. The obedience stemmed from Temuchin's initial successes in uniting the Mongol tribes. He had placed himself under the overlordship of Toghrul Khan,[2] the ruler of the Keraits, but in 1203 he overthrew them and by 1206 was in supreme command.[3] Around this time he adopted the name of Genghis Khan.

Horses were the Mongol's inseparable companions, his wealth, his transport. Ownership of sufficient numbers indicated his social standing and success at raiding.

The Secret History of the Mongols shows the importance of horses in Genghis Khan's early life. He and his brothers owned nine horses, of which eight palomino, or isabelle, geldings were stolen by strangers. Temuchin and his friend Bo'orcu set out in pursuit, Temuchin mounted first on a chestnut, Dargï; when Dargï became exhausted after a three-day chase, Bo'orcu (also riding a chestnut) gave his friend a white horse with a black back. After many adventures, they recovered the stolen geldings. Later Temuchin's wife was captured by the Merkits because she was travelling in a slow-moving ox-cart, while the rest of the party was on horseback.[4] These incidents show Temuchin's resources were still meagre. Among domestic animals the horse headed the list in order of importance.[5]

Before tribal unification each clan fought under its own chieftain. The first evidence of Genghis Khan organizing his troops from tribes adhering to him came in 1203 after his victory over the Keraits, and before he subdued the Naiman. His followers were divided into units of 1,000 (*ming'yan*) and to each he appointed a chiliarch (*ming'yan-u noyad*). These were subdivided into 100s (*ja'un*) and 10s (*harban*). In 1206 the Mongol army was re-organized into 95 chiliarchies under 88 *noyad*, and the myriarchy of 10,000 (a *tumen*) was created, with the army divided into three sectors. That of the right hand was under Bo'orcu, the left under Muqali, the centre under Naya'a.[6] These divisions were based on territorial distribution, not their position during battle.[7] Disaffected tribes had their warriors shared among other clan divisions, while tribes able to muster more than 1,000 men were dispersed into several chiliarchies. The smaller tribes were augmented by additional men, retained their own war captives, and/or acquired reinforcements from distant relatives belonging to other tribes. To each of the chiliarchies specific grazing grounds and watering places were assigned. With the reorganization went strict discipline. Juvaini notes that absolute obedience to the Great Khan was enforced. To stop desertions no man could transfer to another unit, nor could he seek refuge elsewhere, instant execution being the punishment for desertion; abetting desertion earned severe punishment.[8]

By the time of Genghis Khan's death in 1227 the number of chiliarchies had grown to 129, of which 28 were assigned as fiefs to members of his own family. Among the original 95 were 5 of Ongut Turks, the rest being Mongolians. Soon 'foreign' troops were increasingly absorbed into the Mongolian army. In the North China campaign of 1211 Kitans defecting from the Chin army went over to the Mongols.[9] Muqali had been made commander-in-chief of all the forces in China in 1217,[10] and in 1218 when he was ordered to re-attack the Chin he had contingents of Jurchat, Kitan and Ongut Turkish troops.[11] In the war against Khwarazm in 1219, in addition to the 70,000 Mongol troops, there were contingents from the Uighur, Qarluqs, Qirghiz, Solon, Kitan and Ongut peoples under Mongol subjection.[12]

The Mongols were never able to muster much more than the 129,000 they fielded by the time of Genghis Khan's death as their nation was small, numbering only a million.[13] Even this Mongolian core included several thousand Ongut Turks. Army amplification using subjugated peoples was necessary to continue their expansion, but the 'foreign' units were always officered by Mongolians.[14]

The horse facilitated this expansion, and for an almost entirely mounted army a plentiful supply under a well-managed horse policy was essential. Mongols initially rode the stocky, hardy Mongolian horse, whose ancestor was the Asiatic wild horse, known in the local languages as *Kertag*, *Tach*, or *Taki*. Its scientific name is *Equus Przevalski Poliakoff*.[15]

Genghis Khan and his Mongol warriors. From a Persian manuscript. Note how the Mongol ponies are shown as Persian horses. (Ms Suppl. Pers. 1113, f. 72r)

The Mongolian horse has hardly changed since the hordes rode out of the Mongolian steppes. It stands between 13 and 14 hh high, with an upwards and downwards limit of an inch or two. Bay, chestnut, grey, dun, piebald and skewbald occur. It appears a rather coarse, big-headed, straight-necked, heavy-boned animal with a very trappy way of going which gives a short stride and uncomfortable ride. Friar William of Rubruck travelled to the court of Mongke Khan (1251–9) and became used to the gaits of the mounts provided by the *Yam*, the Mongolian postal and courier system (see below, p. 139). He said he dared not complain if he got a horse that 'rode hard', referring to the section of his journey through the country of the Cangle or Qangli Turks.[16] This area would have produced ponies similar to those of the Mongols.

The Mongolian steppeland afforded excellent grazing and as the herbage was never overgrazed it did not become horse-sick with parasites which debilitate livestock. Due to its extent the land could support more head per *yurt*, the family unit named from the Mongol's felt tent, than would be possible in more populated country. Figures from a 1918 animal census highlight Mongolia's pasture availability, especially when shown alongside that of one of Europe's best-known areas for horse-raising, the Älfold Plain in Hungary. The Mongolian People's Republic had a grazing area extending to 1,252,000 km² (about 308,800,000 acres); in 1918 this supported 3,895,200 animal units (five sheep per unit). This was shared by 1,150,500 horses, 1,078,400 cattle, 228,700 camels and 7,188,000 sheep. The Älfold is 100,000 km² (24,710,400 acres). It was estimated that 48.5 hectares (120 acres) were needed per animal unit on range grazing.[17] The Hungarian plain would not long have supported the huge herds that travelled with the Mongol warriors. The impressive Mongolian equine heritage is shown by the 6 million head the republic supplied to the Russians in the Second World War.[18]

The Mongolian pony, in common with many native ponies, can subsist solely on grazing, unlike its kindred horse cousins who would be very debilitated if left outside in all weathers with no supplementary feeding. Meng Hung, a Chinese general and contemporary of Genghis Khan, who met the Mongolian general Muqali in 1221, noted that the Mongol ponies were not fed beans or grain. A little later another writer in the *Hei-Ta Shih Lüeh* remarked they had no fodder, only grass.[19] When Friar John of Plano Carpini arrived at Kiev on his way to the court of Kuyuk Khan (1246–8), he was advised to change to 'Tatar' horses as they knew how to dig for grass beneath the snow, unlike his western horses, which would die if he continued his journey on them.[20] Grain was not available to nomadic pastoralists like the early Mongols, but later, under the Yuan dynasty, provision was made for both fodder and grain.

To the Europeans, Mongols appeared as undisciplined hordes of uncouth barbarians. Their way of waging war was strange; they conducted campaigns in winter, an almost unheard-of thing. They travelled with herds of horses; and sometimes with flocks of sheep as well as their families, speed being restricted to the slower pace needed to herd animals along,[21] but on major campaigns they could cover 80 miles (130 km) a day on good going, and 60 (95) in the mountains as did Batu Khan's army negotiating the Carpathians in the winter of 1241 to invade Hungary.[22]

Right from the early conquests other stock augmented, and in many cases improved, the herds of Mongolian horses. When the Mongols took Peking in 1215 they seized most of the imperial herds of horses, thus depriving the Chin of cavalry remounts.[23] Most Chinese horses were similar to Mongolian animals as the Chinese purchased horses from the Uighur Turks, another steppe people. However, they still bred from a strain first introduced into China by the Emperor Wu Ti in the late second century BC. The emperor had sent an expedition to Ferghana in 106 BC to obtain what are termed 'the blood-sweating horses of Ferghana'. The

Chinese returned empty-handed, so in 102 BC a 100,000-strong force was sent to bring the Ferghana horses back. At a cost of half this army a few dozen prized Ferghana horses, as well as other less noble animals, which were still considerably better than the Chinese stock, did arrive in Shansi province.[24] An official document of the first century AD asserted the horses of Ferghana were 'all seven ch'ih in height' which measures a hair's-breadth under 16 hh. Nearly a millennium later a document of the tenth century AD said 'official horses' were still of the Ferghana breed, which was extremely large. In the eleventh century warhorses purchased by the Chinese government ranged up to 57.73 inches in height, or approximately 14.1¾ hh.[25] This is a fair-sized animal. That the Mongols desired better-bred stock is shown in Rashid al-Din's history, when he refers to Ogodei Khan's request for 'precious clothes, jewel-studded objects such as are brought from Baghdad and Bukhara, Arab horses, and other valuable things'.[26] Other translators of this work have read the same passage as 'tall horses with long necks of western breed'.[27] Western in this sense meant Turanian horses. It was a common error to translate any oriental horse as Arabian.[28]

After his successes in China Genghis Khan set his sights westward, extending his empire to the Pamirs and the Syr Daria (Jaxartes) by 1217. When he moved against the Khwarazmians in 1219 their ruler Mohammad Shah II headed the strongest Muslim state, having driven the Seljuks from Central Asia, but at this critical time they were militarily overextended.[29] The campaign took three years and had been well planned by Subudei, Genghis Khan's most famous general and commander-in-chief. Now the Mongol army numbered 150,000, of which 140,000 were cavalry, the rest being siege engineers from recently subdued China. The army was divided into four sections.[30]

The conquest of Khwarazm opened the way into Asia Minor and Europe, and showed the sheer endurance and speed of men and mounts. When Subudei was called from his winter quarters on the delta of the Rivers Kura and Araxes on the Caspian Sea he rode over 1,200 miles (1,950 km) in seven days to Genghis Khan's newly conquered Khwarazmian capital at Samarkand. He returned to rest in winter quarters before embarking on a two-year reconnaisance in force into Europe (during which he would cover 5,500 miles (8,850 km) and fight over a dozen battles).[31] As he had been summoned to Genghis Khan after Muhammad Shah died on 10 January 1221, ridden over 2,400 miles (3,900 km) by his return and was ready to leave with the reconnaissance force by late February, Mongol rest must have differed from our perception of the term.

Khwarazm's main cities fell: Otrar in autumn 1219, then Senjar, Khojend and Jend all in Transoxiania, followed by Bokhara and Samarkand both in March 1220. Tabriz, rather than be taken by Subudei and Jebe, surrendered and bought its safety with silver and thousands of horses.[32] These would have been Turanians from the high Ferghana valley into which the Mongols had debouched after crossing the Tien Shan mountains.

The oriental horse is better adapted to hot dry climates whereas the Mongolian pony, with its coarser conformation inclining to fat in non-working conditions, its heavy coat so well adapted to the cold, would have sweated condition off. The oriental horse is designed to dissipate heat quickly with a light, spare-fleshed frame and a long neck set into the head at an angle that permits maximum utilization of lung capacity.[33] From the end of Genghis Khan's life onwards the Mongol armies would have presented a mixed equine make-up, though the Mongolian pony still predominated. In the *Naceri* Abou Bekr says 'the Tatar horse rarely has any noble characteristic'.[34]

The Mongol pony had brought Genghis Khan and his sons Juchi, Ogodei, Chagatai and the youngest, Tolui, who accompanied him on the Khwarazmian campaign, to overlordship of Mongolia, China and the Khwarazmian empire. Only efficient central organization could have achieved such swift and complete success, backed by stringent laws.

A Mongolian pony. The rider is carrying a bamboo lasso. This type of pony has not changed since the days of Batu Khan in the thirteenth-century

THE HOUSEHOLD GUARD

The Mongol army maintained its decimal structure throughout its history. The most prestigious division was the *Kesig*, the khan's imperial guard. It is first recorded in 1203 and was comparatively small, numbering 80 guards by night, and 70 by day. To this were added 400 archers and another 1,000 men of the personal guard who formed the advance unit in battle. In 1206 when Genghis Khan achieved Great Khan status he increased the *Kesig* to 10,000.[35] The heads of important administration departments were appointed from among the *Kesig*, including the equestrian establishment in charge of the imperial geldings, and the wagons or transport.[36]

The *Kesig* had strict duties and many privileges. Guarding the khan at all times and accompanying him into battle or attending him in the hunt were personal duties. Others included monitoring all traffic in and out of camp, overseeing distribution of clothes, military equipment and food, and assigning general camp guard duties, plus judging legal cases alongside Genghis Khan's adopted son Chiqi-Utuqu.[37] From the *Kesig* were chosen the military officers of Mongol and 'foreign' units. Initially units from which guardsmen were chosen supported the appointee.[38]

MONGOLIAN HORSE POLICY

The Mongolian horse policy evolved out of Genghis Khan's *Yasa* or code of laws, many of which were relevant to horse-management, and from the frequent *Yarlighs* (rescripts) concerning horses. One of Genghis Khan's earliest moves was to appoint several of his own companions to manage vital supply systems. His brother Bälgütaï and his companion Qaraldaï-Toqura undertook management of the geldings; Tayïčï'udai, Qutu-morïčï and

Mulqaqa managed the horse herds.[39] This outlines the cavalry supply system. Keeping all males entire would have led to absolute chaos in the droves of horses that travelled as back-up mounts in a Mongol army. The system revealed by the *Secret History*, Meng Hung, and the commentators P'en Ta-Ya and Hsü T'ing taken as a whole is excellent for managing herds, controlling and riding youngstock, training and maintaining campaign horses and preventing the bickerings which lead to damaging fights rendering animals useless.

Meng Hung comments on the ideal well-watered Tatar grazing lands.[40] According to the *Yuan-Shih* these extended to 10,000 li (1 li = ⅓ mile or about ½ km) and supported so many head that the horses could not be counted.[41] He outlines early training of war mounts, and although modern practice condemns riding horses hard as yearlings and two-year-olds, Meng Hung's phrase 'ridden hard' can be understood as 'green breaking' which makes them obedient before further education.[42] This obedience was commented on by contemporary authors; Juvaini remarked that complete submission was required, even from a senior commander, who must yield to the khan despite the fact that doing so might mean his death as punishment for an offence.[43] Therefore complete submission would have been expected from horses too, otherwise they would have been a liability in warfare. Leaving the serious work till they were five meant the horse's working life was considerably lengthened, and lessened breakdowns due to strains, lamenesses, etc., any of which could hamstring an army's efficiency.

The early backing moulded the horses into civil behaviour, noted by Meng Hung as an absence of kicking and biting.[44] Later commentators note the practice of gelding. P'en Ta-Ya says they were gelded when they got four teeth; Hsü T'ing only comments on the practice, saying the strong ones were kept as stallions for breeding, each entire having a fifty- to sixty-strong band of mares to run with, which he kept in order, fighting off incursive stallions and bossing back any mare who tried to leave the herd.[45] Gelding all but the best colts meant a constant quality check was maintained. Limiting the mare band to fifty or sixty

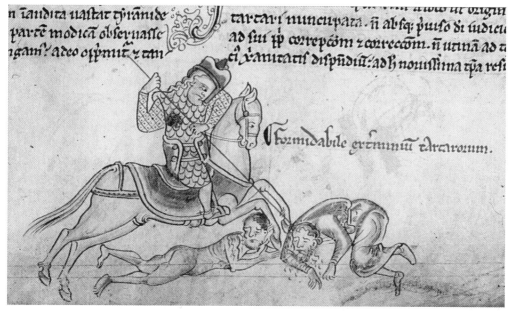

A Tartar on the warpath. The saddle is occidental and the horse so Europeanized it indicates that the artist had never seen a Mongolian pony (Corpus Christi College, Cambridge, Ms 16, f. 145r)

was what one stallion could achieve in fertility and herd control. Removing all colts and gelding them or putting them with new mare bands stopped incestuous breeding and degeneracy of stock. Gelding also helped to control kicking and biting, the latter being common with entires, and to curtail straying and neighing, two points the general did commend. Neighing although common to all is more so between breeding stock – a challenge to other entires, or a form of vocal communication during the covering season. Gelding kept the warband horses quieter, particularly for ambushes, and not so likely to neigh if enemy stallions and/or mares were nigh.

Hsü T'ing describes the year-round fitness regime for a Mongol warhorse. The Mongols turned their horses out to grass during spring and summer when they were not ridden. This allowed the horse to rest its whole system and abate all stresses and strains from campaigning. When taken up from grass they were tethered around the tents and grazing was rationed. When the fat dropped away they were ridden and Hsü T'ing says they would not then sweat over several hundred *li*; in fact a pony would have sweated, but not as copiously as if it had fat- and water-laden tissues, sweat drying quickly in the crisp Mongolian autumn and winter. The commentator said the Chinese followed an opposite system and as a result the horses fell sick.[46] In the muggy southern Chinese climate sweating would have been profuse, and the southern Chinese were not noted for horse-raising.

P'en Ta-Ya noted that Mongol horses had a capacity for endurance, plus other assets. He compared the geldings' docility with the stallions' wildness and unsettled manner. All Mongol horses were able to withstand cold and wind. Prior to a fast sortie food was kept to a minimum, almost the same practice noted by Hsü T'ing. Unsaddling was followed by racking the horse's head up high to prevent his eating until his breathing calmed and the hooves got cold.[47] Controlling eating is one of the soundest methods of after-ride management, preventing colic and laminitis.

There are many references to the usual practice of Mongol horses going unshod. Thomas, Archdeacon of Spalato (1268), noted that in the invasion of Hungary in 1241 the Mongol horses 'ran around on rock and stones without horseshoes as if they were wild goats', and an anonymous poem in Latin written about the same invasion also remarked this fact.[48] Hooves of horses raised in a dry climate, such as that of Mongolia, are much harder and resist abrasion better than those of horses raised in a damp climate. That the Mongol horses sometimes needed shoes, particularly outside their native steppeland, is shown by the levying of one iron horseshoe, among other taxes, on each person on the poll tax list in the Persian Il Khanate from Hulegu's time (1256–65) onward.[49] P'en Ta-Ya mentions a simpler method of shoeing, one which was long in use in China where the soft southern climate rendered hoof laminae more susceptible to breakdown. He describes the thin plate-like shoes of iron or board used to guard against stones. Called 'foot rough', they were tied to the hooves by thonging through holes bored in the hoof (this made for easy removal of the boards when not needed).[50] They were not suitable for constant use because foreign bodies trapped between plate and sole would have caused sole bruising.

When horses reached maturity at five years of age their military use began. All men between fifteen and sixty-one[51] were conscripted at need, but their acquaintance with horses began early. Meng Hung said children of four or five were given tiny bows and arrows and expected to ride and hunt as often as possible.[52] Each Mongol's equipment included a string of horses which facilitated speed by frequent change of mounts before tiredness set in; the number has been variously given. Marco Polo said eighteen head;[53] Hsü T'ing that at different times there were two to three, or six to seven;[54] Meng Hung that six or seven spares were led on occasion;[55] others note specific numbers required as noted below.

Horse levies were raised in several ways, notably by breeding on a large scale; the imperial herds are frequently mentioned in documents of the period. Marco Polo describes the 10,000 white mares owned by the Great Khan Kublai which were kept for their milk.[56] The annual increase would have been approximately half colts which, once cut, went into the gelding herds. When Subudei conducted the successful Russian winter campaign of 1237–8, in which Moscow, Vladimir and Kozelsk fell, the army then proceeded to the Lower Don basin where the cavalry horses rested, grazing and recovering from a harsh campaign. Their numbers were heavily augmented by whole herds driven off from the Cumans, and others were appropriated from Kazakstan.[57]

On private herds of over 100 horses a levy was taken, 1 animal in every 100; smaller herds of between 30 and 100 animals also had to contribute; below this the owners were exempt. However, in Ogodei's time a decree of 1233 stated that the lower limit was 1 in 10 – a pointer to the difficulty of getting adequate numbers. If frontier patrols needed extra horses in an emergency a heavier levy was exacted, and horses paid for at a fixed government price. In 1250 a much harsher tax was levied of a straight 10 per cent. This was relaxed in 1252 by Mongke who was elected Great Khan in 1251, the rate falling back to 1 in 100.[58]

In Mongolia the military cost was negligible. The yearly increase kept a sufficiency forthcoming. Even the toughest wars did not deplete the foundation stock on the steppe. The core of the Mongol army was run on the basis that, when required, each district supplied its quota of men and mounts, all fully equipped with arms and tack. For every 1,000 men, 2,000 to 5,000 horses were required.[59]

HORSES' TACK AND ARMOUR

Mongolian tack consisted of a snaffle bridle and a short-treed deep-seated saddle with very short stirrups. The noted authority on oriental and occidental archery, Mr Edward McEwan, has a collection of Asiatic saddles. Most date from this century but are identical to those used by the Inner Asian warriors. Basic construction is of leather and wood – flat bars, high pommel and cantle, the whole leather-covered. The gullet gives good wither clearance; the short straight seat and centrally hung stirrups put the stockily built Mongol rider in a balanced position. The saddles needed a thick pad, no doubt of felt, a Mongol product. The bridle consisted of an ordinary jointed ring snaffle which, because it is thin, is far more severe than most snaffles. The noseband was linked to the cheekpieces so that when the reins were pulled the horse not only felt pressure via the bars of the mouth, lips and tongue, but also over the nose. The throat latch was fixed to the upper part of the cheekpiece and went around the jowl preventing the horse opening his mouth to avoid bit action.

The Mongols fashioned their own saddles and bridles,[60] so it would be reasonable to suppose leather from their flocks was used as much as possible.

An excellent description of making armour for man and horse is given by Friar John of Plano Carpini:

The upper part of their helmet is of iron or steel, while that part guarding the neck and throat is of leather. Whereas the majority wear leather armour, some have their harness completely wrought from iron, which is made in the following manner. They beat out in large numbers thin iron plates a finger broad and a full hand long. In each they bore eight small holes, through which they pull three straight leather thongs. Thereupon they arrange these plates one above another, as it were, ascending by degrees, and tie the plates to the thongs mentioned by means of other small and tender thongs drawn through the holes. And in the upper part they fasten a single, small thong, doubled on each side, and sewn on to another, that the plates may be well and tightly knit together. Thus a uniform protection

Edward McEwan demonstrating how to use a Mongolian bow, showing the action and position in the saddle needed to do this. The horse is Russian bred., and shows the lean lines required for a speed horse

is effected by these plates, and suchlike armour is made for their horses as well as for their men. It is so highly polished that a man may mirror his face in it.[61]

Not all horses were armour-clad. It was expensive to make; metal supplies were needed for the lamellar type, and a tremendous quantity of leather skins for the hide type as six layers were boiled (to soften them), moulded and stitched together as required. Once fashioned and hardened it would turn the sharpest blade. Friar John comments on the gifts (tribute) of a provincial governor to Kuyuk: 'many camels . . . and many horses and mules covered with armour, some of hide, others of iron'.[62] The two front ranks of the shock division had complete armour for both man and horse, while the rear ranks did not wear armour.[63] The lighter-armed cavalry were able to manoeuvre better without the weight or restrictions of total armour. Vincent of Beauvais said archers withdrew their right arms from their armour prior to loosing a shot, and only the higher-ranking men in the army wore armour, 'so it is believed that not a tenth part of them have it or wear it'. Friar William confirms shortage of armour among the Mongols when he describes his return from Mongke Khan's court and the escort he was given through the country of the Alans in the Iron Gate region of the Caucasus Mountains. Of the twenty-strong escort only two had haubergeons and these they had got from the Alans.[64] Friar John describes the cavalryman's accoutrements:

all of them have at least the following arms; two or three bows, at least one good one, three big quivers full of arrows, an axe and ropes to pull machines. Their helmets are of iron or steel on top but that portion which goes round the neck and throat is of leather . . .

some of them have spears and at the lower end of the head is a hook to pull people out of the saddle. Their arrows are of two feet one palm and two fingers long . . . the heads of their arrows are very sharp and they always carry files to sharpen them . . . they have shields made of wickerwork, but I do not think they carry any except in camp, and when on guard over the Emperor and the princes and then only at night.[65]

On the ropes for pulling machines, I think this is most unlikely, but a lasso for use on either men or animals, was standard nomad equipment.

That there were Mongol horses bulky enough to be successfully used for roping, and heavy enough to carry full armour, is shown by those intrepid friars. Friar William, who was extremely overweight by his own admission, said he was always provided with a strong horse,[66] and Vincent of Beauvais remarked on the 'big stout palfreys the rich Mongol ladies rode'.[67]

MONGOL TRAINING AND CONDITIONING

Very little is given of specifics in training the Mongol warhorse, but because equestrian equipment and methods have remained little changed current practice is a guide to earlier methods. Mongolian horses and riders were bred tough and inured to privation. Some small measure of a Mongol's toughness can be gauged by the trip undertaken by a civil servant called Adalbish who was working in Ulanbaatur in the 1960s. Not accustomed to daily riding, he undertook a 1,200 mile (1,930 km) trip to the Russian border and back during his annual month's leave. One other modern practice that may throw a little light on the obedience of horses who did not wander off, noted by Meng Hung, comes from the same source. A Mongol lad studying at Leningrad University visited his herdsman grandfather, and after a ride was told to 'pat the horse's shoulder and let him go', which he did to his grandfather's chagrin as the horse took off and to recover it needed a three-day chase in the steppes. The grandfather had been using Mongol idiom for hobbling the horse to prevent it straying.[68] Marco Polo was impressed by the Mongol horse's agility noting that 'their horses are so well trained they can turn as quickly as a dog'.[69] This needs superb control to manoeuvre at high speed at the touch of rein or leg. A horse lugging on the rider's hands just cannot turn sharply; one reason why the Mongol bridle was augmented by nasal and jaw control. Nimbleness is partly natural ability, partly training. The stocky build and comparatively heavy head of a Mongol horse meant training was vital as his conformation predisposes him to being on the forehand. Marco Polo's observation is the key to what is lacking in contemporary writings which merely mention training. To achieve these rapid turns the Mongol horse had to have been worked on the circle and in decreasing sizes till he was so well balanced that rapid turns came easily.

The Mongol horse was trained so that his rider could shoot a bow in each and every direction while travelling at a flat-out gallop. Mr McEwan practised what was a natural ability, albeit honed to perfection, of the Mongol archer. Although the Mongol's mount stood only in the region of 14 hh in comparison with its rider's shorter stature there was not that much difference in the proportion of man to horse in the modern experiments. Mr McEwan used a cob of 15.3 hh and a lightweight Russian-bred horse of 17 hh, but he himself is well over 6 feet (1.8 m).

Training started with the horse at a standstill, getting him accustomed to the bow, accompanied by much noise; next, movement with the equipment – different angles for shooting, moving the drawn bow around the horse, withdrawing arrows from the quiver, etc. The time taken varies according to the animal's temperament. A phlegmatic horse tolerates

A Mongolian horseman. Compare this Mongolian depiction with the Persian one on p. 125

considerable activity easily; a nervous animal takes much longer to defuse. While the horse was stationary a slapping noise was made to simulate release of bowstring, prior to using the strung bow. The horse had to learn to keep straight while receiving body weight and leg signals only, as the reins were not held but knotted. He was also trained to verbal commands. Accurate shooting was much easier at full gallop than at canter; to steady his aim Mr McEwan stood in his stirrups just prior to shooting.

At a gallop a horse on a free rein lowers its whole topline, extends and lowers its neck and head, thus giving the archer an interference-free field of fire. It invariably moves straighter even without rein guidance. The gait is smooth giving a steadier platform to fire from. The photograph shows how the rider's lower body and leg position maintain him in good balance; turning in the saddle comes from the waist and hips, leaving the legs undisturbed, and not liable to send the horse off-course by an inadvertent signal.

Other training would have been by steady increments of action until the mount was undeterred by a rope being thrown, bow shot, lance or javelin cast, or sword used, even in close proximity to his head. Lassoing needed a horse to brace away from impact, and a close order charge the reverse with the horse impelling his weight into any riding off dictated by the rider.

HUNTING

Linked to military efficiency and used to prepare men and horses for the rigours of war was the annual hunt or *nerge*. Rashid al-Din[70] refers to the *nerge* formation which encircled the prey; it was used by cavalry as well as hunters. The Mongol hunt was a huge affair employing thousands of men organized as an army. The Great Khan took the centre position, and the wings were each under command of a 'keeper of hounds' (*kuyukchi*) with 10,000 men, 2,000 of whom handled the mastiffs, three to a man. The hunt spread out over a day's marching distance. Using the enveloping wing formation the line was drawn steadily inward. When encirclement was complete, prey was brought down by a combination of hounds and marksmen. Not all hunted animals were graziers, as bear, wild boar, wild oxen, wild asses and wolves were among them. Leopards (cheetahs) were used to bring down prey. They rode pillion behind a horseman until unleashed and set on quarry. Most dangerous of all the hunters were the orange, black and white striped 'lions', which must mean tigers, transported to the hunt on wagons. Unfortunately Marco Polo omits to say how these were recaptured after they had brought various animals down. By the time the season's hunting was over the horses were 'bomb proof' as many of the animals hunted were a horse's natural enemy.

Hunting was incumbent on all within a thirty-day distance of the khan's residence, the best proceeds of the chase being sent to the khan for his encampment's groceries. Folk further off also hunted, sending the cured hides for making army equipment.[71] The Mongol hunt was similar to the Byzantine hunt, and for the same reasons: military manoeuvres, and provision of meat and hides.[72]

Strict discipline was maintained and the 'close season' rigorously enforced during the breeding season. In the hunt a horse learned to watch the prey's movements, anticipating evasive action – invaluable when he later turned to harrying beaten enemies.

FIELD MANAGEMENT

Once fit, horses were well tended. One of Genghis Khan's admirable laws enjoined soldiers:

> Take care of the led horses in your troop, before they lose condition. For once they have lost it, you may spare them as much as you will, they will never recover it on campaign. . . . You will encounter much game on the march. Do not let the men go after it . . . do not let the men tie anything to the back of the saddle. Bridles will not be worn on the march – the horses are to have their mouths free. If this is done the men cannot march at a gallop. If an order has been given, then those who disobey it must be beaten and put under arrest. But as for those who have disobeyed my personal orders, send those who are worth serious consideration to me. The rest, the unimportant ones, are to be beheaded on the spot.[73]

After a long march bringing them close to their target horses were given time to recuperate prior to the last stages and eventual conflict. This is illustrated by the Khwarazmian campaign beginning in 1219. Genghis Khan had spent the summer building up his cavalry horses' reserves by grazing them along the Qara Irtish and Urungu Rivers where grass was abundant in riverside meadow land.[74] He realized that after the 1,000 mile (1,600 km) push to the borders of the Khwarazm Shah's country his horses would not only have burned up reserves of fat but been mentally exhausted and leg-weary; this is when lamenesses occur through stress breakdowns.

THE INVASION OF EUROPE

The invasion of Europe under Batu Khan and Subudei was the most outstanding campaign undertaken by a medieval army. Conceived years before its actual start, it was prefaced by a two-year reconnaissance by Subudei and Jebe. The campaign was meticulously conducted with interaction between army divisions superbly co-ordinated. An unprepared Europe reeled at the devastation's suddenness. Used to summer campaigns conducted under individual commanders, often with little or no cohesion between contingents, the notion of Asiatic barbarians under total discipline and obedience to one overlord was incomprehensible to the bulk of European military.

At the Great Khan's death his empire was divided among his relatives on the basis of allotments of *yurts*, each with their respective herds. His mother Ielun and his uncle received 10,000 households, his son Juchi 9,000, his son Chagatai 8,000, his sons Ogodei and Tolui 5,000 each, his brothers Khazar and Bïlgütaï 4,000 and 1,500 respectively, and his nephew Alchidai 2,000.[75] All these were under the supreme command of the Great Khan; at the time of the European invasion this was Ogodei. As Juchi's son, Batu's inheritance stretched from the River Irtysh to the Aral Sea, but it was in need of consolidation.[76] Subudei, the commander-in-chief, pressed for tightening the Mongol hold on Russia and furthering the push into Europe.[77] However, Batu's troop strength was insufficient for this huge task and Ogodei ordered the other *ulus* under princes of the Chingisid house to boost his forces.[78]

The campaign began with a move against the Kipchaks on the Volga river in 1236 conducted by Mongke and Budek. Early in spring 1237 Batu and Subudei attacked the Bulgars on the

Mongolian heavy cavalry in lamellar armour, from a manuscript of c. 1306 in the Edinburgh University Library

Middle Volga region. Later in the year, at the beginning of winter, the Mongols crossed the Volga into Russia and began the systematic reduction of the Russian provinces, starting with Riazan and its cities, followed by Suzdalia. After the fall of Vladimir in 1238 the army split, Subudei going north and taking Yuriev, Rostov and Yaroslav, and Batu north-east reducing Dmitrov and Tver. In March 1238 the Novgorodian city of Torzhok fell. Spring thaw put an end to campaigning and Novgorod itself was spared. The army summered in the Russian steppes west of the River Don where the horses recuperated, fleshing out, ready for the next stage of conquest. Meanwhile remounts were herded in from Mongolia and horse recruitment aided by herds captured from the Cumans and other nomad tribes which were systematically brought under the Mongol yoke. Human recruitment was bolstered by a huge intake of captives from the wide-sweeping raids. The Mongol armies were getting steadily closer to the Russian/Hungarian border, but for a while there was a respite. In 1240 the assault on the remaining Russian provinces began, ending with the fall of Kiev on 6 December 1240.[79] The gateway to Europe was open but in front of the Mongols lay the Carpathian mountains and months of bitter winter weather. Here the hardiness of man and horse was really put to the test. Although long periods of grazing time had been wisely allotted to the herds, the Mongols had spent the previous summer of 1240 under arms, so the animals would have gone into the winter of 1240/1 in leaner than normal condition. The closest of the modern Russian breeds to the types the Mongols would have acquired in addition to their own animals for this particular campaign, are the Kazakh, Altai, Trans Baikal, Yakut and Kirgiz. All have great similarity to the original Mongolian horse. They have exceptionally strong hooves – which explains much of why the extensive mileage inherent in Mongol conquests was possible.

In the old USSR the State Research Institute of Horse-Breeding was formed to conduct research into Russia's equine resources. The following examples will highlight equine capabilities and why the Mongol army moved so rapidly when necessary.

Russian records show that a Kazakh horse covered more than 66 miles (106 km) in 4½ hours, and another Kazakh horse 33 miles (53.5 km) in 1 hour 58 minutes. Many steppe ponies can pace, which gives a very comfortable ride, less taking for the rider. Modern steppe ponies measure 13–14 hh, with the Kazakh being in the upper height range.[80]

When the Mongols advanced on Hungary they left three *tumens* behind to keep Russia subdued, and to guard their backs. Subudei's strategy was to advance on a front 600 miles (965 km) wide. Two *tumens* under Baidar and Kadan were detached to subdue Poland and Lithuania, while the rest of the army was split three ways to cross the Carpathians by different passes. Batu took the centre position with the 40,000 bulk of the forces; the northern flank with one *tumen* was under Siban, the southern flank under Subudei and Kuyuk held three *tumen*.[81] King Bela IV of Hungary hoped to be able to repulse Batu with the aid of the 40,000-strong force of Cumans under their leader Kotian who had been granted refuge after fleeing from the Mongols in Russia.[82]

In March 1241 Vladimir, the Palatine of Craców, was ambushed by Baidar at Chmielnik and his force almost totally annihilated by arrow fire, the Mongols going on to burn Craców itself. On 9 April following, the army of Baidar, joined now with the *tumen* of Kadan, met the combined forces of western Poland, Wrocław, Oppeln, Moravia and Osterna, plus contingents from Prussia and the Teutonic Knights, who had established themselves at Maalbork. At Liegnitz the combined forces of Poland are said to have numbered 20,000, mostly light cavalry. The Polish horse charged twice and were repulsed. On the flanks the Mongol archers cut the Poles down and forced a rout in which thousands were slain,[83] although the Mongols also took heavy losses.[84]

Meanwhile in Hungary Batu and his other commanders had brought their three contingents down through the Carpathians at the rate of 60 miles (96.5 km) a day in the last of the bitter winter snows, and reaching the foot of the mountains were faced by the River Sajo. Simultaneously Bela was coming up from the other bank into the area around Mohi. Batu reconnoitred and then retired out of sight into the woods of Diosgyor before the Hungarians arrived. They in turn sent a scouting force over the bridge spanning the river, and finding nothing, returned. Meanwhile Batu had sent a force of three *tumen* under Subudei to cross the River Sajo upstream and come round in a wide sweep to take the Hungarians in the rear. Batu himself attacked just prior to dawn with four *tumen*, confident he had the Hungarians trapped. According to contemporary chroniclers the Hungarian forces totalled 100,000.[85] Batu found himself hard-pressed, and with only a narrow access via the bridge over the Sajo brought his artillery up and bombarded the Hungarians across the river in order to keep the passage open. Once across, his 40,000 were vastly outnumbered. In the Hungarian ranks was the finest cavalry in Europe which charged repeatedly, causing Batu heavy losses. Even so and under immense pressure Batu took a seeming chance and spread out into two thin extended wings encircling the Hungarian forces. In their rear Subudei had at last arrived and started to complete the total encirclement of the Hungarian force. Just in time the Hungarians re-formed and conducted an orderly retreat to their camp.

Even though Batu had sustained massive losses Subudei would not allow him to withdraw, so the Hungarian camp was bombarded by artillery and destroyed. The Mongol troops rallied and prepared to deliver their heavy cavalry charge, at the same time leaving a narrow escape route via the same passage they had themselves debouched into from the battlefield the day before. Only the Templars, the troops of Bela's brother Koloman, and the fighting Archbishop Hugolin stood fast. The rest broke and fled through the supposed escape route to be cut down on both sides by a hail of Mongol arrows. In the battle and ensuing rout contemporary chronicles recorded 65,000 dead along the way to Pest 30 miles (48 km) away.[86]

After the battle of the River Sajo the Mongols spread out, pillaging and destroying as they went, resistance being met with wholesale terror and massacres, but after a season of marching and fighting the Hungarian plain offered the best chance for cavalry mounts to recuperate. Reconnaissance patrols were sent into Italy and Austria, and the Mongols marched to the Dalmatian coast. Further conquests were planned, but several factors halted European expansion. Mountainous terrain was unsuitable for massed cavalry and the remount system to operate efficiently; grazing was inadequate; in addition Europe had a far greater number of stone-built cities and fortified castles than any of the territories Batu's armies had marched through. Horses would starve, and siege warfare was the weakest part of Mongol tactics. The political factor intervened. The death of Ogodei Khan on 11 December 1241 meant a *Kurultai* was convened to elect his successor in Karakorum. Mongke, Kadan and Buri had already returned. Batu favoured the election of Mongke who, after the short reign of Kuyuk, did succeed, but Batu himself returned as far as Sarai on the Volga where he had established his base and capital. Still under the nominal command of the Great Khan, Batu was the first khan of the Golden Horde, and was strong enough to be to all purposes independent. In 1260, after the death of Mongke Khan, Berke, the third khan of the Golden Horde, did proclaim his independence from Mongolia.[87]

In the years since 1236 Mongolian cavalry had covered an incredible distance, much of it in harsh winter weather when the horses had to scratch for poor grass beneath the snow, and the ground was frequently frozen. In mountains and stony tracts they went hungry. An accurate idea of the mileage covered is impossible but the direct passage was over 4,000 miles (6,400 km) from Karakorum to the Dalmatian coast. This must have been at least quadrupled with the return trip, variations in routes, and circumvention of geographical barriers, plus the constant fanning-out to subjugate countries in their path. Western horsemen may see the Mongol horse as a scruffy, ill-conformed equine lacking visual symmetry in motion, but without him the Mongols' warlike and acquisitive natures would have availed them nothing.

THE YAM

Rashid al-Din gives us one of the earliest accounts of the Mongol *yam*, dating it to the reign of Ogodei. Persons entitled to use the facilities were ambassadors and couriers, and the stations were known as *Tayan yams*.[88] Other types were the *Morin yam* (horse station), *Tergen yam* (wagon station) and *Narin yam* (secret station), the latter for urgent military communications.[89] Marco Polo gives the most complete picture.

In the time of Kublai Khan there were over 10,000 post stations, supplied by over 200,000 horses. Distances between stations ranged from 25 to 40 miles (40 to 65 km) according to population density, and each station had up to 200 head ready, and a further 200 at grass on a monthly rotational system. The upkeep of the stock was a charge on the local community who had to provide fodder, etc. Horses were supplied on the same basis. However, if post stations were situated at a great distance from the Great Road the khan provided part of the stations' stock, the locals the rest. To ensure adequate management of stock and facilities a monthly inspection was carried out. While on duty horses were ridden hard. When necessary a post rider could cover up to 250 miles (400 km) per day and such riders were highly esteemed.[90]

Abuses crept in; during the unsettled period between Kuyuk Khan's death and Mongke's accession too many *paizas*, or tablets of authority, were being issued and horses commandeered from ordinary folk by ambassadors, who were also demanding too many *yam* horses.[91]

Under certain conditions, especially that of a harsh winter, a traveller deprived of his horse could easily die. The horse provided transport and, in an emergency, food; the custom was to slit the vein in a horse's leg, draw blood, mix it with iron rations, or take it neat, and plug the slit. Therefore stealing a horse was a capital offence. Unless the thief returned the stolen horse and with it nine others, execution followed, the thief being split in two, one of the Mongol (and Mamlūk) forms of execution.[92]

EIGHT

The Importance of the Horse in the Crusades

A quarter of a century after Manzikert, east met west in two centuries of warfare.

The horse played a vital part in the armies of both orientals and occidentals. Indeed without horses, and to a lesser extent mules and donkeys, it is doubtful if these interminable conflicts would have taken place. Infantry was greatly used, more so in Christian than Islamic armies. A significant part of Islamic forces came from Turkish tribes whose livelihood centred around horses. Ibn Battuta says it was from raising horses that Turks made their living, breeders often numbering herds in the thousands, marking the tally by one felt pennant attached to a rod for each thousand. Some breeders had up to ten pennants. The method of catching a horse from the herds is still used by the Mongol pastoralists today – a rod with a noose attached.[1] Syria raised excellent horses from Seleucid times onwards.[2] Other horses available to oriental cavalry have been discussed in Chapter Six.

Opposing Islamic cavalry were smaller Christian contingents. Without the knights' leadership and financing from landed estates, there would have been no Christian army. By this period no knight went to war on foot, and laws had long been enacted over the part the wealthy, and their men-at-arms, played as mounted men in feudal armies. At the start of each crusade Christian cavalry was mounted on horses brought from the Occident by overland routes, and to a lesser extent by sea. The oriental horseman despised the *Afrendji* or Frankish horse. In listing ten breeds, Abou Bekr noted the *Afrendji* was the 'softest and worst'.[3] This disparaging description is a key to the long-term utility of crusading cavalry. In equestrian terms 'soft' is unfit, but in the narrower sense it means lacking in endurance. The *Afrendji* warhorse was unsuited to the climate, had less dense bone structure than an oriental horse and was therefore more susceptible to lameness and locomotor breakdown; its larger structure, coarser, more porous bone, and heavier flesh were unsuited to the swift skirmish warfare employed by the Muslims. Although in a massed charge the Franks were both feared and effective,[4] the horse's impetus was soon spent. In addition to substandard physiological traits the *Afrendji* easily fell victim to diseases endemic in the Levant;[5] he needed more food than the oriental horse, not only because of the difference in size, but also because of the relative metabolic rates of different types of equine and the European habit of overfeeding warhorses. The Arabian horse is a good doer and when adequately exercised does not run to fat as is common with many heavier European types of horse.[6]

The preferences of different races have remained constant over the ages and although six centuries separate the following comments, they are apposite. Bertrandon de la Brocquière, who travelled among the Turkish people in the early 1400s, remarked that the Turks 'keep their horses very low, and never allow them to get fat'.[7] The modern parallel concerns an

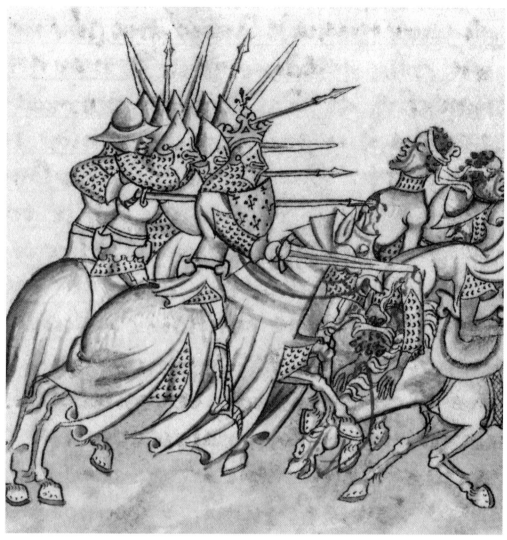

Crusader knights charge against their Arab opponents (British Library, Add. MS 21143, f. 90)

equestrian photographer who overheard a visiting Arab prince comment on the obesity of some Arabians being shown in the USA, querying, 'What do you do with your horses, eat them? We use ours for riding.'[8] De la Brocquière noted the ability of the Turkish horses to keep up a fast gallop for great periods, and the fact that they had wide nostrils[9] (an attribute of the Arabian and other oriental horses, allowing better air intake and therefore increased capacity for sustained speed). Another contributing factor only recently scientifically proven is muscle fibre proportion. In brief the spare-framed oriental horse has more long-twitch muscle fibres and the chunkier European more short-twitch muscle fibres, the former being better adapted to sustained endurance.[10] Lady Anne Blunt[11] noted the bedouin horror of becoming fat and also the perpetually poor condition of many horses. She also describes traditional Bedouin breaking-in methods and the warfare of the nineteenth century. These echo medieval Turkish methods and show that whereas European horsemanship was constantly modified in changing social conditions, that of the bedouin and Turk was not, mainly because they still used horses primarily for warfare.

The human, military and religious aspects of the wars of the crusades/jihad have been extensively written about by contemporary Arab and Christian men of letters, and by eminent modern historians. Most Muslim authors were trained for important civil posts or as historians. Ibn al-Qalānisī (1073–1160) was the first Arab historian of the crusades, his work covering mainly Syria and Damascus in the era of the first and second Crusades. 'Imad ad-Din al-Isfahani (1125–1201) was secretary to both Nur ad-Dīn and Saladin; Behā ed-Dīn (1145–1234) was Saladin's Qadi (army judge); ibn al-Athir (1160–1233) was the foremost Arab historian of the era; Usāmah ibn Munqidh (1095–1188), Amir of Shaizar, was a man of letters, a warrior and a huntsman.

For the Christian record we must rely on chronicles written by clerics. Among the best of these are the works of William, Bishop of Tyre who wrote of the First Crusade. Equine participation is shown far better by Arab historians than the Christian clerics, with the exception of the perceptive Raymond of Aguiliers. For the later crusades we have the secular chronicles of Villehardouin (born c. 1150–4) and Joinville (born c. 1224–5). Both were fighting participants in the events they chronicle and give us significant equestrian details. The best Muslim source for the full implication of the horse's part in jihad is that of Usāmah ibn Munqidh. For the Christian equine elements we cannot improve on the Rule of the Templars, plus the Rules of the Hospitallers, which mainly mirrored the Templars' on equestrian matters.

THE PRELUDE

The crusading era began in 1095 at the Council of Clermont when Pope Urban II called for armed aid to be given to the Christians of the east.[12] This was in response to an appeal from the Byzantine Emperor Alexius Comnenus I for military assistance to bring his wars against the Seljuks to a final and successful conclusion.[13] An eloquent orator, Urban fired the Franks[14] with religious zeal aimed at wresting the Holy Land, and Jerusalem in particular, from Muslim tenure, even though the Muslims tolerated Christians in the population and allowed Christian pilgrimages, for a price.

The Pope set 15 August 1096 as the departure date for the armies[15] which were to converge on Constantinople. Alexius was alarmed by the size of the approaching Frankish armies in place of the mercenaries he had requested. His concern was to be more than justified. The first to arrive after a hazardous sea journey, followed by a courteous but confining escort through Byzantine territory, was Hugh of Vermandois, youngest brother of Philip of France.[16] He was followed by Godfrey of Bouillon, Duke of Lower Lorraine, whose troops ravaged the pasture lands and environs of Adrianople, and when removed to a more confined area outside Constantinople overran the suburbs, stealing stores, herds, flocks and baggage animals, until they were allowed their own market.[17] Anna Comnena makes much of the hooliganism of Godfrey's troops and gives us the first look at equine losses. To break the force of the Franks' charge the Byzantines shot at the Franks' horses.[18] These chargers had already been weakened by insufficient fodder, Alexius having cut off supplies in an effort to persuade Godfrey to swear allegiance to him. That, combined with the Byzantines' superior military skill, brought Godfrey to his senses, and after he had taken an oath to restore to Alexius any lands he conquered that had previously been in Byzantine possession, his army was ferried across the Bosphorus.[19] Other contingents soon followed Godfrey under the nobility of France and Norman Italy, the foremost among the leaders being the Normans Bohemond and his nephew Tancred, and Raymond of St Gilles, Count of Toulouse. To emphasize the religious nature of the crusade the Pope had set Adhemar, Bishop of Le Puy, in overall authority.

Godfrey of Bouillon, one of the leaders of the Crusades. At one stage his army numbered not more than 5,000 cavalry and 15,000 infantry. (Ms Fr. 9084, f. 20v)

SHIPPING AND ITS EFFECTS ON WARHORSES' SERVICEABILITY

One of Alexius' concerns was to prevent crusading forces uniting at Constantinople,[20] and the ferrying of troops and horses across the Bosphorus to the Asian side was mutually advantageous. The Byzantine experience in shipping large numbers of horses over long distances influenced much of the later European horse-transport design.

As each contingent left for the East animals came with them, at first mostly by land, but as transports improved and capacity increased more by sea. Records exist detailing shipments; the Templars made regular importations, and chroniclers give an idea of numbers, costs and embarkation and landing procedures. Records of ships' specifications show how the animals were carried inside the ships, and from the room allotted to each animal comes the size of the crusaders' destriers. In Byzantine writing horse transports are referred to as *Dromons*, *Triremes*, and *Chelandia*; in Muslim works as *Taride (Tarida)* and *Usari*, and in the Christian sources as *Uscerii*, *Uissiers* and *Salandria*, which were evolved from the Arabic and Greek names.[21]

As early as 1038 Byzantine shipping carried their Norman mercenaries' warhorses across the Straits of Messina to fight Sicilian Muslims. Thereafter Normans often plied their own transports from Italy in their expansionist exploits against Sicily, Malta and the Byzantine Balkans. At that time the horse-carrying capacity was about twenty-one animals per vessel.[22] Anna Comnena records that in the First Crusade a three-masted pirate vessel had transported 1,500 men and 80 horses from Italy to Illyria.[23] At this stage of shipbuilding such a number is exaggerated, the meaning being a greater number than normal was carried in this large vessel. Shipping considerable numbers of horses from Italy across the Adriatic was within maritime capabilities, but the longer voyage across the Mediterranean was not practicable, and Fulcher of Chartres noted that in 1101 those coming direct to Jerusalem by sea were unable to bring horses with them.[24] Long-haul capability had improved by 1123 when horses were transported direct to the Levant but frequent landings were necessary to take fresh water on board for them.[25] Sea travel was dangerous, to be avoided where possible. In 1097 one of the ships carrying horses and mules for Stephen of Blois and Robert of Normandy broke up at sea.[26] En route to Jerusalem in 1101 those without horses went by sea, and those with by land.[27] Also recorded are the types of horse transport constructed by the Byzantines and used to ship Frankish horses from Acre to Damietta in the 1169 assault on Egypt by combined crusader and Byzantine forces. They were fitted with large openings in the stern and had ramps for easy embarking and disembarking.[28]

The pages of Villehardouin's *History of the Fourth Crusade*, which started auspiciously in 1199 with French nobility flocking to take the Cross, degenerated into war with the Byzantine Greeks and was destined never to reach the Holy Land, describe the overall problems of shipping large numbers of horses. The Venetians, Genoans and Pisans were the leading medieval maritime people. For the Fourth Crusade a deal was struck between the French and the Doge of Venice for shipping the entire estimated army of 20,000 foot, 4,500 knights, 9,000 squires and 4,500 horses, plus fodder and victuals, to the Levant. Special transports were promised for the horses and attendant squires. The total cost was 85,000 marks, each man costing 2 marks and each horse 5.[29] The best-laid plans went awry as many contingents chose to go by other routes, leaving a shortfall of 34,000 marks from the original agreed sum.[30] After renegotiation which entailed crusaders retaking the Venetian city of Zara off the Illyrian coast the fleet sailed at the latest by 8 October 1202[31] and offloaded at Zara on St Martin's day, 11 November. The horses had been loaded below decks.[32] Once they were on board the entrance hatches were caulked to make them watertight.[33] Unloading warhorses was effected by lowering ramps from the side of the ships.[34, 35] Either the knights quickly mounted once the horses were unloaded,[36] or, as Robert of Clari states of the landing at Constantinople in July 1203, the knights rode down the ramps; we do not know which is accurate.[37]

On-board stabling arrangements are given in several contemporary documents of ships' specifications. For King Louis IX's crusade a contract was made with Genoa on 13 September 1246, for twelve round ships and twelve oared *taride*. The round ships were to be provided with mangers, stall rails, bedding of esparto grass, rope and ringbolts to secure the stabilizing underbelly slings. It is certain that the slings were not intended for raising horses off their feet. No horse would survive other than a very short time in suspension.[38] Other ships leased by the nobility also had rope slings for horses, and on one ship, the *Bonaventura*, sixty horses were to be provided for.

Another contract for twelve oared *taride* built specifically for horse transports gives the first known dimensions:

overall length	48 *cubiti* (35.71 m [approx. 115 ft])
width on floor at waist	13½ *palmi* (3.48 m [nearly 10 ft])
headroom in hold at waist above keel	9 *palmi* (2.25 m [6⅔ ft])
camber in the deck from centre line to gunwale	½ *palmus* (0.125 m [about 3½ in])
beam in waist at the wale before the tumblehome	16½ *palmi* (4.10 m [about 13¼ ft])

Stern ports were to be incorporated. This shows these ships were to be backed on to the beach for disembarkation. Carrying capacity was twenty per vessel.

The Statutes of Marseilles of 1253 stipulated each horse was to be allotted 3 Marseillese *palmi* (0.75 m [about 2 ft]). If this measurement was used the twenty horses could be stabled in one row in the centre of each ship. The headroom of 2.25 m (6⅔ ft) was just sufficient to ride a horse out of the ship.[39] In 1278 Charles I of Anjou, King of Sicily, had a *taride* built at Brindisi in which the stabling deck measured 18 *canne* (1 *canna* = 2.10 m [6¾ ft]). Only 10 *canne* were actually used for carrying the thirty horses, gear being stowed in the rest. Three horses were allotted 7½ *palmi*, a *catena mortua* (a large post) being set between each group of three. The stern ports at 2.23m (about 6⅔ ft) were slightly lower than those of Louis' ships.[40]

These specifications indicate the approximate size of horses used by crusaders, and here I differ from my source in using measurements other than those given in the article, which are those of a modern shire, standing up to 18 hh in height, greater in stature than his near kin of the period between the two world wars. Horses of that size had not been developed in the Middle Ages. Old-fashioned draught-horse collars can sometimes be picked up by collectors at farm sales; one from the 1920s or 1930s would not fit the modern heavy horse.[41] With three horses per 7½ *palmi*, or 1.97 m (about 6 ft), each horse had 0.66 m (nearly 26 in) room widthways. However, although the horses were stabled very close together there had to be room for a man to pass between them, even at a tight squeeze, in case any animal needed individual attention. My horse trailer, which is of a standard two-horse type designed to carry two 16.2 hh horses, has a compartment 2½ ft (0.75 m) wide for each horse. It is just possible to squeeze past a horse of that size, provided it is reasonably lean.

Using the above statistics I made some calculations, bearing in mind several important points. I used three of my own horses:

Granicus	standing 16.1 hh (i.e. 5 ft 5 in [1.67 m] at the withers)
Khusrau	standing 15.3 hh (i.e. 5 ft 3 in [1.59 m] at the withers)
Katchina	standing 14.3 hh (i.e. 4 ft 11 in [1.24 m] at the withers)

and a rider 5 ft 9 in (1.75 m) tall to ride Granicus and Katchina.[42] The location for measuring was my barn doorway which is exactly 7 ft 10 in (about 2.35 m) high. The crusading ship's stern port was 7 ft 4 in (2.25 m). There were other ships noted in the Pryor article with maximum head room of just under 6 ft 6 in (1.98 m). I marked the height of the *taride* hatch at 7 ft 4 in (2.25 m). The next measurements taken were the height of the horse's ears when erect and the head held naturally, neither lowered to duck or high in alarm:

Granicus   6 ft 11½ in (about 2.1 m)
Khusrau   6 ft 5 in (about 1.9 m)
Katchina   6 ft (1.8 m)

Next was the height of the rider sitting erect with a riding hat on. A medieval helmet or casque, depending on its variety, would have been several inches taller:

Granicus plus rider 8 ft 1 in (2.45 m) (the rider had to dip his head to get under the 7 ft
                     10 in [2.35 m] lintel of the door)
Katchina plus rider 7 ft 9 in (2.32 m)

With the rider bending down, his head alongside the horse's neck, the highest part was the curve of the rider's back:

Granicus   6 ft 8 in (2 m)
Katchina   5 ft 11 in (1.7 m)

I had a jumping saddle on Katchina which allowed the rider to crouch much lower. Realizing that a medieval saddle sat higher on the horse's back and had high front and rear aches, I used my endurance saddle which is similar in concept on Granicus.

The reason for taking measurements at the horses' ears was because most horses are nervous of going under a low door-frame and their normal reaction, other than balking, is to raise their heads. They have to become relaxed and accustomed to lowering their heads and necks, and even then often barge through. Both Granicus and Katchina were measured widthways at the widest part of the barrel. Neither horse was overweight from grazing, but both were in good flesh:

Granicus   28 in (0.4 m)
Katchina   25½ in (0.33 m)

These measurements show that early medieval destriers were of a very moderate size! I estimate the build as stocky, and a height range of between 15 and 15.2 hh. Of course other sizes occurred with exceptional horses as noted by Usāmah ibn Munqidh.

With these dimensions and the provisions carried, including water, conditions were uncomfortable but sustainable. Each horse on Louis IX's 1270 crusade was to have four *modia* of barley by the measure of Acre, a barrel of hay 3 ft 3 in by 5 ft (about 1 m by 1.5 m) and just over 6 imperial gallons of water (27.9 l).[43] These are extremely generous rations but certain points have to be understood. Modern bailers compact hay to a much greater degree than medieval workers could achieve, so the amount seems larger than it was; a percentage would have been spoilt by on-board conditions;[44] many horses waste hay and will not eat trampled fodder. Most horses drink 4 gallons (18.1 l) per day. Working up a sweat, either in hard work and hot conditions, or on board a ship which would have been very humid with twenty-plus horses confined in a small space, would force water consumption up; large hay intake increases water needs, or the horse suffers from impaction of the gut. A horse is fussy and may refuse stale or putrid water, although with a raging thirst he will drink even bad water. The barley ration was far too much for an idle horse. Excess grain consumption allied to no exercise would have caused azoturia on disembarkation when coupled with sudden violent exercise. However, one has to take into consideration that veterinary dental care was unlikely to have been

The Westminster Psalter depicting a crusading knight from c. 1250 (British Library, Royal MS 2A XXII, f. 220)

carried out so teeth would not have ground barley efficiently and much would have passed through the gut whole.[45] Horses cannot be sick but are adversely affected by sea travel, especially if the rider wishes to use them efficiently on landing. There would have been considerable muscle wastage through enforced inactivity.[46] Mental stress is also involved and rough sea conditions would have heightened this.[47] Horses landing in the East would have been in poor health and the reasons for and underlying causes of many losses would have gone unrecorded because they were not fully understood. The horses would have been very vulnerable in battle because of debility, and also even more susceptible to local diseases. The effects of enforced bad management on board would have exacerbated their debility.

Horses were on board for five weeks before they were disembarked at Zara. They re-embarked at Eastertide. They were next unshipped at Corfu for an airing. After three weeks' recuperation at Corfu, which was well supplied with food, they left at Pentecost in May for Scutari. This meant it had taken them about three weeks to get to Corfu, Pentecost being six weeks after Easter. They arrived at Constantinople on the Eve of St John the Baptist's day, 23 June.[48] Therefore in the spring and early summer of 1203 the horses had spent many weeks on board ship. It takes at least five days for a horse to get back to full fitness after even a short 24-hour, albeit very rough, North Sea crossing, as I found when shipping fit endurance horses to Germany for a 100-mile race. Crusaders' horses must have felt the effects much more in medieval vessels. Even with sailings occurring in the better weather months frequent storms still sprang up.

ACQUISITION OF REMOUNTS

Acquiring horses from Europe often depended on the goodwill of a ruling sovereign of a particular country. It was common practice in medieval times to forbid export of horses except under licence; warhorses were regarded in much the same way as weapons and their falling into enemy hands was to be avoided. Unlike weapons it took many years to produce a warhorse of fighting age so warhorses were a very valuable commodity. The *Rule of the Templars* indicates mounts were procured on a regular basis from overseas, either as direct shipments,[49] or as part of a secular knight's equipment when he 'joined up' for a specified time.[50] There are records of licences being issued to Hospitallers and Templars by Charles I of Anjou in the latter years of the thirteenth century.[51] This implies that licences were issued over the whole of the crusading era, although records have not survived. In 1129 Hugh de Payens, the first Master of the Templars, on returning to the kingdom of Jerusalem from a visit to Europe, brought a large contingent of cavalry, horses and infantry.[52] Shipments from Europe were never enough to supply all remounts and baggage animals for the crusaders. The supply was augmented by purchase, capture, battle spoils, the occasional gift, payments for prisoners released, and as rents for land. Even so there were many occasions when mortality was so high that cavalry was forced to fight on foot, and in some cases to use donkeys and other baggage beasts as transport. When Saladin sent fruit to an ailing Richard I at Jaffa, the bearer returned with the information that Jaffa was manned by 300 knights; in a subsequent engagement his Qadi noted that these knights were mostly mounted on mules.[53]

There was also the much better horsed Muslim cavalry and on occasion the two sides benefited from each other's mounts, so it may be that there was no hard dividing line between the animals used by either side, except when a new wave of Franks, or a welcome and large enough shipment, arrived from overseas.

THE HORSE AND THE MILITARY ORDERS

Although the following is largely drawn from the *Rule of the Templars*, the general aspects apply to all crusader cavalry, even though the secular arm was not so rigidly controlled. Arabic and Christian sources are also instructive. The information obtained gives us a surprisingly detailed picture. Much of what pertains to Frankish horses would also have applied to those of the Muslims. Most Christian writings when mentioning horses give sparse notes on numbers and when they were used. A few illustrate the privation the animals suffered. In Arabic sources the horse appears in a far more personal light; descriptions are varied enough to show differences in type; one is aware the horse was part of Islamic warrior culture, often valued for himself, and his owner expressed his feelings for him which is something that is almost totally lacking in Frankish sources. One reason for this is that many Arab authors were also warriors; many Muslims came from a horse-oriented culture. Among the Franks nearly all who could write were clerics, and fighting clerics, of which there were many, spent their literary talents on less interesting ecclesiastical works.

How important the horse was to the Templars is shown by the fact that he, or some part of his equipment, maintenance, breeding and/or acquisition features in over a hundred of the rules of the Temple. The only other sector of the knights' lives that receives such importance is the 'praying factor'.

The Templars took their name from their first convent which was given to them by King Baldwin II in 1118, and was situated adjacent to the Temple at Jerusalem. Funds to maintain

A twelfth-century portrayal of an episode from the Arturian legend showing fully equipped mounted warriors. (From the archivolt of the Porta della Pescheria, Modena Cathedral)

The Castle of Marab, the Hospitallers' stronghold in Syria. Its superb location gives an overview of the surrounding territory

them were also made available; their main duty was 'that, as far as their strength permitted, they should keep the roads and highways safe from the menace of robbers and highwaymen, with especial regard for the protection of pilgrims'. Nine years later the knights were still wearing secular clothing, but a council was held at Troyes in 1128 where a Rule for the Order was drawn up and a habit of white assigned to them. At this date the Order was small, only 9 members, but soon began to grow, numbers soon reaching 300. The Order rapidly acquired possessions in the Levant and Europe. For a long time the Templars adhered to their protective role, but as they grew stronger they became independent, acquisitive and proud.[54] Their role expanded into a purely military one and such was their prowess that they became the most feared and effective of the Christian fighters.

The Hospitallers formed the other major military Order. Originally founded at Jerusalem in 1070 to care for sick pilgrims it started to become militarized in 1118 under its second Grand Master, Raymond of Le Puy.[55] Although we do not have specific numbers of either Order, both were rich and powerful, and capable of furnishing sizeable contingents of mounted fighters. In 1158 the Hospitallers provided a total of 1,000 knights, brother sergeants and men-at-arms or Turcopoles, who were light cavalry formed from native-born men with a Latin father and a native mother. For the Egyptian campaign, and in 1187, the year of the fateful battle of Hattin, the Templars furnished in the region of 300 knights, all drawn from the kingdom of Jerusalem.[56]

The Templars, although numerically smaller, were the elite of the crusading task force. Islamic historians paid tribute to both Orders: ibn al-Athir called them 'the backbone of the Frankish armies', and Imād ad-Din 'infernal Templars', along with a gory account of the execution of Templars and Hospitallers after the battle of Hattin.[57]

The Rule of both Orders was strict, that of the Templars stipulating the retinues and beasts – as horses were unsympathetically termed – which each member should have for his personal use. In addition there was a general pool known as the 'caravan' from which additional mounts were drawn. There were also other 'caravans', such as the Marshal's in which horses newly arrived from overseas were kept till the Master of the Order had inspected them and chosen any he needed. The Marshal could then issue horses to knights needing new mounts, but retained a few for use of 'secular friends of the house being used as heralds'.[58] Pack animals had their own remuda; if the Master went on a ride or progress he was entitled to two sumpters, if on a raid or to war, four. During these expeditions they were to be grazed on a tether. Once finished with they had to be returned to the caravan for the general use of the house.[59]

The types of animal to be found in Templar caravans were:

1. destriers or warhorses
2. Turcoman or Turkmene horses
3. palfreys
4. mules for riding
5. sumpters or pack horses
6. rouncies.[60]

The senior officers of the Templar Order were:

1. the Grand Master of the Temple in overall charge[61]
2. the Seneschal, who in battle carried the Order's main black and white standard or gonfanon[62]
3. the Marshal in charge of horses, arms and armour[63]
4. the Commanders of the various territories:
     Jerusalem,[64] City of Jerusalem,[65]
     Antioch and Tripoli[66]
5. Drapier in charge of clothing[67]
6. Turcopolier in charge of the brother sergeants, men-at-arms and Turcopoles.[68]

The basic allocation for senior officers was four horses plus a mount for ordinary riding, which could be a palfrey, mule, rouncy, or Turcoman. A Turcoman was stipulated for the Marshal, and the Turcopolier and the Commander of the City of Jerusalem could, if they wished, have Turcomans. This suggests that these three positions – in the front line as it were – were supplied with more robust horses that could double if necessary as warhorses in battle. They would have been larger than palfreys and mules. This is strengthened by the specific order regarding the role of the Turcoman horse in the Master's retinue, which is worth setting out in full for the equine content:

The Master of the Order shall have four beasts and one brother chaplain; and one clerk with three beasts, and a brother sergeant with two beasts; one gentleman valet to carry his shield and lance with one beast; a farrier and an interpreter, a Turcopole, a cook, two boys on foot, and a Turcoman horse kept in the caravan. The Turcoman shall be led on the right by a squire and by a horse from the caravan [i.e. alongside the squire's allotted horse]. When the Master returns it [the Turcoman] must be put back in the caravan. In war it is to be held on the rein [i.e. led to battle and held in reserve at the ready by the squire].[69]

This is a minimum of fifteen saddle horses allowing one horse for each member of the retinue entitled to one. The farrier in this instance may not be the house farrier, but an extra one so he would rate one horse. In addition there were pack animals.[70]

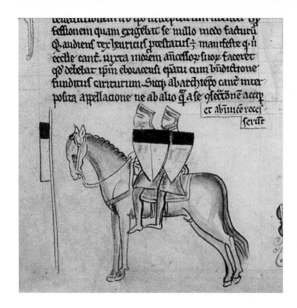

Two Templars on one horse as depicted by Matthew Paris. In accordance with their vows of poverty, the Templar knights often shared their horses. (Corpus Christi College, Cambridge, Ms 26, f. 110v)

The number of animals allowed to Grand Commanders and Priors of the Hospitaller Order varied according to where their bailiwick was. They ranged from twenty for the Grand Commander of Spain down to the Prior of Lombardy and the Commander of the Morea who were both allowed five. These included chargers, palfreys, mules and pack animals.[71]

Horse allocation to other Templars in descending order of rank was:

1. knight commanders of Templar houses, four horses[72]
2. brother knights, three mounts; and at the discretion of the house an extra one for the squire[73]
3. brother sergeants, one permanent horse; and one other if the house deemed it necessary[74]
4. five brother sergeants with special duties, two permanent horses; among these were the front-line brothers – Undermarshal, *gonfanonier*, and farrier; if they were transferred to another house one mount was surrendered to the Marshal.[75]

Presumably the extra horses were allocated in time of war, of if an animal was unfit for duty through sickness, injury, or lameness. There also had to be enough horses to mount the Turcopoles and servants of the house.

Shipments from overseas were insufficient. In addition to normal wastage the Marshal's caravan would have suffered continual depletion in times of war or raiding as Templars were at the sharp end of any engagement. Frankish camps and grazing areas were also pillaged of horses and mules on many occasions. Saladin hired 300 Arab bandits to do just this.[76]

Levantine supply is shown by references in the Rule, and by mention in Christian and Islamic chronicles. Booty or prize horses were put in the Marshal's caravan, and he had the right to buy horses and mules at any time and in any location.[77] Horses were also paid to Franks as ransom. After Richard I had taken Acre Seif ed-Dīn el Meshlat had included them in his ransom payment.[78] As there was a perpetual shortage of horses this would not have been an isolated incident.

Templars had their own farms, and farm managers, or brother kasaliers, were entitled to two mounts.[79] The plan of Acre at the end of the thirteenth century, which is kept in the

Vatican, shows two such establishments which were used as stables and cow parks.[80] The reference to colts which could be allocated from the Marshal's caravan implies that young horses were both purchased and bred on the farms, and subsequently came under the Marshal's jurisdiction.[81] The term colts was translated from the medieval French to mean foals. Whichever meaning is used – foals or colts – it shows youngstock was produced.[82] Young colts were given to brother knights and sergeants to feed,[83] showing some warhorses were allocated before riding age. A good partnership could thus be formed and a brother train the horse to his particular way of riding. The most telling reference to Templars' breeding stock comes from the rule forbidding commanders of houses to take a brother's horse away and send it to stud, unless permission had first been obtained from the Master and the full chapter.[84] There would have been occasions when certain stallions proved to be exceptional and were worth more at stud than in battle.

Warhorse equipment was purely functional. Silver mountings were forbidden on bridle, stirrups or spurs – i.e. on any metal parts of the tack. Any silver or gold decoration was to be scraped off leatherwork unless tarnished or dull when it was deemed permissible to retain it.[85] If a saddle had precious stones on it permission to use it had to be sought.[86] The war-saddle was reserved for fighting and permission needed to use it.[87] Turkish saddles were used for ordinary riding and we find reference to them as gifts from the Commander of Jerusalem to the brothers.[88] They were often flamboyant; Usāmah describes several. The rules of the Hospitallers, as shown by the Chapter General held at Limassol on 8 October 1292, stated that if used they must be covered with black or white leather.[89] Saddle pads were provided,[90] and were necessary to keep the back in good condition under the hard saddle bars and given the violent movements of a fully accoutred fighting Templar.

As seen from a list of things not to be loaned to another brother, hobbles and muzzles were standard equipment.[91] This highlights horse-management on campaign and is a guide to temperament and sex of horses. A hobbled horse cannot stray far and is easy to catch again. Muzzles indicate use of entires as stallions frequently attack other stallions with their teeth – not a petty nip either. Usāmah describes two horses who continued to fight each other even though their riders were unhorsed.[92] Other essential tack was a longe, here meaning a lead line or even a tether; and two girths, one with and one without a buckle.[93] The different means of securing girths gave added security. In a violent fighting situation air intake could suddenly expand the horse's ribcage, causing a buckle to rip through leather. Safety depended on the extra girth, probably used as an over girth secured with a flat knot.[94] Night blankets were provided and on manoeuvres when the horse was 'eased', i.e. unsaddled, brothers needed permission to put them on.[95] Permission had to be sought for almost every action, and there was a host of prohibitions. One of the few freedoms was to miss prayers if a Templar had to take his horse to the farrier for shoeing.[96]

The one item missing in the extensive list of equestrian equipment is horse armour. Arms and armour are referred to in a general way under sections dealing with the Marshal.[97] The only specific reference to horse armour is in the section covering manoeuvres when a knight may dismount to adjust saddle or barding.[98] This leaves us wondering whether or not Templar horses were armoured in the conventional sense; was it cloth, leather, or mail housing? Saladin's Qadi, Behā ed-Dīn, describes 'a man of high rank among the Franks who rode a great charger covered with a hammer cloth of chain mail that reached down to its hoofs and he was apparelled in most extraordinary fashion'.[99] The surprised tone of the remark shows that although some horses

Christ leading the crusaders (British Library, Royal MS 19B XV, f. 37)

were protected, it was unusual. Equipping all knights' and sergeants' mounts with mail bardings would have been too costly. However, an incoming knight who was rich enough would bring such equipment with him. There would also have been horse armour among spoils as orientals and Byzantines had been barding their heavy cavalry for centuries.

The Templars' Rule states that an incoming secular knight had to buy his own horse and arms and have it valued and recorded. Once enrolled his needs were provided for, plus those of his squire and his horse, including horseshoes. When his term was up half the value of the horse was paid to the knight and half to the Temple. If the horse died in service the Temple paid its value.[100] This implies the horse never returned home, unless the knight paid half its value to buy it back. The Hospitallers' Rule sets out what a knight should bring when he 'joined up'. Although the Templars' Rule does not state what the brother knight should bring, except in the case of a secular knight, it was probably similar to that of the Hospitallers. They were adamant over the value of the knight's equipment. From the Statutes of the Chapter-General of 1292: 'It is decreed that all the brother knights, who shall come from beyond the sea, should bring with them all their equipment [arnois] complete, that is to say, three beasts; and he who shall bring less, that the said brother be taken and sent back beyond the sea.' In the Statutes of 1260, No. 261 states: 'If he be a knight and lacking in equipment let him take with him 2,000 deniers Tournois and said Tournois be placed in the Treasury.' Again, if he did not have the cash either, he was to be sent back. Later, in 1302, the number of horses required was reduced to two.[101]

DIFFICULTIES IN MAINTENANCE OF MOUNTS

The feeding of Templar horses was well organized with a combination of barley, hay, straw and grazing. On campaign it was common practice to go out foraging for food (i.e. cut grass or hay) and water, but permission had to be obtained before brothers could leave camp and they were supposed to stay within earshot.[102] When Templars were resident at their respective house, horses were either stabled or alternatively let out to grass. Then they went in an orderly group in the care of the squires, conducted out to and back from pasture by the *Gonfanonier*.[103] Presumably he supervised the squires as they guarded the grazing horses. Each Templar had a basin to measure and a sieve to sift his horse's grain ration.[104] The sieve indicates the grain was poorly harvested and contained a lot of husk and other debris. In wartime, or on campaign, barley came out of a general supply and was a measured amount, rations being increased or decreased only by order of the whole chapter. However the Master could reduce the ration if the grazing was good. When that failed the ration was again raised.[105] When the horses were fed straw on campaign the brothers were not allowed to augment their horses' food with grass.[106] Straw is less nutritious than good hay, but given primitive harvesting methods may have retained some grain. The 'straw' of the Curzon translation could be cut hay. Other feeding rules applied in stables. A granatier doled out rations and no brother's horse was to have extra feed to the disadvantage of another horse; nor was any brother to purchase barley himself for his horse unless permission was granted. Stockpiling of rations while still getting the normal dole was forbidden. Horses not working and kept in the caravan were on half rations.[107]

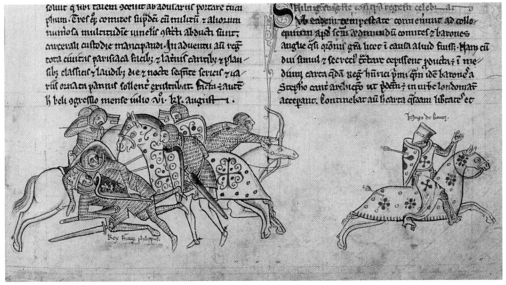

A knight forced to take to flight – Hugh de Boves at the battle of Bouvines. (Corpus Christi College, Cambridge, Ms 16, f. 41r)

A vivid scene of the reality of cavalry combat in the eleventh century is portrayed in this depiction of the Holy Lance being borne in battle outside Antioch by Adhemar, Bishop of Le Puy. (British Library, Ms Yates Thompson 12, f. 29)

These were sensible precautions, especially that of reducing hard feed for idle horses. The penalty for not doing so could have been azoturia. However, it is normal horsemen's practice to try to get that extra feed for a hardworking favourite mount. Templars were probably no different, and the incentive to boost a horse's energy and stamina would have paid dividends in increased safety in a hard-fought battle. The horses would have received adequate but not generous rations. Fodder supplies, especially in times of heightened and prolonged military activity, would have been erratic, and frequently insufficient.

Raymond of Aguiliers gives graphic accounts of the deprivation of men and mounts, especially after the city of Antioch had fallen to the crusaders under the leadership of Bohemond on 3 June 1098. The crusaders' elation was short-lived. Kerbogha, Atabeg of Mosul, arrived with his army only four days later and laid siege to Antioch.[108] Penned inside the city and with the citadel still in Muslim hands the crusaders were soon desperately short of food. A tongueless head of a horse cost 2 or 3 *solidi*; a goat's intestines 5; a hen 8 or 9. Green figs were boiled, as were hides of horses and cattle, to extract what little nutrition they contained. Most knights refused to kill their horses but did drink their blood.[109] The siege lasted till 28 June when Bohemond drew up the crusading host in six divisions and faced Kerbogha whose army was riven by dissatisfaction and desertions.[110] Indeed it was difficult to keep a Muslim army together for a lengthy period. Much of the cavalry was formed from men granted *Iqtas*, the near equivalent of European fiefs, and men under arms were always anxious to return home to attend to them. The standing armies were the Askars of individual towns and the leader's Mamlūk guards. Once in the Levant the Christians had to stay, at least until seasonal sea-passages provided a way out for the wealthy; or unless one was a leader and could pull out at will, as Stephen of Blois did the day before Antioch fell, taking with him a large body of northern French.[111]

Raymond of Aguiliers comments on a providential shower, saying it affected the horses miraculously, and although they had eaten only bark and tree leaves for eight days, the crusaders broke Kerbogha's Turks, who fled and were chased till sundown:

the Lord laboured surprisingly well with men and horses, for the men were not deterred by avarice, and those famished horses scarcely led from their scanty provender into battle by

St George portrayed as a knight, c. 1100. The carving shows St George attacking Saracens on the right, while Christian knights pray on the left. (From the church of St George, Fordington, Dorset)

their masters, now pursued without difficulty the best and fleetest Turkish steeds. . . . Kerbogha fled. Few Turkish knights perished, on the other hand hardly a footman survived.[112]

In 1133–4 during a period of truce between Shams al-Mulk of Damascus and the Franks, a duel ensued when the Franks broke the treaty, ravaged estates in Hawran, and fought for two days with the Muslims penned inside their camp. Finally Shams al-Mulk and part of his Askar broke out and in turn ravaged the Frankish towns of Akka (Acre), Nazareth and Tiberias, looting and burning. The prolonged retaliatory raids eventually ceased towards the middle of October 1134.[113] Shortly after, it was the Franks' turn to be raided. In 1136 the Amir of Aleppo, Mas'ud Sawar, invaded the Frankish-controlled district of Al Ladhiqiya (Latakia) with 3,000 Turkish horsemen. Over a hundred villages were devastated and every movable possession pillaged, including 7,000 captives and 100,000 head of livestock.[114] The Damascus chronicler says this information, contained in a letter from Shaizar, was much exaggerated, but it shows how a massive raiding expedition could strip a countryside of growing crops and every other asset, including horses vital to the conduct of warfare. The movables were replaced to some extent by retaliatory raids, but burnt crops and felled orchards were gone till time and sufficient peaceful interlude promoted regrowth.

The few battles that punctuated the era were costly in lives, but formed only a small part of the overall picture of the crusades; most was taken up with countless skirmishes, planned raids, attacks on pilgrimage trains, and general hooliganism by the crusaders. On the Muslim side, the fighting against enemy crusaders was in addition to constant tribal warfare and the struggle for supremacy by various Islamic chieftains. Treaties were frequently struck between Muslim and Frank, always for a designated period, and just as frequently broken when the pillaging urge became too strong, or the right opportunity offered an easy victory. When one part of Frankish territory was under arms, another area could be enjoying a

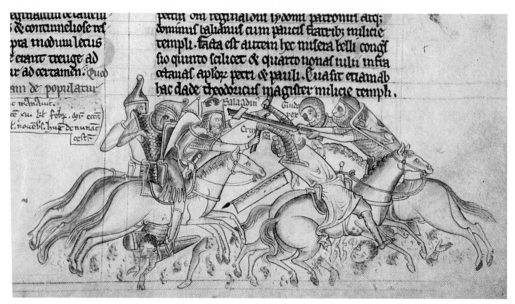

King Guy of Jerusalem's failed attempt to conquer Saladin and the Saracens (Corpus Christi College, Cambridge, Ms 16, f. 139v)

peaceful interlude, in which friendships were made between Muslim and Frank. Usāmah Ibn Munqidh had many Frankish friends, among whom he counted the Templars at Jerusalem who used to let him pray in a little oratory in what had been a Muslim mosque, but was currently in the Templars' hands.[115]

During military action such friendships were suspended and Usāmah's autobiography is full of incidents of mounted fighting between Muslim and Frank. He details the exploits of many of his top Arabian horses and those of his compatriots against the Franks who 'were, of all men, the most cautious in war'.[116] 'Cautious' can be supplanted by 'discipline', given a further look at the core of the Templars' rules.

THE TEMPLARS ON CAMPAIGN

Important leaders of crusading contingents, the most successful of whom carved out their own principalities, such as Bohemond of Antioch, Raymond of Tripoli and the Kings of Jerusalem, pursued conflicts between themselves which were damaging to the presence of Latins in the East. The main constants in the era were the Templars and Hospitallers and, briefly, the Teutonic Knights. They owed their military efficiency as much to their strict codes as to their undoubted courage. The Templars' Rule shows the Order's equestrian establishment was geared to war, and that horses' energies were to be conserved for the battlefield.

No specific battle training is outlined, but that need not surprise us. A knight learned to ride a warhorse as a matter of course; even if he did not initially break it in he would have seen the job was done to his satisfaction.

The undoubted bravery shown in the feared Frankish charge is commendable, but to a horsewoman the action was a waste of precious ammunition. Although frequently successful it was costly. Al-Qalānisī refers to horses with so many arrows sticking out of them that they looked like hedgehogs,[117] following the battle of Cerep on 28 June 1119.[118] Usāmah refers to Tancred wasting seventy destriers in an unsuccessful attempt on Shaizar.[119]

The Turks on the other hand, and particularly the Arabs who hated risking their precious Faras steeds, usually softened the enemy up with continuous arrow fire before risking an expensive charge.

Hunting, so often a schooling ground for cavalrymen, was forbidden to Templars.[120] A limited amount of pleasure riding was allowed but hemmed in by restrictions. Horses were not to be raced without permission, but a brother could sprint his horse to test it two or three times. When carrying lances and riding against each other only a half-speed run was allowed, and permission needed first. In any case if they mock jousted (bohourd) no lances were to be thrown. At half-speed a brother was not required to don chausses, but these were obligatory at top speed – obviously when the danger element was great. Other than the above incidents all pleasure riding was at a walk or amble.[121]

Testing a horse's speed ensured it was fit and responsive; the mock joust and half-speed lance attack without casting weapons taught the rider to place his horse accurately; if the horse jinked off target the rider had advance warning of how his horse would react under pressure and could have reflexive counter-measures ready in battle. Horses who shy from a frontal object nearly always do so to the same side. This exercise built the horse's confidence to charge as he never got hurt. Repeated often enough, with no harm ensuing, it could help restore a charger's shattered confidence. Also any bloody-minded horse would have the nonsense knocked out of him by a skilled rider. Such trials were a way of monitoring the safety and ongoing usefulness of a charger. Worn-out horses had to be replaced by the Commander of the house applying to the Marshal for replacements. The borrowed horses had to be returned and a brother's own horse taken back once it was recovered in health.[122]

Individual brothers could not request a specific horse, but if they had one that was restive, i.e. unsettled to the point of being uncontrollable, or if it was a puller, rearer, or stumbler, the rider could complain to the Marshal. Once the Marshal had ascertained that the horse had any of these vices he could let the brother change it. If the Marshal refused to do so he could not force the brother to ride the horse.[123] It was important that horses were always under control. The cited faults would put a Templar at great risk. Rearing is especially dangerous because once a horse goes up beyond a certain height he becomes unbalanced by the weight on his back, exacerbated when carrying an accoutred man, and he goes over backwards. A puller can usually be counteracted. A stumbler can be held up unless it is very bad and goes on to its knees; some horses stumble because they are idle-minded, some because they are unsound in the legs. All such serious faults would have impaired the knight's safety in battle.

How much pleasure riding was enjoyed depended largely on the attitude of the squadron leader. If racing was permitted, and from the many rules guarding against speed riding it is clear Templars loved a challenge, no wagering was allowed.[124]

Penalties for rule infringements were severe. For a serious infringement a brother lost his habit and could be placed in irons. If the offence was minor, the penalty might be left to the discretion of the brothers in chapter. When a brother was defrocked, which was not always permanent, his arms went to the armoury and his horse to the caravan.[125] Many misdemeanours centred around the horse. In addition to doing any of the above without permission, killing, losing, or injuring a saddle horse,[126] or loaning without permission a horse which was then injured,[127] entailed a Templar's losing his habit at the brothers' discretion. Several occasions when automatic loss occurred are worth noting:

Jaque de Ravane, Commander of the Palace of Acre, was defrocked and placed in irons for leading a troop against Saracens at Castle Robert, between Nazareth and Tiberias. He had done so without permission and suffered defeat.[128]

The rule makes it clear that disobedience was worse than defeat.

A series of major misdemeanours led to the same punishment for the Commander of the Templars' house at Cyprus. A rich layman had left a sick horse at the house to recuperate. When the horse had recovered the Commander went hunting on it; the horse fell and died from its injury. Brothers from Cyprus went to the Acre chapter to intercede, saying the horse was not Templar property, and that when they received it into care it was valueless. Their intercession was to no avail.[129]

At Fontaine Barbe the Turcopolier leading a detachment got caught between two Turkish ambushes. It seemed to the ten knights under Brother Mago that the Turcopolier was about to be overwhelmed, so without permission four brothers went to his aid and two lost their horses. In chapter all were reprimanded, and for a while it seemed that the two who lost horses would be defrocked. However, because the skirmish had ended to their advantage and the Turcopolier had been at great risk they received a lighter punishment.[130]

What these lighter punishments were is not stated, but in the Rule of the Hospitallers there were five punishments:

1. to be deprived of wine, and possibly of cooked food as well, for trivial offences
2. the Septaine for more serious offences
3. the Quarantaine for more serious offences
4. defrocking temporarily, and a possible prison sentence
5. defrocking permanently with a possible prison sentence.[131]

Horse-orientated offences were considered serious enough for the Septaine or the Quarantaine, the first a sentence of seven days, the second of forty, during which the offender ate on the floor apart from the others, and also underwent the discipline (scourging) in front of the brothers in the church on Wednesdays and Fridays.[132]

There were many similarities between the Orders and occasionally members fought together. When a Templar, separated from his squadron, was near a Hospitaller squadron he was to remain and fight under their banner.[133] It is to be expected that punishments, though not necessarily identical, were similar. If a Templar was undergoing penance he could not fight under arms, unless an emergency occurred when he could be loaned horse and arms to fight. When the emergency ceased, horse and equipment had to be returned. Permission for such a loan had first to be sought in chapter.[134] The Templars' prowess, hemmed in by strictures, says much for their discipline and their love of the Order's honour.

All actions undertaken on campaign were done in strict military fashion, either promptly on the order being given, or in compliance with a regular routine. This heightened efficiency, improved security, and added greatly to group and individual Templar safety as there were contingency plans for the occasions when things did not go according to expectations. This cohesion was remarkable in an era when discipline and adherence to strict military procedures were often more notable by their absence. It gave the Templars their supremacy in battle and must have been responsible for much of the admiration, possibly unwilling but clearly honest, Behã ed-Dīn showed for Frankish 'excellent judgement' in military actions,[135] allied to bravery and fearlessness, and 'wonderful self-control'.[136] In these instances he was not referring specifically to either Templars or Hospitallers. As these Orders were to the forefront of any fighting their example must often have stiffened ranks which wavered. Saladin's Qadi who was present at many of the engagements between Franks and Muslims describes the series of engagements from 12 July 1191, when Acre fell to Richard I, to 2 September 1192, when both sides sued for peace and a treaty was signed to run for three years from that date.[137]

A squadron of Turkish cavalry, depicted in a Muslim manuscript of the thirteenth century

Sahyun, Saladin's castle, Syria

The battle of Arsuf, 7 September 1191, was a victory for the Franks and is graphically described, with a deal of information as to battle formations and Frankish vigour. Although the Hospitallers initiated the charge from the rear it was the Templars who led the van once they had erupted from the protecting circle of infantry. Behind came the Angevins, Bretons, King Guy (of Jerusalem), Normans, English and Poitevins, with Hospitallers closing the rear. The combined weight of Frankish cavalry put the Muslims to flight, and a second charge completed the victory, the Muslims fighting as they fled to eventually regroup and count their losses. Both sides had high casualties, many men and horses dead and a large number injured.[138] The Arabs who later went over the battlefield counted more than a hundred dead Frankish chargers.[139]

The Templars' premier position was hard won. It must have come hard for a knight not used to obsolute obedience to knuckle under to authority. Manoeuvres started with Templars arraying in marching order on the command to mount.[140] Proceeding at the walk or amble, each knight was followed by his squire. Once *en route* the knight then placed his squire(s) in front of him with his war gear – armour, weapons and spare horse(s). Marching was done quietly and, unless speech was absolutely necesssary, in complete silence on night moves. Wind direction was noted and as far as possible anyone having good cause to get out of line had to do so with the wind to avoid making a mess of the route.[141] In dry weather the dust would have alerted the enemy.

To drink water – for both man and horse – required permission. However, if the march was through peaceful countryside it was permissible to take advantage of a running stream so long as the column was not disrupted. On a reconnoitring mission watering was possible only if the standard-bearer called a water halt. If the alarm was raised close by, those nearest could arm and mount and wait for the Marshal's order.[142]

The above account indicates several points. Obviously *en route* the warhorses were led by the squires, and the knights rode mules or palfreys. In the Rule of the Hospitallers it was decreed that except for helmet and leg armour all other armour was to be carried at the cantle when out on a raid.[143] The not watering rule was very sensible. An apposite modern example concerns Noel Carney, whose son John related the incident to me. In the 1920s as a member of the Middlesex Yeomanry he was stationed in Palestine to keep Zionists and Palestinians from their interminable warfare. On a patrol with full arms strapped behind their saddles, the column dismounted at a desert rill. Shots rang out. The whole troop of horses bolted, and for weeks after Arabs proudly paraded captured British chargers and firearms. A very successful razzia; the lieutenant in charge was later court-martialled.[144]

At all times Templars had to be prepared and observe cautionary measures. When waiting in ambush, guarding foragers, or on watch, they were to keep their horses saddled and bridled, and not to feed them unless authorized.[145] Other than feeding making a horse unready for action, a horse with a full stomach can colic if asked for strenuous exertion, the pain causing him to seize up.

Once established in their respective squadrons the brothers remained with that group. They armed when ordered, placed their squires leading spare warhorses behind them, and kept their ranks, quiet and ready.[146] The only reason for getting out of line was to sprint a horse to make sure it was fit, i.e. responsive, or to check tack – the saddle and barding.[147] It was not considered necessary to detail types of horse armour, just as a bridle was referred to simply as that, not as a particular type.[148] Trying the tack would normally have meant tightening the girth. The only time a brother could charge out of ranks on his own decision was if a confrère was being attacked and in danger of being killed by a Turk.[149]

The rallying point in any engagement was the Templar black and white gonfanon. Sometimes it was carried by the Undermarshal,[150] sometimes the Marshal elected to carry it.

The standard was always surrounded by a select guard of ten knights, and a spare standard was kept ready furled round the lance of one of the guards. If the Marshal was killed or injured and his standard downed, the squadron rallied to the spare gonfanon and operated in the same manner.[151] Templars were the very last to leave the field of battle. No brother was to quit while the Templar standard still flew. If it was downed and irrecoverable he had to go to the nearest Hospitaller or other Christian standard and remain with it until it too was irretrievably lost. Only then could he return to the garrison, unless the pressure was so great it was obvious that no one could hold out.[152] Such rules show the essence of the military Orders: how much was demanded of them, and why such a toll was taken in men and horses killed and injured. The fact that these two Rules were so explicitly framed shows that a fight to the 'outrance' was not a rare occasion. Of the knights' valour we are left in no doubt. They have received admiration from contemporary Christian and Arabic chroniclers, and from historians ever since. The valour of the horse too should be lauded. It was in the Muslim camps! After the great battle of Acre on 4 October 1189, Saladin's Qadi reported that from the Frank left wing alone 4,100 dead were counted by an eye-witness, but he could not verify the dead from the right wing, although he thought the total to be less than the reported 7,000. According to him the Muslims lost only 150.[153] In the aftermath Saladin paid tribute to the horses saying they too had had their share of the fighting and were worn out after being fifty days under arms, but after a rest their spirits would revive. With winter setting in, activities were halted,[154] and the battle for Acre was temporarily deferred.

Horses that could be used in battle were either the very stupid, so thick that they did not flinch at most batterings (this type has slow responses and would hardly have been ideal) or

Saladin. The Sultan of Egypt from 1175, Saladin made peace with Richard I in 1192, following the Third Crusade (1189–92). This work dates from c. 1180 and is the oldest extant Arabian portrait of the Khalifate period

the courageous, a real partner to his rider. Close order combat, in which the Templars excelled, was undertaken aboard stallions, whose natural aggression was an asset. This trait, coupled with noise, sudden movements, speed and the challenge of other stallions present in the heightened atmosphere of a rapidly moving maelstrom, would have worked to the horse's advantage by keeping its courage, i.e. aggression, flowing during combat. Non-crippling injuries would not have registered while the aggression manifested itself;[155] yet at all times the mastery of the man, instilled through years of training and association, would have allowed this volatility to be channelled at the rider's command.

THE HORSE'S VALOUR AND IMPORTANCE

References to specific Frankish equine losses in Christian chronicles are scarce, most being mentioned in multiples of hundreds, more often in exaggerated thousands. In the Arabic sources there are more concrete facts. For example, 400 were lost on the day when the Franks started their march to Ascalon after taking Acre (12 July 1191), a depletion that continued as Frankish horses and soldiers on the march were riddled with up to ten arrows apiece from Muslim fire.[156] The most graphic accounts concerning the part played by horses in the crusades come from Usāmah who was a natural horseman and a warrior, and fully appreciated the courage shown by his, and other, Arabian horses. He shows what risks a charger took when in close order combat; how the animals responded; and how very heavy losses could be. Although the frequent incidents he relates were mostly personal, their sad cavalcade down the years exposes a chilly reckoning and is applicable to both sides.

He gives perceptive insight into equine mentality according to breed which offers a good link to my remarks above. When his father was hunting roe deer on a black Arabian mare, and got thrown when the mare put a hoof into a pit dug for a boar, he contrasted the mare's behaviour with that of a berdhun who had shied and thrown its rider. The berdhun took off and cost half a day's chase before it was caught; the Arabian mare returned to watch over her master until help came.[157] The translator calls the berdhun a hackney, another breed entirely.

Usāmah recounts excursions not only against Franks but also against towns and districts held by other Muslims. The Arab attitude to war, hunting and horses comes out clearly with the quote about him by his Egyptian host on a hunting trip: 'And what other business has this man but to fight and hunt?'[158] and with a line from the poet Antarah ibn Shaddad: 'For why should I ride a horse unless I am going to fight on its back.'[159]

Usāmah's horses were constantly tested in hunting and fighting, his first experience of the latter being in a skirmish outside Afamiyah (Apamea) in August 1119. Sent to Afamiyah to raise troops and pillage the crops in the Frankish-held territory, and thinking it devoid of troops, he was surprised to be set upon by a reinforcement troop of sixty horse and sixty foot and driven back upon the Muslim pillagers already harvesting grain. In retreat, 'with a mare under me as swift as a bird', Usāmah turned on a pursuing Frank who had divested himself of his mail coat to lighten his horse's burden so it could chase more effectively. He thrust him through the chest with his lance, killing him instantly. With the roles reversed and the Franks now in flight, Usāmah pursued another Frank 'on a black horse large as a camel' and was worried that he was being drawn into an ambush until he saw the black begin to flag with exhaustion. His mare charged, and he spitted the Frank on the lance, which stuck out a cubit in front of the enemy, the force of the blow pushing Usāmah back over the cantle. Later it transpired that the lance had gone through a double thickness of mail shirt only grazing the Frank's side as it came out in front of him.[160]

Other near misses came from close order combat. Desperate attacks and ripostes occurred when either Frank or Muslim was in flight, as at Antioch when Franks pursued Usāmah's detachment. Usāmah jumped a sizeable wall and found himself faced with a fully armoured Frank. Avoiding him, or, as he put it, 'letting him pass', he turned, rejumped the wall and hit the Frank so hard with his lance that he knocked him sideways; the Frank's head was thrust down to his stirrup and he lost shield, lance and helmet, but eventually managed to haul himself upright.[161]

Not all engagements ended without serious injury and there were several instances of horrific wounds to horses. Among the Shaizar troops was a Kurd named Kāmil al-Mashtūb who rode 'a horse of solid black colour as big as a camel'.[162] In an encounter with a Frank his horse was hit beside the throat-latch and its head skewed to one side, the lance coming out at the lower end of the neck (near the withers) and piercing Kāmil al-Mashtūb's thigh. Both horse and rider survived; the horse was again injured severely in a later engagement by a lance thrust into the frontal bone (of the forehead) which forced it inward. Even when healed, the hole was big enough for a man's fist. This same horse later formed part of a rent paid for a village to a Frankish knight from Kafartab, and when it died a year later the Frank complained, saying it had been poisoned (the translation says 'Because it had been given something to drink'), hoping to get double pay for it.

Other horses suffered mortal wounds. One had its heart pierced in combat at Hims, and while arterial blood was pumping out still carried Usāmah out of danger before collapsing and dying. Others were wounded several times in one battle; yet another succumbed to a mere arrow scratch, repeatedly falling, much to the disgust of Usāmah. An Arabian of the Banu-Numayr tribe used in a local battle showed extreme courage while mortally wounded. Even with its entrails spilling out, and strapped up by a surcingle to stop it treading on them, it stayed on its feet throughout the battle between the Banu-Numayr and Shihāb-al-Dīn Mālik-ibn-Shams-al-Dawlah, brother of the Governor of Al-Raqqah whom the tribe had killed.[163]

SUPPLIES AND LOSSES

Throughout the unfolding of the crusades one of the major problems for the cavalry was to keep itself mounted. Figures abound in the chronicles of both sides, but in common with all other medieval historians, crusader chroniclers showed unreliable arithmetic. Behā ed-Dīn strikes one as being the most reliable because he will occasionally report figures, and if he was not himself present at an engagement sometimes says he thought them inflated.[164] However, he tends to diminish Muslim losses and inflate Christian ones; on the other hand there are instances when it is clear he is accurate. He is unusual in giving low odd number assessments, such as the small body of men under Richard I outside Jaffa in 1192, which Richard was trying to relieve. Attacked by Saladin, Richard repulsed him with only 1,000 foot and at the most seventeen horse, at the least nine.[165]

There are no accurate records for how many horse and foot actually took part in the crusading era. For the First Crusade Sir Steven Runciman has estimated that the cavalry taking part totalled approximately 4,200–4,500, and the infantry 30,000, which included civilians who could be armed if necessary.[166] To this figure should be added the extra horses taken by wealthier knights. We have seen that Hospitallers and Templars, according to rank, had up to four horses each, of which at least two were battle chargers. The majority of knights or men-at-arms would be lucky to have had just one. However, leaders and senior knights could have sizeable pools. In Louis IX's first crusade Joinville recalls landing in 1249 at Damietta where one small ship was carrying eight of his horses; this implies that Joinville had others, too.[167] No doubt some of these were supplied for his own retinue. On the other hand Villehardouin, when discussing the logistical arrangements for shipping horses, notes contracts for 4,500 horses and the same number of knights.[168]

The thirteenth-century Chertsey tile showing Richard I and Saladin

Horse losses quickly whittled down the original numbers. Once the Latins were established in their newly won principalities of Tripoli, Antioch, Acre and Jerusalem, together with satellite towns, and were able to enjoy the more settled life many achieved in the Levant, a limited amount of stock breeding was possible, as suggested by the reference to the Templars' stud horses. Even so there were frequent outbursts of warfare between Frank and Muslim, and Frank versus Frank, in which precious remounts were at risk. This is highlighted by the conflict between Tancred and Baldwin, who had taken Tarsus. Tancred sent a group of archers with the express purpose of either wounding Baldwin's horses grazing outside Mamistra or if possible capturing them and driving them off. He was unsuccessful in the ensuing fight, and although prisoners were taken on both sides he retired to the city.[169] Tancred was luckier after his conquest of Cilicia as surrounding rulers, both Turk and Armenian, seeking his favour, sent drafts of horses and mules among their precious gifts.[170]

On the march to Jerusalem the remount situation was temporarily eased, as towns such as Shaizar, Hama and Emesa, and other fortified towns, in order to escape unscathed gave herds and flocks to the crusading army which was then able by purchase and gifts to build up horse stocks.[171]

After a battle one of the prime assets was the means of horse replenishment. Crusaders especially valued the top-quality Arabian horses which the Syrians also prized. Al-Qalānisī makes several references to 'swift Arabian horses';[172] Usāmah also refers to horses of Arabian breeding, such as one of the Khafā'jah strain, and others of the 'best breed' or of 'great value'.[173] A horse of the Khafā'jah strain was demanded by Tancred as part ransom for a Muslim named Hasanum. Tancred already had acquired a valuable fleet horse from the Munqidh family.[174]

There is a cross-reference to the best type of horses available to the crusaders of the first and subsequent crusades in Syria in the works of Raymond of Aguiliers from the First

Crusade and Usāmah whose life spanned the greater part of the twelfth century and who served under Saladin's predecessor Nur ad-Dīn. Raymond also refers to the crusaders' trip to Shaizar, Usāmah's home town, and Camela (Emesa/Homs), but gives more information than William of Tyre, and slightly different facts regarding the herds. The capture of Marratt an Numan on 11 and 12 December 1098, and the seizing of a huge herd of cattle, 'caused our knights and more affluent people to go to Shaizar and Camela with their money to buy Arabian horses . . . and so we had almost 1,000 of the best warhorses'.[175]

At the subsequent siege of Arqah Raymond of Tripoli's entourage boasted of their 'Arabian horses and riches'; two of these horses formed part of a gift to Tancred from Raymond for his services during the fighting and sieges en route to Jerusalem.[176] It would appear Tancred was a connoisseur of Arabian horses.[177] He was not alone in his appreciation. Earlier in the protracted siege of Antioch which lasted from 20 October 1097 to 3 June 1098, after one of many encounters the crusaders celebrated a victory and haul of spoils, including many horses, by running back and forth between their tents on Arabian horses showing new

The battle of Dorylaeum, 1097, from a fourteenth-century history by William of Tyre. The date of the illustration is indicated by the Christian horses, almost all of which are barded. This would have been most unusual at the time of the battle itself (Ms Fr. 352, f. 49)

riches to their friends.[178] Raymond of Aguiliers' short account has many references to Arabian horses, and to the crusaders replenishing their stocks by gift, purchase, theft and booty.[179] He also gives brief but vivid accounts of the downside of equine stocks, showing that mortality was high and the conditions and numbers, prior to sporadic replenishments, frequently depleted. For two days after the crusaders' victory at the battle of Dorylaeum on 1 July 1097 the ground was covered with dead horses and men.[180]

At the seige of Antioch horses were dying from hunger.[181] In the Provençal camp there were hardly a hundred left, and they were scrawny and feeble, and similar conditions prevailed in the camps of all the other leaders.[182] After the city of Antioch, but not the citadel, fell, more than a hundred Christians and a greater number of horses died at one entrance to the city alone.[183] During the journey to Jerusalem 'many gave up hope and turned back on account of scarcity of horses, the absence of Godfrey and the exodus of many knights to Baldwin of Edessa'.[184]

Although replenishments were frequent, losses were greater. This is not surprising and no doubt more died from starvation, or by being so debilitated they could not withstand work and the injuries during the conflict, than from outright death on the battlefield. In the two years' bloodsoaked journey to Jerusalem there would have been scant edible provender after armies had repeatedly trampled it underfoot; any agriculture that survived the constant upheavals and depredations along the route and its environs would have been minimal. Indeed the picture of the host arriving at Jerusalem is pitiful. It might have been the ultimate goal for the crusaders but it had cost their livestock dear. By the Pool of Siloam at the foot of Mount Zion outside the city, 'in the fields stood horses, mules, cattle, sheep and many other animals too weak to take another step. There they shrivelled, died from thirst, and rotted in their tracks.'[185]

The original cavalry may have brought their 4,500 warhorses with them, plus reserve warhorses, baggage animals and riding hackneys and palfreys, but how many thousands perished in addition? From first to last an ongoing wastage in horseflesh littered the battlefields and depleted the breeding stocks. In that one aspect of the economy the cost was enormous; the pain unforgivable. Behind the so-called chivalry lay the unwarranted cruelty to men and animals. The cost was to continue. In the Orient the horse was in his heyday as a tool of war. In the Occident his heyday had yet to come, although cavalry momentum was gathering.

Glossary of Terms

aid	instruction given to horse by hand, leg, whip or spur (last two known as false aids)
ala	Roman cavalry regiment (literally wing)
alod	land held in absolute ownership
amble	two-beat lateral gait
azoturia	a build up of lactic acid in the horse, causing swelling of the muscle fibres, followed by degenerative changes, locomotor inability, passage of myoglobin into blood plasma and its excretion into the urine
bard	housing for horse of mail, leather, lamellar, plate, or cloth
bars	(1) gums between molars and incisors in horse's mouth
	(2) part of saddle tree that sits each side of horse's spine
blood	(1) coldblooded – refers to horse of draught horse type
	(2) hotblooded – refers to horse of oriental ancestry, i.e. thoroughbred
	(3) oriental – Arabian, Akhal Teke, Turcoman, Berber
	(4) warmblood – cross of hot and cold, and/or cold and oriental
cantle	back part of saddle
carty	of either pure or partial draught horse physique
cataphract	heavy-armoured trooper whose horse may also be armoured
chamfron	horse's head armour
caltrop	three-pointed metal devices, a few inches in size, that when strewn on the ground always have one point uppermost so horses' hooves get pierced and internal bones suffer massive damage
clenches	the turned down part of the horseshoe nail that grips the hoof
curb	(1) a type of bit which acts on poll, chin groove and mouth
	(2) a swelling on the calcaneo-cuboid ligament on the inside of the leg below the hock
dehydration	loss of fluids in a horse – very dangerous if excessive
entire	ungelded male horse
ergot poisoning	a fungal disease of grain which causes encephalitis in horses, termed 'blind staggers'
farcy	highly contagious disease of lymphatic system manifesting itself in nodules, ulcerations, and degenerations in respiratory passages or in the skin
girth	leather or fabric around horse's body to secure saddle. Also measurement around body in that area
glanders	as for farcy
greenbreaking	basic training for horse to make it rideable
green horse	one who only has the basic education
gullet (of saddle)	part over the withers – underneath of pommel
hackamore	English language term for a bitless bridle that works by nasal control, originally from the Spanish and Arabic. Spanish – *Jaquima*; Arabic/Moorish – *Hakamah*; Roman – *psalion*
hand (hh)	a means of measuring horses, 4 in being the approximate width of a man's hand
hybrid vigour	where the offspring of two different breeds of horse is a larger and/or superior animal than either parent

jihad	Islamic holy war
laminitis	hoof ailment where the laminae of the hoof become damaged as a result of internal fever in the hooves usually due to overfeeding and/or overwork and too sudden a cooling down by offering the horse cold water while he is in an overheated condition
lead	horse's leg that extends furthest when in canter stride (to be absolutely correct the horse on the left lead actually struck off into that stride with the right hind leg, but visually it is easiest to appreciate the leading foreleg)
lead change	when a horse in canter switches his leads from left to right or vice versa
martingale	leather strap from noseband to girth to prevent horse from throwing his head, or holding his head too high. Can also be run from rein to girth; former is a standing, latter a running martingale
oestrus/non oestrus	when a mare is receptive/not receptive to the covering stallion
pelham	a curb bit using four reins, two attached to the branches of the bit on each side. Mouthpiece comes in many varieties
pommel	front part of saddle over the withers
razzia	raid
remuda	stock of spare horses travelling with mounted men on herd patrol. In context of this book, the extras to replace dead or injured warhorses held behind the lines in reserve group, or by squires
roach backed	horse's spine raised in convex form towards the loin area – bad conformation
snaffle	a bit using single rein, working on the tongue and bars of the mouth and lips. Comes in many varieties
splints	bony enlargements on cannon bones, can cause lameness
staggers	ataxia, incoordination
suppling	training the horse so that he manoeuvres smoothly at all paces, and especially in circling and turning exercises
touched in the wind	impaired lung capacity
trappy	short, choppy gait, usual in chunkier type horse with poor conformation
tushes	teeth (one each side in lower jaw) between molars and incisors

Notes

Abbreviations

AHR	American Historical Review
al-Ansari	'Umar Ibn Ibrahim al-Awsī al-Ansarī
ANS	Anglo-Norman Studies
ASC	Anglo-Saxon Chronicles
BAR	British Archaeological Reports
Behā	Behā ed-Dīn Abu el Mehāsan Yūsuf
CAP	Capitularies of Charlemagne
CAS	Central Asiatic Studies
De V.	'De Villis' (Loyn and Percival)
EHR	English Historical Review
HJAS	Harvard Journal of the Asiatic Society
Ibn al-Athir	'Izz ad-Din Ibn al-Athir
Ibn Hodeil	Aly Ben Abderrahman Ben Hodeil El Andalusy
Jahiz of Basra	Amr. b. Bahr. b. Mahbub Abu Othman al-Jahiz
JAOS	Journal of the American Oriental Society
JRAS	Journal of the Royal Asiatic Society
Naceri, Le Naceri	Le Naceri of Abou Bekr Ibn Bedr
RFA	Royal Frankish Annals
Taybugha	Taybugha al-Baklamishi al-Yunani
Usāmah	Usāmah Ibn Munqidh

Introduction

1. From *Le Naceri*, trans. M. Perron (Ministry of Agriculture of France, 1860), 3 vols, Vol. II, p. 380.

1. Medieval Equestrian Cultures

1. A. Hyland, *Equus* (Batsford, London, 1990), pp. 183–6.
2. ibid., p. 40.
3. ibid., pp. 148ff.
4. C.M. Trevelyan, *English Social History* (Pelican, Harmondsworth, 1967; first pub. Longmans Green, 1942), p. 393.
5. Hyland, *Equus*, p. 44.
6. S.I. Rudenko, *The Frozen Tombs of Siberia* (J.M. Dent, London, 1970), p. 56; recent Russian findings now date these burials between the third and first centuries BC, but the redating does not alter the equestrian significance.
7. Herodotus, *The Histories*, trans. A. de Selincourt (Penguin, Harmondsworth, edn), 1954; citing 1974 Book VIII.41, p. 459F and Book VII.88, p. 471.
8. A. Dent, contribution to *Encyclopedia of the Horse* (Octopus, London, 1977), p. 13f.
9. N.H.H. Sitwell, *The World the Romans Knew* (Hamish Hamilton, London, 1984), p. 100.
10. H.W.F. Saggs, *The Might that was Assyria* (Sidgwick & Jackson, London, 1984), p. 169.
11. Strabo, *Geography* (Loeb Classical Library, Heinemann, London, 1961), 11.3.9.
12. A. Hyland, *The Endurance Horse* (J.A. Allen, London, 1988), p. 13.
13. ibid., p. 11.
14. Hyland, *Equus*, p. 148ff.
15. Ammianus Marcellinus, *The Later Roman Empire, AD 354–378*, trans. W. Hamilton (Penguin, Harmondsworth, 1986), 24.6 and 25.1.
16. M. Jankovich, *They Rode into Europe*, trans. Anthony Dent (Harrap, 1971), p. 35.
17. Julius Caesar, *De Bello Gallico: The Gallic Wars*, trans. J.J. Edwards (Loeb Classical Library, Heinemann, London, 1955), Book IV.2.4.
18. ibid.
19. Hyland, *Equus*, p. 77.
20. Vegetius Publius Renatus, *Digestorum Artis Mulomedicinae*, ed. Ernestus Lommatzsch (Leipzig, 1903), III.VI.
21. W.M. Leake, *The Edict of Diocletian AD 303* (John Murray, London, 1826).
22. Rudenko, *Frozen Tombs of Siberia*, p. 133.
23. Caesar, *Gallic Wars*, Book IV.4.2.
24. P. Connolly, 'The Roman Saddle', in *Roman Military Equipment: The Accoutrements of War: Proceedings of the Third Roman Military*

Equipment Research Seminar, *British Archaeological Reports* [hereafter *BAR*] *International Series*, 336 (1987), p. 7ff.

25. Leake, *Edict*.

26. Hyland, *Equus*, pp. 130–4.

27. G. Vernam, *Man on Horseback* (Harper & Row, New York, 1964), *passim*.

28. M.D. Bishop, 'Cavalry Equipment of the Roman Army in the 1st century AD', in Military Equipment and the Identity of Roman Soldiers, *BAR International Series*, 394.

29. Vernam, *Man on Horseback*, pp. 56–7.

30. M.S. Merwin, contribution to *The Horse through Fifty Centuries of Civilization*, pr. A. Dent (Phaidon Press, London, 1979), p. 29.

31. Ammianus Marcellinus, *The Later Roman Empire*, 19.1., 24.5.

32. *The Holy Qu'ran*, trans. A. Yusuf Ali (Sh. Muhammad Ashraf, Lahore, Pakistan, 1975), Sura XVI, n. 81.

33. The conformation of oriental horses, other than Nesaean, differed from those raised in Europe. The Arabian does have a larger brain than other breeds.

34. Bigger horses are not necessarily stronger than small wiry ones. Huge horses are more prone to breakdown.

35. E. Oakeshott, *A Knight and His Horse* (Lutterworth Press, London, 1962), pp. 36f.

36. Vernam, *Man on Horseback*, p. 134.

37. ibid., p. 141.

38. ibid.

39. J. de Joinville, see *Chronicles of the Crusades*, trans. M.R.B. Shaw (Dorset Press, 1985), p. 273.

40. J. Froissart, *Chronicles*, trans. and ed. G. Brereton (Penguin, Harmondsworth, 1968; rep. 1983), pp. 411, 414.

41. Maurice, *Maurice's Strategikon: Handbook of Byzantine Military Strategy*, trans. George T. Dennis (University of Pennsylvania Press, 1984), Book I, Ch. 2.

42. A.D.N. Bivar, 'The Stirrup and its Origin', *Oriental Art*, new series, 1, no. 2 (1955), pp. 61–5.

43. M. Grant, *Dawn of the Middle Ages* (Weidenfeld & Nicolson, London, 1981), p. 66.

44. Abou Bekr Ibn Bedr, *Le Naceri*, trans. M. Perron (Paris, 1860), Vol. II, p. 183.

45. Museum of London, Medieval Catalogue (catalogues, no. 7) (HMSO, 1940), Fig. 18, nos 2 and 3, p. 78.

46. Showing it was no small pony.

2. Byzantium and her Enemies

1. Hyland, *Equus*, pp. 192ff and Chapters 1 (Breeding), 3 (Veterinary Medicine), 5 (Supply of Equines), 15 (Racing) and 17 (*Cursus Publicus*).

2. ibid.: Syria, pp. 179, 75; Phrygia, p. 238; Cappadocia, pp. 11, 19, 213. A. Hyland, *Training the Roman Cavalry from Arrian's Ars Tactica* (Alan Sutton, Stroud, 1993), on Cappadocian horses, pp. 9–13 *passim*.

3. H.G. Creel, 'History of the Horse in China', *American Historical Review*, LXX, 3 (April 1965), pp. 647–72. This measurement is taken from the *Yang K'uan-Chung-Kuo Li-Tai Ch'in-yu-K'ao* (a study of the history of measures).

4. Marco Polo, *The Travels of Marco Polo*, trans. Teresa Waugh from the Italian translation by Maria Bellonci (BCA edn, 1984; Sidgwick & Jackson, London, 1984), p. 30, XXXIII.

5. Strabo, *Geography*, Nesaean/Persian 11.13.7, Armenian 11.14.9. Xenophon, *The Persian Expedition*, trans. Rex Warner (Penguin Classics, Harmondsworth, 1986 [1949]), on Armenian horses Book IV, Chap. 5, p. 201.

6. Dede Korkut, *The Book of Dede Korkut*, trans. Geoffrey Lewis (Penguin, Harmondsworth, 1982 [1974]), p. 18f.

7. ibid., pp. 34–5, especially, and *passim*, p. 191.

8. ibid., p. 123.

9. Many Akhal Teke horses have gold coats and black points, i.e. mane, tail, lower legs. The uncertain temperament sometimes attributed to the modern breed may be linked to the literary reference on p. 191 (note 7).

10. Jankovich, *They Rode into Europe*, drawing from Hancar (1955) on p. 37.

11. ibid., p. 33.

12. Marco Polo, *The Travels of Marco Polo*, trans. William Marsden, from the Italian translation by Remusio (Cox & Bayliss, 1818), p. 129. See also Polo, *Travels*, trans. Waugh, p. 42, XLVIII.

13. V. Kalinin, trans. H.P. Fox, 'Horse Breeding in the Soviet Union', in *The Book of the Horse*, ed. B. Vesey-Fitzgerald (Ivor Nicholson & Watson, London and Brussels, 1947 [1946]).

14. Procopius, *The History of the Wars*, trans. H.B. Dewing. (Loeb Classical Library, Vols I–V, Heinemann, London, 1914–1928) Vol. II, Book III, Ch. xii, p. 6.

15. ibid., Vol. I, Book I, Ch. i, p. 9f.

16. J.C. Coulston, 'Roman Archery Equipment' in The Production Distribution of Roman Military Equipment, Proceedings of the Second Roman Military Equipment Research Seminar, ed. M.C. Bishop (*BAR International Series*, 275, 1985).

17. Personal discussion with Edward McEwan, an expert in all forms of archery, especially oriental and Mongolian methods.

18. Procopius, *History of the Wars*, Vol. I, Book I, Ch. xviii, p. 24ff.

19. ibid., p. 9ff.

20. ibid.

21. Procopius, *Secret History*, trans. G.A. Williamson (Penguin Classics, Harmondsworth, 1987 [1966]), note by translator, p. 19. Belisarius was born about AD 505.

22. Procopius, *History of the Wars*, Vol. I, Book I, Ch. xii, p. 20f and Ch. xiii, p. 9f.

23. ibid., Ch. xiii, p. 19ff.

24. ibid., Ch. xiii, pp. 25–30.

25. The Immortals, so called because always kept up to strength.

26. Procopius, *History of the Wars*, Vol. I, Book I, Ch. xiv, pp. 1–55.

27. L.H. Fauber, *Narses, Hammer of the Goths* (Alan Sutton, Stroud, 1990), p. 189. Procopius, *History of the Wars*, Vol. IV, Book VII, Ch. i, pp. 16–21.

28. Fauber, *Narses*, p. 189.

29. Procopius, Vol. II, Book III, Ch. ix, p. 25f; Ch. xi, pp. 2–21; Ch. xii, p. 6f.

30. ibid., Vol. III, Book V, Ch. iii, p. 22f. Hyland, *Equus*, p. 171f.

31. Procopius, *History of the Wars*, Vol. II, Book III, Ch. xvi, p. 12.

32. ibid., Vol. II, Book III, Ch. xiv, p. 17; Ch. xvii, pp. 7–17.

33. ibid., Vol. II, Book III, Ch. xxv, p. 10ff.

34. ibid., Vol. II, Book IV, Ch. ii, p. 1ff.

35. ibid., Vol. II, Book IV, Ch. iii, pp. 2–28.

36. ibid.

37. ibid., Ch. xiv, p. 17ff.

38. ibid., Ch. vii, p. 20f.

39. ibid., Vol. III, Book V, Ch. v, p. 11.

40. ibid.; ibid., Ch. vii, p. 26.

41. ibid., Ch. xiv, p. 1; Ch. xiv, p. 14.

42. ibid., Ch. xvi, pp. 5–11.

43. ibid., Ch. xviii, pp. 2–27.

44. ibid., Ch. xix, p. 19.

45. ibid., Ch. xxvii, pp. 1–23.

46. ibid., Ch. xxvii, p. 27f.

47. ibid., Ch. xxix, pp. 13–49.

48. ibid., Vol. IV, Book VI, Chs i and ii *passim*.

49. ibid., Vol. III, Book V, Ch. xi, p. 1.

50. ibid., Vol. IV, Book VI, Ch. iii, pp. 23–32; Ch. iv, p. 1f.; Ch. v, pp. 1–4; Vol. V, Book VII, Ch. xiii, pp. 20–1.

51. ibid., Vol. IV, Book VI, Ch. x, p. 1; Ch. xii, p. 26f.

52. ibid., Ch. xiii, pp. 16–18.

53. ibid., Ch. xviii, pp 1–19; Ch. xxi, pp. 13–42.

54. ibid., Ch. xxii, p. 4.

55. ibid., Ch. xxx, p. 1.

56. ibid., Ch. ix, p. 22f.

57. ibid., Vol. V, Book VII, Ch. ii, p. 7.

58. ibid., Ch. viii, p. 20.

59. ibid., Ch. iv, pp. 10–12.

60. ibid., Ch. xl, p. 19.

61. ibid., Vol. V, Book VIII, Ch. xxi, pp. 5–22.

62. ibid., Ch. xxii, p. 1f.

63. ibid., Ch. xxvi, pp. 5–6.

64. ibid., Ch. xxvi, pp. 7–13.

65. ibid., Ch. xxxi, pp. 1–8.

66. ibid., Ch. xxx, p. 17.

67. ibid., Ch. xxxl, p. 1ff.

68. ibid., Ch. xxix, pp. 16–21.

69. ibid., Ch. xxxl, pp. 2–16.

70. ibid., Ch. xxxl, pp. 18–21.

71. ibid., Ch. xxxii, pp. 5–10.

72. ibid., Ch. xxxii, p. 20; ibid., pp. 20–8.

73. ibid., Ch. xxxv, p. 18f. Fauber, *Narses*, p. 104f.

74. Procopius, *History of the Wars*, Vol. V, Book VIII, Ch. xxxv, p. 36ff.

75. Fauber, *Narses*, p. 125ff.

76. Maurice, *Strategikon*, p. xvi (Dennis).

77. ibid., pp. xvi and xvii for possibilities of authorship.

78. ibid., Book I, Ch. 1.

79. ibid., Ch. 9.

80. ibid., Ch. 1.

81. ibid., Book II, Ch. 17.

82. A.D.N. Bivar, 'Cavalry Tactics and Equipment on the Euphrates Frontier', *Dunbarton Oaks Papers* [hereafter *DOP*], 26 (1972), pp. 273–91.

83. Maurice, *Strategikon*, Book I, Ch. 1.

84. Taybugha al-Baklamishi al-Yunani, *Saracen Archery*, trans. J.D. Latham and W.F. Paterson (Holland Press, London, 1970).

85. Maurice, *Strategikon*, Book I, Ch. 2.

86. ibid.

87. On lasso: such stockmen's methods would go unremarked, but can certainly be considered as part of nomadic tactics.

88. Maurice, *Strategikon*; most of the pack animals were horses, judging by references in the text. See Book XII, Ch. 6 for packhorses and Book XII, Ch. 22 for packhorses and camels.

89. ibid., Book I, Ch. 2.

90. Procopius, *History of the Wars*, Vol. II, Book III, Ch. xii, p. 6.

91. *The Theodosian Code*, trans. C. Pharr, (Princeton University Press, Princeton, 1952), Imperial Herds Title 6.4.19, communication dated 13 April 372.

92. ibid., Title 6.10.6.1, under 30 November 396/7.

93. Maurice, *Strategikon*, e.g. Book III, Ch. 5; ibid., Ch. 15.

94. ibid., Book I, Ch. 8, p. 16.

95. ibid., Book VII, Ch. 17.

96. ibid., Book III, Ch. 5.

97. ibid., Book I, Ch. 4.

98. ibid., Ch. 5.

99. ibid., Book II, Ch. 1.

100. ibid., Ch. 13.

101. Bivar, 'Cavalry Tactics', p. 283.

102. Maurice, *Strategikon*, Book II, Ch. 13.

103. ibid., Book III, Ch. 12.

104. ibid., Book II, Ch. 3.
105. ibid., Book III, Ch. 12.
106. ibid., Chs 13, 14, 16.
107. ibid., Book XI, intro.
108. ibid., Book XII, Ch. 7.
109. ibid., *passim*.
110. ibid., Book XI, Ch. 1, *passim*.
111. ibid., Ch. 2, *passim*.
112. Bivar, 'The Stirrup and its Origin', pp. 61–5.
113. D. Obolensky, *The Byzantine Commonwealth* (Weidenfeld & Nicolson, London, 1971; Sphere Cardinal edn, 1974), p. 72.
114. ibid., p. 72f.
115. ibid., p. 75ff.
116. Maurice, *Strategikon*, Book XI, Ch. 2.
117. ibid.
118. ibid., Book II, Ch. 1.
119. ibid., Book XI, Ch. 2.
120. ibid., Book IX, Ch. 2.
121. ibid., Book XI, Ch. 2.
122. ibid.
123. ibid., Book I, Ch. 2.
124. ibid., Book XI, Ch. 2.
125. ibid., Book IX, Ch. 2.
126. ibid., Book XI, Ch. 2.
127. Russell Robinson, *Oriental Armour* (Herbert Jenkins, London, 1967), illustration p. 58.
128. S. Jagchid and C.R. Bawden, 'Some Notes on the Horse Policy of the Yuan Dynasty', *Central Asiatic Studies* [hereafter *CAS*] (1965), pp. 246–65 (p. 257).
129. Maurice, *Strategikon*, Book XI, Ch. 2.
130. ibid.
131. ibid.
132. ibid.
133. ibid.
134. ibid., Book VII, on 'Strategy before the Day of Battle'.
135. S. Bökönyi, *History of Domesticated Mammals in Central and Eastern Europe* (Akadémiai Kiadó, Budapest, 1974), pp. 267ff.
136. Maurice, *Strategikon*, Book XI, *passim*.
137. ibid., Book XII, Ch. 22.
138. ibid., Book IX, Ch. 3.
139. ibid.
140. ibid., trans. Dennis, introduction, p. xvi.
141. ibid., Book VIII, Ch. 1, p. 30.
142. ibid., e.g. Book IX, Ch. 3; Book VII, Ch. 10.
143. ibid., Book V, Ch. 3.
144. ibid., Ch. 4.
145. ibid., Book VII, Ch. 10.
146. ibid., Book XII, Ch. 22.
147. ibid., Book VII, Ch. 9.
148. ibid., Book XII, Ch. 22.
149. ibid., Book III, Ch. 8.
150. ibid., Book V, Chs 1 and 2.
151. ibid., Book IX, Ch. 5.
152. ibid.
153. Hyland, *Equus*, p. 50.

154. Maurice, *Strategikon*, Book IV, Ch. 3.
155. ibid., Book II, Ch. 9.
156. Note: it is not the weight they object to but the heaving up of the object.
157. Maurice, *Strategikon*, Book IX, Ch. 5.
158. ibid., Book XII, *passim*, no. D.
159. Most Arabs were not equestrians at the outset of their conquests but rapidly became so.
160. Obolensky, *Byzantine Commonwealth*, p. 106ff.
161. L. Brehier, *Les Institutions de L'Empire Byzantin* (Editions Albin Michel, Paris, 1949), p. 356.
162. Strabo, *Geography*, 11.13.9. and 11.14.9. Xenophon, *Persian Expedition*, Book IV, Chap. 5, p. 201. Plutarch, *Lives*, trans. W. and J. Langhorne (Chandos Classics, Frederick Warne, London, 1884), Vols 1 and 2, Roman, Life of Crassus. Saggs, *The Might that Was Assyria*, p. 169, noting King Sargon II (721–705 BC) on the cavalry horses of Urartu (Armenia).
163. Brehier, *Les Institutions*, p. 356.
164. F. Lot, *L'Art Militaire et les armées au moyen âge en Europe et dans le proche orient* (Payot, Paris, 1946), Vol. I, p. 174.
165. Brehier, *Les Institutions*, p. 360.
166. C. Oman, *A History of the Art of War in the Middle Ages*, Vol. I (Burt Franklin, rev. edn, 1924), p. 182.
167. ibid., p. 184.
168. ibid.
169. Brehier, *Les Institutions*, pp. 363 and 347.
170. ibid., p. 363.
171. C. Porphyrogenitus, *De Administrando Imperio*, trans. R.J.H. Jenkins from Greek text ed. Gy Moravcsik (Budapest, 1949), nos 51 and 52.
172. Hyland, *Equus*, pp. 157–9 *passim*.
173. Brehier, *Les Institutions*, pp. 374–5.
174. ibid., p. 329.
175. Procopius, *Secret History*, 7.30.13f.
176. Brehier, *Les Institutions*, p. 329.
177. Procopius, *Secret History*, 30.2ff.
178. Brehier, *Les Institutions*, p. 330f.
179. A. Comnena, *The Alexiad*, trans. E.R.A. Sewter (Penguin Books, Harmondsworth, 1987 [1969]), Book XII, Ch. ix.
180. Obolensky, *Byzantine Commonwealth*, p. 76.
181. S. Vyronis, *Byzantium and Europe* (Thames & Hudson, London, 1967), p. 38f.
182. N.H. Baynes, 'The Campaigns of Heraclius against Persia', *English Historical Review* [hereafter *EHR*], 19 (1904), pp. 694–702.
183. Vyronis, *Byzantium and Europe*, p. 60.
184. Obolensky, *Byzantine Commonwealth*, p. 77f.
185. Vyronis, *Byzantium and Europe*, p. 60f. Obolensky, *Byzantine Commonwealth*, p. 227.
186. J.B. Glubb, *The Great Arab Conquests* (Hodder & Stoughton, Sevenoaks, 1963), p. 280.

187. Obolensky, *Byzantine Commonwealth*, pp. 227–34 *passim*.

188. C.A. Macartney, *The Magyars in the Ninth Century*, (Oxford University Press, Oxford, 1968 [1930]), pp. 194, 196, 199, 200.

189. Obolensky, *Byzantine Commonwealth*, p. 221.

190. Marco Polo, *Travels*, trans. Waugh, p. 42, XLVII, on Bactrian horses.

191. Sitwell, *The World the Romans Knew*, p. 178. Hyland, *The Endurance Horse*, p. 22f.

192. Glubb, *Conquests*, p. 280.

193. D.R. Hill, 'The Role of the Camel and the Horse in the Early Arab Conquests', in *War, Technology and Society in the Middle East*, ed. V.J. Parry and M.E. Yapp (Oxford University Press, Oxford, 1986), p. 36.

194. Lady Wentworth, *The Authentic Arabian Horse* (Allen & Unwin, London, 1945), p. 29ff. Abou Bekr, *Le Naceri*. Ibn Hodeil, *La Parure des cavaliers et l'insigne des preux*, trans. Louis Mercier (Librairie Orientaliste, Paul Geuthner, Paris, 1924).

195. W. Ridgeway, *The Origins and Influence of the Thoroughbred Horse* (Cambridge Biological Series, Cambridge University Press, Cambridge, 1905), p. 245.

196. Hyland, *Equus*, pp. 25, 173ff, 210f.

197. Lady Wentworth, once she leaves the very early period, can be accepted as an authority, especially when using the records of her mother, Lady Anne Blunt (see below, note 233).

198. W. Keller, *The Bible as History*, trans. W. Neil (BCA edn, London; Hodder & Stoughton, 1956), pp. 270, 231, 210. *Catholic Bible*, ed. Rev. J.P. O'Connell (Harwin Press/Virtue, London, 1956), I Kings 10.26–9.

199. Abou Bekr, *Naceri*, Vol. I, Ch. IV, p. 122.

200. Ibn Hodeil, *La Parure*, p. 317.

201. *Cambridge Encyclopedia of Archaeology*, ed. A. Sherratt (Cambridge University Press, Cambridge, 1980), p. 213.

202. Ibn Hodeil, *La Parure*, p. 317.

203. Our own queen frequently receives horses as gifts.

204. Lady Wentworth, *Authentic Arabian*, p. 88.

205. Glubb, *Conquests*, p. 116.

206. Ibn Hodeil, *La Parure*, pp. 309–12 *passim*.

207. Abou Bekr, *Naceri*, Vol. I, pp. 99–102, except Mourtediez, p. 79.

208. Marco Polo, *Travels*, trans. Waugh, CLXXV.

209. ibid., CXCV and CXCVII.

210. ibid., CXCV; and Marco Polo, *Travels*, trans. Marsden, p. 726.

211. E.W. Bovill, *The Golden Trade of the Moors*, 2nd edn (Oxford University Press, Oxford, 1978), p. 168.

212. Note: this is not always the case in other texts, where oriental horses are frequently called Arabs (Arabians) and may have no Arabian blood.

213. Abou Bekr, *Naceri*, Vol. I, p. 77.

214. Glubb, *Conquests*, p. 68.

215. ibid., p. 61ff.

216. Hill, 'Camel and Horse', p. 36.

217. ibid., p. 36.

218. ibid., p. 37.

219. Note: more likely lack of water, which is far more important than lack of grass.

220. Glubb, *Conquests*, p. 84f.

221. ibid., p. 99.

222. ibid., pp. 108–12.

223. ibid., p. 146ff.

224. Lynn White, Jr, *Medieval Technology and Social Change* (Oxford, Clarendon Press, 1962), p. 18.

225. Robinson, *Oriental Armour*, p. 75.

226. Glubb, *Conquests*, p. 174.

227. Robinson, *Oriental Armour*, p. 17.

228. ibid., p. 83.

229. Glubb, *Conquests*, p. 274.

230. ibid., p. 218f.

231. Hill, 'Camel and Horse', p. 38.

232. Glubb, *Conquests*, p. 218.

233. Note: Lady Anne Blunt was fluent in Arabic and had access to many original manuscripts and to the oral history of the bedouin.

234. Wentworth, *Authentic Arabian*, pp. 109–13f.

235. ibid., p. 107.

236. Glubb, *Conquests*, pp. 150, 159f.

237. ibid., p. 173ff.

238. Hill, 'Camel and Horse', p. 37.

239. ibid., p. 35.

240. Glubb, *Conquests*, p. 184.

241. Hill, 'Camel and Horse', p. 39.

242. Glubb, *Conquests*, p. 193ff.

243. Hill, 'Camel and Horse', p. 36.

244. Glubb, *Conquests*, p. 203.

245. ibid., p. 247.

246. Hill, 'Camel and Horse', p. 36.

247. Brehier, *Les Institutions*, p. 375, note 3.

248. Hyland, *Equus*, p. 14.

249. Vyronis, *Byzantium and Europe*, p. 83.

250. H.M. Hayes, *Veterinary Notes for Horse-owners* (Stanley Paul, London, 1976 edn), pp. 220–62. Hyland, *Equus*, p. 129.

251. Brehier, *Les Institutions*, p. 375.

252. Obolensky, *Byzantine Commonwealth*, p. 67f.

253. ibid., pp. 91–6 *passim*.

254. ibid., pp. 116f and 124f.

255. ibid., p. 129 (the reasons have nothing to do with this book, although the wrangling between the two Christian sects caused a lot of military activity and sparked off many wars, as is the case with all unnecessary religious confrontations).

256. ibid., p. 145f.

257. Porphyrogenitus, *De Administrando Imperio*, p. 49, no. 1.

258. ibid., p. 49, no. 2.
259. ibid., p. 51, no. 3.
260. ibid., p. 51, no. 4.
261. ibid., p. 53, no. 5.
262. ibid., p. 65, no. 13.
263. Macartney, *Magyars*, p. 69f.
264. ibid., p. 76f.
265. Jankovich, *They Rode into Europe*, p. 23.
266. D. Sinor, 'The Inner Asian Warriors', *Journal of the American Oriental Society* [hereafter *JAOS*], 101 (1981), pp. 133–44.
267. Oman, *Art of War in Middle Ages*, Vol. I, p. 206.
268. Jankovich, *They Rode into Europe*, p. 66.
269. Also under Turks come Pechenegs and Bulgars.
270. Oman, *Art of War in Middle Ages*, Vol. I, p. 206.
271. Jankovich, *They Rode into Europe*, p. 97.
272. ibid., p. 94.
273. Obolensky, *Byzantine Commonwealth*, p. 146.
274. ibid., p. 206.
275. Oman, *Art of War in Middle Ages*, Vol. I, p. 122ff.
276. Jankovich, *They Rode into Europe*, p. 60.
277. Obolensky, *Byzantine Commonwealth*, pp. 150–5 *passim*.
278. ibid., p. 173ff *passim*.
279. M. Psellus, *Fourteen Byzantine Rulers*, trans. E.R.A. Sewter (Penguin Classics, Harmondsworth, rev. edn 1966), Book I, 34, p. 47.
280. Obolensky, *Byzantine Commonwealth*, p. 178f.
281. T. Talbot Rice, *The Seljuks* (Thames & Hudson, London, 1961), p. 36f.
282. Psellus, *Fourteen Byzantine Rulers*, Book 7, 4–9, pp. 352–4.
283. Oman, *Art of War in Middle Ages*, Vol. I, p. 288ff.
284. Talbot Rice, *The Seljuks*, p. 37.
285. Oman, *Art of War in Middle Ages*, p. 220f.
286. Talbot Rice, *The Seljuks*, p. 38.
287. Vyronis, *Byzantium and Europe*, p. 133.
288. Oman, *Art of War in Middle Ages*, p. 221.
289. Note: a fleshy horse always tires more quickly than a lean animal, and it also loses more fluid from its tissues which can put it into a serious clinical state if carried to excess.

3. Western Europe in the Eighth and Ninth Centuries

1. Fauber, *Narses*, p. 173f.
2. Procopius, *History of the Wars*, Vol. V, Book VIII, Ch. xxxii, pp. 7–14.
3. ibid., Vol. IV, Book VII, Ch. xxxiv, pp. 40–6.
4. ibid., Vol. V, Book VII, Ch. xxxix, p. 20.
5. ibid., Book VIII, Ch. xxvi, pp. 7–12.
6. ibid., Ch. xxvii, pp. 7–8.
7. ibid., Ch. xxxl, pp. 1–2.
8. ibid., Ch. xxxiii, p. 2.
9. Hyland, *Equus*, p. 183ff.
10. ibid., pp. 22–3. The Akhal Teke is of a lean build when fit. Oriental horse breeds are perfectly capable of carrying considerable weight.
11. ibid., pp. 11–29, *passim*.
12. Oman, *Art of War in Middle Ages*, p. 48f.
13. S. Loch, *The Royal Horse of Europe* (J.A. Allen, London, 1986), pp. 50 and 51, quoting d'Andrade.
14. W. Montgomery Watt, *A History of Islamic Spain* (Edinburgh University Press, Edinburgh, 1965), pp. 27ff.
15. R. Dykes Shaw, 'The Fall of the Visigothic Power in Spain', *EHR*, 21, 82 (April 1900), pp. 209–28.
16. Loch, *Royal Horse*, p. 58.
17. Montgomery Watt, *Islamic Spain*, pp. 81–6 *passim*.
18. Loch, *Royal Horse*, p. 59.
19. D.J.A. Ross, 'L'Originalité de "Turoldus": le maniement de la lance', *Cahiers de Civilisation Médiévale*, VI (1963), pp. 127–38.
20. Personal discussion with Henry Deptford who breeds and uses Quarter horses which are the breed most used in this task.
21. The upper weight limit is more suitable for roping. My own horse Jacobite once roped a pony out of a New Forest quagmire. He weighed 1,200 lb (440 kg) and needed all his weight to free the mare from sucking clay.
22. Bökönyi, *History of Domesticated Mammals*, p. 271.
23. Oman, *Art of War in Middle Ages*, Vol. I, p. 58.
24. White, *Medieval Technology and Social Change*, pp. 3–4.
25. This is of course the case in most European climates. In hotter eastern provinces the flush would be somewhat earlier.
26. *Royal Frankish Annals* in *Carolingian Chronicles*, trans. Bernhard W. Scholz with Barbara Rogers (Ann Arbor Paperbacks, University of Michigan Press, Ann Arbor, 1991 [1972]) [hereafter *RFA*] under year 758, p. 42.
27. Lot, *L'Art militaire*, Vol. I, p. 93.
28. ibid., p. 91. P. Contamine, *War in the Middle Ages*, trans. Michael Jones (Basil Blackwell, Oxford, 1984), p. 24.
29. Lot, *L'Art militaire*, p. 93.
30. In the *Roland* the 'Moors' are actually 'Basques'.
31. Notker, the Stammerer, 'Charlemagne', in *Two Lives of Charlemagne*, trans. and intro. Lewis Thorpe (Penguin Books, Harmondsworth, 1969), II.17.

32. ibid., II.12.
33. ibid., II.9.
34. Thorpe, *Two Lives of Charlemagne*, introd., p. 5ff.
35. *RFA*, as above, under years 788 to 796, pp. 66–75.
36. Einhard, 'Life of Charlemagne', in *Two Lives of Charlemagne*, II.6.
37. ibid.
38. ibid., II.8.
39. ibid., II.9.
40. ibid.
41. ibid., II.11.
42. ibid., II.13.
43. ibid., II.14.
44. ibid., III.22.
45. ibid., IV.32.
46. Nithard, 'Nithard's Histories', in *Carolingian Chronicles*, III.6.
47. *RFA*, the year 782, p. 186, note 1. The alternative ms, shown as *R*, notes: 'At the beginning of the summer, when sufficient fodder was available to take the army to Saxony . . .'
48. ibid., under, year 782, pp. 59–61.
49. ibid.
50. H.R. Loyn and J.R. Percival, *The Reign of Charlemange* (Edward Arnold, 1975), 'Capitularies of Charlemagne' [hereafter Cap.] 'De Villis' [hereafter De V.], 10.
51. ibid., De V.50.
52. ibid., De V.13.
53. This is unusual even today, but provided stallions have equable natures and mares are not around to incite fights it is perfectly possible. My own stallion runs with three geldings.
54. Cap., De V.13; very old stallions lose fertility.
55. ibid.
56. Cap., De V.14.
57. ibid.
58. Cap., De V.15.
59. Because stallion is more accurate than stud groom in choosing the right time, except where veterinary surgeons do internal examinations.
60. Cap., De V.13.
61. ibid., 23.
62. ibid., 27.
63. ibid., 62.
64. Oman, *Art of War in Middle Ages*, Vol. I, p. 79, where Cap. Aquisgranense No. 5 is quoted.
65. Cap., De V.64.
66. ibid. De V.13, 23.
67. ibid., 24, 34, 41, 48.
68. ibid., De V.46.
69. ibid., 37.
70. ibid., 69.
71. Contamine, *War in Middle Ages*, p. 25.
72. B.S. Bachrach, 'Animals in Warfare in Early

Medieval Europe', *Septimane*, XXXL (1983), pp. 707–64.
73. My stallion Nizzolan when doing 100-mile race training during which he travelled at a high average speed ate 15 lb of grain and about 12 lb of hay per day. Cavalry horses would not have had anything like his sustained energy expenditure.
74. *RFA*, year 783, p. 61.
75. Oman, *Art of War in Middle Ages*, Vol. I, p. 81f.
76. Bachrach, 'Animals in Warfare', p. 784.
77. *RFA*, under year 786, p. 63.
78. ibid., under year 787, pp. 64–6.
79. ibid., under year 788, pp. 66–8.
80. Vegetius, *Digestorum*, III.VI.
81. *RFA*, under year 791, pp. 60–70.
82. Contamine, *War in Middle Ages*, p. 25.
83. This was most likely the disease we call strangles. Although today it is rarely fatal, my veterinary surgeon, Russell Lyons, MRCVS, considers that in the historical context we are discussing it would have been the cause of many fatalities.
84. *RFA*, the years 805 (p. 84f), 811 (p. 93f).
85. Contamine, *War in Middle Ages*, p. 27.
86. Nithard, in *Carolingian Chronicles*, I.2.
87. ibid., I.3.
88. ibid., II.1.
89. ibid., II.3.
90. ibid., II.6.
91. ibid., II.7.
92. ibid., II.8.
93. ibid., II.9 and 10.
94. ibid., II.10.
95. *Carolingian Chronicles*, trans. Scholz, p. 210, note 5.
96. Lot, *L'Art militaire*, p. 105.
97. Nithard, in *Carolingian Chronicles*, IV.3.
98. Lot, *L'Art militaire*, p. 106.
99. ibid., p. 110.
100. Contamine, *War in Middle Ages*, p. 28.
101. Oman, *Art of War*, Vol. I, p. 108.

4. The Anglo-Saxon Period

1. Caesar, *Gallic Wars*, V.IV.33ff, V.V.15ff.
2. Dio Cassius, *Dio's Roman History*, 9 vols, trans. E. Cary (Loeb Classical Library, Heinemann, 1961–70), Vol. 3, Book 5, and XL.3.
3. Hyland, *Equus*, p. 88.
4. ibid., p. 192.
5. ibid., p. 183ff.
6. Vegetius, *Digestorum*, II.VI.
7. Hyland, *Equus*, p. 28.
8. E. Birley, *Housesteads Roman Fort* (English Heritage, Historic Buildings and Monuments Commission for England, HMSO, London, 1985; first published by the National Trust, 1936), p. 7.

9. A.L.F. Rivet and C. Smith, *The Place-Names of Roman Britain* (Batsford, London, 1981, Book Club Associates edn), p. 238.

10. ibid., p. 220.

11. S. Frere, *Britannia* (Routledge & Kegan Paul, London, 1987, Book Club Associates edn), p. 167.

12. Rivet and Smith, *Place-Names*, pp. 220 and 221.

13. Hyland, *Equus*, p. 25.

14. Loch, *Royal Horse of Europe*, p. 63.

15. John Mann, personal comment.

16. G. Webster, *The Roman Army* (Grosvenor Museum, Chester, rev. edn, 1973), p. 5.

17. Giraldus Cambrensis, 'The Journey through Wales', in *Gerald of Wales*, trans. with an intro. by Lewis Thorpe (Penguin, Harmondsworth, 1978), Book I, Ch. 12.

18. New Forest ponies of 13 hh and 14 hh are customarily ridden on colt hunts and cattle drifts by farmers, many of whom are not exactly lightweight.

19. Giraldus Cambrensis, 'Description of Wales', in *Gerald of Wales*, Book I, Ch. 9.

20. ibid., Ch. 8.

21. ibid., Book II, Ch. 7.

22. Bede, *Bede's Ecclesiastical History of the English People*, ed. Bertram Colgrave and R.A.B. Mynors (Oxford University Press, Oxford, 1969), p. 259.

23. ibid., p. 466.

24. G. Fleming, *Horseshoes and Horseshoeing* (Chapman & Hall, London, 1869), pp. 277–8.

25. ibid., quoted from Cotton Mss, Cleopatra B.5 (Department of Mss, the British Museum, London).

26. *Beowulf*, trans. Kevin Crossley-Holland (Folio Society, London, 1973), p. 46, ll. 5–7; p. 47, ll. 25–7.

27. ibid., p. 51, l. 16ff.

28. ibid., p. 61, ll. 31–2.

29. ibid., p. 78, ll. 17–19.

30. ibid., p. 87, ll. 7–11, 20–1.

31. R. Glover, 'English Warfare in 1066' in *EHR* 67, 262 (January 1952), pp. 1–18.

32. *The Anglo-Saxon Chronicles*, trans. and coll. Anne Savage (Phoebe Phillips/Heinemann, London, 1982), the years 868, 869, 870, 871, all on p. 92.

33. Ingulph, *Chronicle of the Abbey of Croyland*, trans. (from the Latin) H.T. Riley (Bell, London, 1893), p. 42.

34. *Anglo-Saxon Chronicles*, the year 871, p. 92.

35. ibid., the years 789–93, p. 73; 794–800, p. 76; 801–36, pp. 82–3; 838–65, pp. 88–9; 866–75, pp. 92–3; 876–93, pp. 96–9.

36. A stallion's 'book' is the number of mares he is contracted to cover.

37. Speeds on competitive trail rides with no race element range from 6 to 8 mph on average.

38. Fleming, *Horseshoes and Horseshoeing*, p. 276.

39. ibid., p. 353.

40. J. Clark, 'Medieval Horseshoes', Department of Medieval Antiquities, Museum of London, Finds Research Group 700–1700, Datasheet 4, reproduced and distributed by Coventry Museums.

41. *Anglo-Saxon Chronicles*, illustration on p. 87.

42. Cotton Mss, Cleopatra C.VIII, folio 4.v. (Department of Mss, the British Museum, London).

43. *Anglo-Saxon Chronicles*, year 937, p. 122.

44. Ingulph, *Croyland Chronicle*, p. 75.

45. *Anglo-Saxon Chronicles*, years 994–1010, pp. 144–51 and 156; years 1011–1015, pp. 156–7 and 160–1.

46. To a horse, working cattle is much the same as harrying people.

47. Ingulph, *Croyland Chronicle*, p. 182.

48. *Anglo-Saxon Wills*, ed. and trans. Dorothy Whitlock (Oxford University Press, Oxford, 1930), p. 3, no. I and note, p. 10.

49. ibid., p. 7, no. II.

50. ibid., p. 13ff, no. III.

51. ibid., p. 27, no. X and note, p. 127.

52. ibid., p. 31ff, no. XIII.

53. ibid., p. 47, no. XVII.

54. ibid., note, p. 153, l. 6ff.

55. ibid., p. 55, no. XIX.

56. ibid., note on p. 166, l. 19f.

57. ibid., pp. 57–9, no. XX.

58. ibid., p. 81, no. XXXI.

59. C.W. Hollister, *Anglo-Saxon Military Institutions* (Clarendon Press, Oxford, 1962), p. 50.

60. ibid., p. 64.

61. ibid., p. 81f.

62. *Welsh Medieval Law*, text of the Laws of Hywel the Good (Hywel Dda), trans. A.W. Wade-Evans (Clarendon Press, Oxford, Harleian Mss 4353, 1909; the British Museum, London), p. xxi.

63. ibid., p. xxiif.

64. ibid., V2a18.

65. ibid., V8b20.

66. ibid., V27a10.

67. ibid., V1b3.

68. ibid., W39a14,ff. (all chief officers noted as having horses supplied).

69. ibid., V3a10; V3b17; V3b19; V3b21; V3b22.

70. ibid., W37b13.

71. ibid., W38b4; V3b24.

72. ibid., V8b20.

73. ibid., V29a3.

74. ibid., W105b13.

75. ibid., V32b11.

76. ibid., W65b21.

77. ibid., V44b15.
78. 'Ancient Laws and Institutes of Wales', in ibid., p. 314/15, I744.
79. ibid., p. 301, I794, W92b, 13–15.
80 *Welsh Medieval Law*, V41a2.
81. ibid., W88b21.
82. ibid., V41a8.
83. ibid., V30a7.
84. ibid., V30a11.
85. ibid., W10496.
86. ibid., V29b15.
87. ibid., U.29 a 15–16 (inter honunt et Runfi, V29b2; 'Ancient Laws', 1.704).
88. ibid., V29a3; W104a6.
89. ibid., V29b2; V29b8; V29b10.
90. ibid., V29b24.

5. *Norman and Early Plantagenet Equestrianism*

1. Contamine, *War in the Middle Ages*, p. 54.
2. ibid., p. 35f.
3. ibid., p. 56.
4. A.J. Robertson (ed.), *The Laws of the Kings of England from Edmund to Henry I*, trans. A.J. Robertson (Cambridge University Press, Cambridge, 1925), p. 263.
5. M. Chibnall, 'Military Service in Normandy before 1066', *Anglo-Norman Studies* [hereafter *ANS*], V (1982), pp. 65–77; and R.H.C. Davis, 'The Warhorses of the Normans', *ANS*, X (1987), pp. 67–82.
6. Chibnall, 'Military Service', p. 67.
7. ibid., p. 70, quoting Orderic Vitalis, II.80–5.
8. ibid., p. 70f.
9. Davis, 'Warhorses of the Normans', p. 77, quoting Orderic Vitalis, III.186.
10. ibid., quoting Orderic Vitalis, III.200.
11. *Liber Quotidianus Contrarotulatoris Garderobae, Anno Regni Regis Edwardi Primi Vicesimo Octavo, AD MCCXIX and MCCC* (Society of Antiquities, London, 1787), p. 168, f. 128; Bishop Winton's palfrey cost £13 6s 8d; destriers ranged from £10 upwards, £20 being exceptional; pp. 170–86, ff. 133–43.
12. Davis, 'Warhorses of the Normans', pp. 67–82.
13. A.J. Brookes, 'The Percheron Horse in Great Britain', in *Book of the Horse*, ed. Vesey-Fitzgerald, p. 625.
14. Lady Wentworth, 'The World's Horse', ibid., p. 37.
15. Giraldus Cambrensis, 'Journey through Wales', Book II, Ch. 12.
16. J. Hewitt, *Ancient Armour and Weapons in Europe* (John Henry and James Parker, Oxford and London, 1855), quoting Wace, ll. 12,673f on p. 173.
17. Contamine, *War in the Middle Ages*, p. 54f.
18. F. Allibone, *In pursuit of the Robber Baron* (Lennard, 1988), pp. 5, 6, 35.
19. J. Beeler, *Warfare in Feudal Europe, 730–1200* (Cornell University Press, Ithaca and London, 1972), p. 70.
20. Contamine, *War in the Middle Ages*, p. 55.
21. Comnena, *Alexiad*, Book I, Ch. xi (p. 54) desc. of Guiscard, Book V, Ch. iv (p. 163) and *passim* on heavy Frankish/Celtic charge.
22. ibid., Book I, Ch. xi (p. 54).
23. Hyland, *Equus*, pp. 73, 171f.
24. Procopius, *History of the Wars*, Vol. I, Book V.iii.22; Book VII.xl.19; Book V.xxvii.1; Book V.xxix.22f; Book V.xxix.35; Book VII.xxxix.20: all *passim* in book on the Gothic wars. Also J.H. Pryor, 'Transportation of Horses by Sea during the Era of the Crusades: eighth century to AD 1285; Part I', *Mariner's Mirror*, 68 (1982), pp. 1–27; 'Part II', ibid., pp. 103–25.
25. See Chapter 2 for the measurements and how they were reached.
26. Beeler, *Feudal Warfare*, p. 75.
27. A 14.2 hh Arabian weighing 750 to 850 lb (340 to 385 kg) in fit condition can carry at least a quarter of its own weight over a 100 mile (160 km) distance and travel at a consistent 6 to 7 miles (9.6 to 11.2 km) per hour (I have done this in Florida frequently).
28. Kai Ka'us Ibn Iskander, *Qabus Nama: A Mirror for Princes*, trans. (from the Persian) R. Levy (Cresset Press, 1951), p. 120.
29. ibid., p. 183.
30. ibid.
31. ibid., pp. 112ff; included with the down-to-earth comments is a cluster of superstitious remarks which I have omitted.
32. Parrot mouth: the top dentition overshoots the teeth of the lower jaw, making it difficult to obtain adequate nutrition.
33. Like a rabbit's, but not so extreme.
34. An open gullet permits good wind.
35. i.e. not pot-bellied; 'fine' here does not mean gaunt or scrawny.
36. i.e. not spindly, but not coarse either.
37. The good solid horn with a decent depth to the foot is a characteristic of oriental horses; a round sole would obviate contracted heels.
38. Overabundant hair on heels is a sign of coarse breeding derived from carty blood.
39. Chibnall, 'Military Service', p. 73.
40. ibid.
41. M. Altschul, *A Baronial Family in Medieval England: The Clares, 1217–1314* (Johns Hopkins University Press, Baltimore, 1965), p. 49.
42. R. Barber and J. Barker, *Tournaments, Jousts, Chivalry and Pageants in the Middle Ages* (Boydell Press, Woodbridge, 1989), p. 177.
43. ibid., p. 21.

44. ibid., p. 140.
45. *Royal Frankish Annals* in *Carolingian Chronicles*, the year 778.
46. W. von Eschenbach, *Willehalm*, trans. C.E. Passage (Ungar, New York, 1977), p. 5.
47. ibid., p. 283.
48. ibid., p. 4.
49. ibid., p. 12f.
50. *Royal Frankish Annals* in *Carolingian Chronicles*, the year 801.
51. Turoldus, *The Song of Roland*, trans. D.L. Sayers (Penguin, Harmondsworth, 1988 [1957]), v. 240, l. 3350.
52. ibid., v. 241, l. 3353; v. 380, l. 3869.
53. ibid., v. 91, l. 1153.
54. ibid., v. 116, l. 1534f.
55. ibid., v. 68, l. 847f.
56. ibid., v. 114, ll. 1490ff.
57. ibid., v. 228, l. 3152.
58. ibid., v. 93, l. 1197.
59. ibid., v. 79, l. 994, triple ring; v. 99, l. 1281f, double ring; v. 97, l. 1269ff, single ring; v. 251, l. 3466, banded steel, which is similar to the laminated armour of a Roman cuirass; v. 124, l. 1647, jazrain or jazerant, jazerant armour being variously described as: laminated (Hewitt, *Ancient Armour*, p. 111); chain mail made in Algiers (*Song of Roland*, trans. Sayers, p. 115); and small metal plates riveted one to the other, or on to a stout lining (*Shorter Oxford English Dictionary*, 1983 edn); v. 247, l. 3426, cordwain (*OED*, goat leather and later horse hide) takes its name from Cordova.
60. ibid., v. 79, l. 994ff.
61. ibid., v. 101, l. 1300.
62. ibid., v. 248, l. 3432ff, helm, cap and coif; v. 249, l. 3449, ventail; v. 124, l. 1645, nasal; and *passim.*
63. ibid., v. 225, l. 3091.
64. William of Malmesbury, *A History of the Norman Kings*, trans. Joseph Stevenson (first pub. in the series 'The Church Historians of England', Seeley, London; facsimile repr. Llanerch Enterprises, 1989), section 2581, p. 31.
65. Florence of Worcester, *A History of the Kings of England*, trans. Joseph Stevenson (first pub. in the series 'The Church Historians of England', Seeley, London, *c.* 1860s; repr. Llanerch Enterprises, nd), the year 1079.
66. Henry of Huntingdon, *The Chronicle of Henry of Huntingdon*, ed. and trans. T. Forester (first pub. 1853; facsimile repr. Llanerch Press, 1991), p. 215.
67. William of Malmesbury, *Norman Kings*, section 309, p. 63.
68. Turoldus, *Song of Roland*, v. 189, l. 2624; v. 196, l. 2730.
69. Pryor, 'Transportation', p. 12, where the Arabic and Latin equivalents are explained.
70. Comnena, *Alexiad*, Book I.xvi; Book 3.xii.
71. David C. Douglas, *William the Conqueror* (University of California Press, 1964), p. 203.
72. Turoldus, *Song of Roland*, v. 201, l. 2781f.
73. ibid., v. 79, l. 994ff.
74. ibid., v. 216, l. 2999.
75. ibid., v. 151, l. 2033.
76. W. von Eschenbach, *Parsival*, trans. Helen M. Mustard and Charles E. Passage (Vintage Books, Random House, New York, 1961), Book II, pp. 69 and 89; Book IV, p. 114; Book VI, p. 156 (twice); Book IX, p. 243.
77. ibid., Book V, p. 142.
78. ibid., Book VI, p. 169.
79. ibid., Book XII, p. 320.
80. ibid., Book VIII, p. 215.
81. ibid., Book II, p. 87.
82. ibid., p. 89.
83. ibid., note; when competing in 100 mile (160 km) races my Arabian stallion Nizzolan had a working weight of about 800–40 lb (360–80 kg) and no matter how many miles he travelled did not alter in girth.
84. Giraldus Cambrensis, 'Journey through Wales', Book II, Ch. 12.
85. Eschenbach, *Parsival*, p. 169, translator's note.
86. Jankovich, *They Rode into Europe*, p. 161, note 34. Budapest Archives, Dl.84214 and 84198.
87. ibid., Kállay family archives 497.
88. ibid., p. 114.
89. Eschenbach, *Parsival*, Book I, p. 22, Book IV, p. 114, Book VI, p. 155, iron armour. ibid., Book II, p. 41, armed to the hooves. ibid., Book IV, pp. 116 and 117, Book V, p. 142, mail armour.
90. J.G. Mann, 'Notes on the Armour of the Maximilian Period and the Italian Wars', *Archaeologia*, 79 (1929), pp. 217–44.
91. Heliodorus, *Aethiopica*, 9.15, quoted in M.I. Rostovtzeff, *The Excavations at Dura Europus, 6th Season, Preliminary Report* (New Haven, Yale University Press, 1936), p. 445.
92. Eschenbach, *Parsival*, Book IV, p. 114.
93. ibid., Book I, p. 21.
94. ibid., Book II, p. 94.
95. Eschenbach, *Willehalm*, p. 81.118, p. 85.128, p. 232.405.
96. ibid., p. 107.172, p. 133.224, p. 140.239, p. 227.395 and *passim.*
97. ibid., p. 401.
98. ibid., p. 232.405.
99. ibid., p. 227.395.
100. 'Umar Ibn Ibrahim al-Awsī al-Ansarī, *Tafrīj Al Kurūb Fī Tadbīr Al-Hurūb: A Muslim Manual of War*, ed. and trans. G.T. Scanlon (American University at Cairo Press, Cairo, 1961), p. 97. See also Ibn Hodeil, *La Parure*, p. 139.
101. Eschenbach, *Willehalm*, p. 331.
102. ibid., p. 188f.333ff.

103. ibid., p. 237ff.417ff.

104. Turoldus, *Song of Roland*, v. 27, l. 347.

105. Eschenbach, *Willehalm*, p. 380.

106. ibid., p. 214.368.

107. A. Hyland, *The Appaloosa* (J.A. Allen, London, 1990).

108. The Arab, Persian, African and Mamlūk saddles did have raised pommel and cantle but were not as high as European saddles. The Spanish saddle had a less accentuated construction than other European war saddles.

109. Ibn Hodeil, *La Parure*, p. 141ff.

110. I can vouch for this, having done experimental riding so equipped.

111. But not as long as the straight-legged style current in Europe north of Spain. Ibn Hodeil, *La Parure*, p. 412, note. Most weight is borne by the horse's forehand, while the hindquarters provide the powerful thrust.

112. Hyland, *Equus*, pp. 140–2.

113. Ibn Hodeil, *La Parure*, p. 141ff.

114. ibid., p. 230ff.

115. ibid., p. 269ff.

116. ibid., p. 264f.

117. Glover, 'English Warfare in 1066', pp. 1–18.

118. Robertson, *Laws of Kings of England*, p. 209ff, Canute II.

119. Ingulph, *Croyland Chronicle*, p. 182.

120. William of Poitiers, contribution trans. Lewis Thorpe, in *The Bayeux Tapestry and the Norman Invasion* (Folio Society, London, 1973), p. 34.

121. A 170 mile (273 km) crow flight trip from Wisbech to Durham is 225 miles (362 km) via the A47 and A1, adding approximately one-third to the total, the proportion needed when checking other distances.

122. Glover explains the *Heimskringla*'s errors over family relationships of the English leaders by noting similar mistakes in the *Anglo-Saxon Chronicles* about Norse leaders, and comments that these errors do not invalidate a nation's documents. See *EHR*, 262 (January 1952), pp. 1–18 (p. 6).

123. S. Sturleson, *Heimskringla: Sagas of the Norse Kings*, trans. Samuel Laing, rev. with intro. and notes Peter Foote (Everyman's Library, Dent, London, 1961 [1930], Ch. XC, p. 229.

124. ibid., Ch. XCI, p. 229.

125. ibid., Ch. XCII, p. 229.

126. Fleming, *Horseshoes and Horseshoeing*, p. 287.

127. Florence of Worcester, *History*, p. 133.

128. ibid., pp. 125, 124, 130.

129. Sturleson, *Heimskringla*, Ch. LXXXIX, p. 229.

130. Florence of Worcester, *History*, the year 1066, p. 133. Florence says that the army was raised *shortly after* the Kalends of May. A comet was seen on 24 April, the eighth of the Kalends of May.

131. *Carmen de Hastingal Proelio*, in *EHR* (R.H.C. Davies), 367 (April 1978), pp. 241–51.

132. William of Poitiers, in *Bayeux Tapestry*, p. 44.

133. ibid., p. 48.

134. ibid., p. 49.

135. ibid., p. 50.

136. ibid., p. 51.

137. ibid., p. 52. Other sources: William of Malmesbury, *History of Norman Kings*, p. 21, also says three; *Carmen de Hastingal Proelio* says two.

138. Douglas, *William the Conqueror*, p. 273.

139. ibid., p. 278ff.

140. ibid., p. 282.

141. Florence of Worcester, *History*, p. 134.

142. ibid., p. 136.

143. Douglas, *William the Conqueror*, pp. 214 and 216.

144. ibid., p. 214ff.

145. William of Malmesbury, *Norman Kings*, p. 24f, section 249.

146. Florence of Worcester, *History*, p. 137.

147. Douglas, *William the Conqueror*, p. 221, quoting Orderic Vitalis, Vol. II, p. 196.

148. ibid., p. 221f.

149. *Anglo-Saxon Chronicles*, the year 1085.

150. *De Gestis Herewardi Saxonis*, trans. Rev. W.D. Sweeting transcr. S.H. Miller (Geo. Carter, Peterborough, 1895), pp. 31 and 60.

151. Richard of Hexham, 'History of the Acts of King Stephen and the Battle of the Standard', in *Contemporary Chronicles of the Middle Ages*, trans. Joseph Stephenson (Llanerch Enterprises, 1988), pp. 60ff.

152. Florence of Worcester, *History*, pp. 194–6.

153. Richard of Hexham, 'History', pp. 66ff.

154. Henry of Huntingdon, *Chronicle*, Book VIII, p. 270.

155. Florence of Worcester, *History*, p. 196.

156. Henry of Huntingdon, *Chronicle*, Book VIII, p. 277ff.

157. William of Malmesbury, 'Historia Novella, or History of His own Times', in *Contemporary Chronicles of the Middle Ages*, trans. Joseph Stephenson (Llanerch Enterprises, 1988), pp. 50 and 51.

158. ibid., p. 54.

159. ibid., pp. 57 and 72.

160. ibid., p. 57.

161. W.L. Warren, *Henry II* (Methuen, London, 1991 [1973]), p. 231.

162. ibid., p. 232.

163. Giraldus Cambrensis, *Expugnatio Hibernica*, ed. Frederick J. Furnivall (Kegan Paul, Trench & Trubner, London, for the Early English Texts Society, 1896), ref. XL and p. 89.

164. John of Marmoutier, 'The Chronicles of the Counts of Anjou', in *The Plantagenet Chronicles*,

ed. Elizabeth Hallam (Guild Publishing, London, 1986, Book Club Associates edn), p. 48.

165. William of Poitiers, in *Bayeux Tapestry*, p. 35.

166. John of Marmoutier, in *Plantagenet Chronicles*, p. 52.

167. William Fitzstephen, 'The Life of St Thomas Becket', in *The Plantagenet Chronicles*, ed. Elizabeth Hallam (Guild Publishing, London, 1986, Book Club Associates edn), p. 98.

168. W. Childs, *Anglo-Castilian Trade in the Later Middle Ages* (Manchester University Press, Manchester, 1978), pp. 12 and 91.

169. Robert de Monte, *The Chronicles of Robert de Monte*, trans. Joseph Stevenson (first pub. Seeley, London, 1856, facsimile repr. Llanerch Publishers, 1991), pp. 66–9.

170. Warren, *Henry II*, p. 47.

171. Heavy-set horses often sweat considerably more than the 'drier' oriental horse. Azoturia, or tying-up syndrome, occurs with animals under extreme physical stress: muscles of hindquarters become rigid; urine appears bloody due to the chemical action of myoglobin present in it due to lactic acid build-up.

172. Warren, *Henry II*, p. 192f. Giraldus Cambrensis, *Expugnatio Hibernica*, pp. 9, 25, 35. P. Roche, *The Norman Invasion of Ireland* (Anvil Books, 1970), pp. 58–86 *passim*.

173. Giraldus Cambrensis, *Expugnatio Hibernica*, p. 35.

174. Roche, *The Norman Invasion of Ireland*, p. 98f.

175. Giraldus Cambrensis, *Expugnatio Hibernica*, p. 11.

176. Giraldus Cambrensis, *First Version of the Topography of Ireland*, trans. J.H. O'Meara (Dundalk, 1951), p. 85.

177. Roche, *The Norman Invasion of Ireland*, p. 71.

178. Warren, *Henry II*, pp. 201 and 204.

179. ibid., p. 205.

180. Giraldus Cambrensis, *Topography of Ireland*, p. 94.

181. I once had a horse that suffered from encephalitis, caused by an excess of selenium; the symptoms were as described – panic, blindness and head-beating, ending in the horse's being destroyed.

182. Warren, *Henry II*, p. 71f, quoting William Fitzstephen, II.20–33.

183. ibid., p. 91.

184. Robert de Monte, *Chronicles*, p. 96.

185. ibid., p. 117.

186. ibid., p. 119f.

187. Warren, *Henry II*, p. 129ff *passim*.

188. Jordan Fantosme, 'Fantosme's Chronicle' in *Contemporary Chronicles of the Middle Ages* (see note 157), ll. 1752–1853.

189. ibid., ll. 1856–63.

190. ibid., ll. 1864–73.

191. ibid., ll. 1874–7.

192. ibid., ll. 1878–90.

193. ibid., ll. 1893–1900.

194. ibid., l. 1810.

6. *Muslim Armies and the Horse*

1. Ibn Battuta, *The Travels of Ibn Battuta*, AD *1325–1354*, trans. H.A.R. Gibb (Hakluyt Society, second series, no. CX issued for 1956, Cambridge University Press, Cambridge, 1958), Vol. II (1962), Vol. III (1971) (Vol. II, p. 478).

2. Ibn al-Qalānisī, *The Damascus Chronicle of the Crusades*, ed. and trans. H.A.R. Gibb (University of London Historical Series, no. V, Luzac, London, 1932), pp. 77, 79, 86ff, 114, 127f and *passim*.

3. Marco Polo, *Travels*, trans. Bellonci, CLXXV, CXCV, CXCVII; trans. Marsden, p. 726.

4. Abou Bekr, *Naceri*, Vol. I, pp. 76 and 97.

5. ibid., Vol. I, p. 118.

6. Jahiz of Basra, 'Exploits of the Turks and the Army of the Khalifate in General', trans. C.T. Harley-Walker, *Journal of the Royal Asiatic Society* [hereafter *JRAS*] (1915), pp. 631–97 (p. 671).

7. Al-Ansarī, *Muslim Manual of War*, p. 113.

8. Abou Bekr, *Naceri*, Vol. I, Ch. I, vii, p. 98.

9. ibid.

10. ibid., Vol. II, Ch. XI, xx, p. 113.

11. ibid.

12. ibid., Vol. I, Ch. I, vii, p. 98.

13. ibid., Ch. III, v, p. 118f.

14. ibid., p. 119f.

15. ibid.

16. David Ayalon, 'Preliminary Remarks on the Mamlūk Military Institution in Islam', in *War Technology and Society in the Middle East*, ed. V.J. Parry and M.E. Yapp (Oxford University Press, Oxford, 1986), p. 44.

17. ibid., p. 46.

18. ibid., p. 46ff.

19. Jahiz of Basra, 'Turks', p. 633.

20. ibid., p. 645.

21. ibid.

22. Abou Bekr, *Naceri*, Vol. II, Ch. XII, ix, p. 149.

23. ibid., Vol. II, Ch. II, i, p. 17.

24. Creel, 'History of the Horse in China', pp. 647–72.

25. Robinson, *Oriental Armour*, pp. 24 and 50.

26. Jahiz of Basra, 'Turks', p. 646.

27. Robinson, *Oriental Armour*, p. 51.

28. Jahiz of Basra, 'Turks', p. 646.

29. Talbot Rice, *The Seljuks*, pp. 25f and 18.

30. Shying, one of the most aggravating habits, is particularly common in cheating and/or nervous horses.

31. Jahiz of Basra, 'Turks', p. 665f.

32. Taybugha, *Saracen Archery*, p. xxv.

33. Jahiz of Basra, 'Turks', p. 666f. In rodeo contests a talented roper can choose which part of the steer to rope; a pair of ropers can simultaneously snare head and heels.

34. British law forbids roping in the American manner.

35. Jahiz of Basra, 'Turks', p. 668.

36. With endurance conditioning a horse's lung and heart capacity can be greatly enhanced.

37. Jahiz of Basra, 'Turks', p. 669.

38. ibid., pp. 670 and 672.

39. ibid., p. 671, lance; p. 667, bows: p. 668, lasso.

40. ibid., p. 647.

41. Turkish archers used a thumb release, Europeans a finger release.

42. Talbot Rice, *The Seljuks*, pp. 28–36 *passim* and p. 39.

43. ibid., p. 43.

44. Comnena, *Alexiad*, Book I, Chs i–ii.

45. ibid.

46. ibid., Book I, Ch. iv.

47. ibid., Book III, Chs. viii–ix, xi.

48. ibid., Book IV, Chs. vi–vii; Book V, Chs vi–vii.

49. ibid., Book IV, Ch. ix.

50. ibid., Book VI, Chs ix–xii.

51. Ibn al-Qalānisī, *Damascus Chronicle*, p. 21.

52. ibid., p. 25.

53. ibid., pp. 25, 31, 34.

54. Comnena, *Alexiad*, Book IX, Ch. iii.

55. ibid., Book X, Ch. vi.

56. William, Archbishop of Tyre, *A History of Deeds Done Beyond the Sea*, Vol. I, trans. and annotated E.A. Babcock and A.C. Krey (Columbia University Press, 1943), Book III, Ch. 2, p. 155.

57. S. Runciman, *The First Crusade*, abridged edn (Cambridge University Press, Cambridge, 1980), p. 122f.

58. Raymond of Aguiliers, *Historia Francorum Qui Ceperunt Iherusalem*, trans., intro. and annotated J.H. Hill and L.L. Hill (American Philosophical Society, Philadelphia, 1968), p. 27.

59. William of Tyre, *Deeds*, Vol. I, Book III, Ch. 13, p. 169.

60. Oman, *Art of War*, p. 272.

61. William of Tyre, *Deeds*, Vol. I, Book III, Ch. 16, p. 174.

62. S. Runciman, *A History of the Crusades*, 3 vols (Cambridge University Press, Cambridge, 1925; Pelican Harmondsworth, 1971), Vol. I, p. 341; Runciman is convinced that Kilij Arslan's army was not as large as the combined Christian forces at Dorylaeum.

63. William of Tyre, *Deeds*, Vol. I, Book III, Chs 13–15, pp. 169–73.

64. Lady Wentworth, *Authentic Arabian*, p. 100.

65. ibid., p. 98.

66. R.C. Smail, *Crusading Warfare* (Cambridge University Press, Cambridge, 1956), p. 65.

67. Abou Bekr, *Naceri*, Vol. II, Third Exposition, Ch. 7, iii, p. 388f.

68. Lady Wentworth, *Authentic Arabian*, p. 35; see letter on the Barb from His Highness E. Sherif Sidi Hassan Raissuli.

69. Abou Bekr, *Naceri*, Vol. II, Ch. 4, x, p. 378.

70. ibid., Vol. II, p. 164.

71. Ibn Hodeil, *La Parure*, pp. 141–57 *passim*.

72. Abou Bekr, *Naceri*, Vol. II, p. 145.

73. Ibn Hodeil, *La Parure*, pp. 141–57 *passim*.

74. Abou Bekr, *Naceri*, Vol. II, p. 175.

75. ibid., p. 151.

76. ibid., p. 153; some horses, feeling a rider disadvantaged, finish the job by throwing the rider.

77. ibid., p. 141.

78. ibid., pp. 141 and 173.

79. Lady Wentworth, *Authentic Arabian*, p. 100.

80. Abou Bekr, *Naceri*, Vol. II, p. 159.

81. ibid., p. 163.

82. ibid., p. 172.

83. ibid., p. 170.

84. ibid.

85. ibid., p. 171f.

86. ibid., p. 164.

87. ibid., p. 183.

88. ibid. Abou Bekr had empathy with his equine charges, but a later deterioration in Arab standards set in, shown in the lengthy notes scattered throughout Perron's translation of the *Naceri*.

89. Taybugha, *Saracen Archery*, Ch. 15, ii, p. 71.

90. Abou Bekr, *Naceri*, Vol. II, p. 253, describes the hakamah but not its action.

91. ibid., Vol. II, p. 249f, bits; Vol. II, p. 181, rein/bit-handling.

92. Ibn Hodeil, *La Parure*, pp. 241f and 246.

93. ibid., p. 244f.

94. ibid., p. 245.

95. D. Nicolle, 'The Impact of the European Couched Lance on Muslim Military Tradition', *Journal of the Arms and Armour Society*, (1980), pp. 7–39.

96. Taybugha, *Saracen Archery*, p. 71.

97. ibid., p. 72.

98. ibid.

99. ibid., p. 73.

100. Ibn Hodeil, *La Parure*, p. 298. 'Conversion' means change of leg at canter.

101. ibid., p. 294; and Abou Bekr, *Naceri*, Vol. II, pp. 138 and 143.

102. Taybugha, *Saracen Archery*, p. 73, iii.

103. ibid., p. 73, iv.

104. ibid., p. 73f.

105. ibid., p. 82f. Jarmaki appears to be a method whereby the archer drew his bow anchoring his

drawing hand in the nape of his neck with the line of arrow displaced to the left of the line of sight in order to shoot at a target unattainable by using normal draw to chin or face. The drawing hand was therefore behind the rider, and accuracy a matter of instinctive skill.

106. ibid., p. 80.3.
107. ibid., p. 74.
108. ibid., p. 91.
109. ibid., p. 137.
110. ibid., p. 29ff.
111. Ibn Hodeil, *La Parure*, p. 230ff.
112. Robinson, *Oriental Armour*, p. 51.
113. H. Rabie, 'The Training of the Mamlūk Fāris', in *War Technology and Society* (note 16).
114. Ibn Hodeil, *La Parure*, p. 239.
115. Kai Ka'us Ibn Iskander, *Qabus Nama*, p. 85f.
116. Hodeil , *La Parure*, p. 399.

7. The Horses of the Mongols

1. E.D. Phillips, *The Mongols* (Thames & Hudson, London, 1969), p. 25.
2. G. Vernadsky, *The Mongols and Russia* (New Haven, Yale University Press, 1953), p. 22.
3. Dr Ch'i-Ch'ing, Hsiao, *The Military Establishment of the Yuan Dynasty* (Council on East Asian Studies, Harvard University Press, 1978), p. 9.
4. *Histoire secrète des Mongols*, trans. (from Mongolian) P. Pelliot (Librairie d'Amérique et d'Orient, Paris, 1949, Sec. Hist. no. 90), p. 140f.
5. Jagchid and Bawden, 'Horse Policy', pp. 246–64 (p. 246).
6. Hsiao, *Yuan Military*, pp. 9–10.
7. H. Desmond Martin, 'The Mongol Army', *JRAS* (April 1943), pp. 46–85 (p. 48).
8. Hsiao, *Yuan Military*, p. 11.
9. ibid., p. 12.
10. Desmond Martin, 'Mongol Army', p. 54, note 1.
11. Hsiao, *Yuan Military*, p. 12.
12. Desmond Martin, 'Mongol Army', p. 47, note 1.
13. Vernadsky, *Mongols and Russia*, p. 4.
14. ibid., p. 118f.
15. Jankovich, *They Rode into Europe*, pp. 13 and 59.
16. William Rubruck, *The Journey of William Rubruck to the Eastern Parts of the World, 1253–55, with two accounts of the earlier journey of John of Plano Carpini* ed. and trans. W.W. Rockhill (Hakluyt Society, Second Series, no. IV), pp. 131–2.
17. Denis Sinor, 'Horse and Pasture in Inner Asian History', *Oriens Extremus*, 19 (1972), pp. 171–83.
18. *Bandung*, Channel 4 TV programme on Mongolia, 26 September 1990.
19. Jagchid and Bawden, 'Horse Policy', p. 248f.
20. Rubruck, *Journey*, p. 4.IV.
21. D.O. Morgan, 'The Mongol Armies in Persia', *Der Islam*, 56 (1979), pp. 81–96.
22. J. Chambers, *The Devil's Horsemen*, (Weidenfeld & Nicolson, London, 1979, Book Club Associates edn), p. 93.
23. Vernadsky, *Mongols in Russia*, p. 33f.
24. Hyland, *The Endurance Horse*, p. 22f, note; the blood-sweating syndrome is normally caused by minute parasites which gorge on the horse's blood in such huge numbers that the horse appears to be sweating blood. However, veterinarians have recorded actual incidents of sweat containing blood.
25. Creel, 'Horse in China', pp. 647–72.
26. Rashid al-Din, *The Successors of Genghis Khan*, trans. (from Persian) J.A. Boyle (Columbia University Press, New York and London, 1971), p. 78.
27. Jankovich, *They Rode into Europe*, p. 64.
28. See Chapter 8, note 177.
29. Vernadsky, *Mongols in Russia*, p. 57ff.
30. ibid., p. 60.
31. Chambers, *Devil's Horsemen*, pp. 16f, 19 and 32.
32. ibid., p. 16.
33. In heavy-bodied horses the internal core of heat is hard to dissipate, thus delaying recovery rates for heart and respiration.
34. Abou Bekr, *Naceri*, Vol. II, p. 18.
35. Desmond Martin, 'Mongol Army', p. 55.
36. Hsiao, *Yuan Military*, p. 35.
37. Desmond Martin, 'Mongol Army', p. 56f.
38. Hsiao, *Yuan Military*, p. 43.
39. *Histoire secrète*, no. 124, p. 157.
40. Jagchid and Bawden, 'Horse Policy', p. 248.
41. ibid.
42. From experience of doing both I prefer to back at two years of age, leave hard work till four.
43. Hsiao, *Yuan Military*, p. 10.
44. Jagchid and Bawden, 'Horse Policy', p. 248.
45. ibid., p. 250.
46. ibid., p. 249.
47. ibid.
48. Sinor, 'Inner Asian Warriors', pp. 133–44.
49. Rubruck, *Journey*, p. 47, note 4.
50. Jagchid and Bawden, 'Horse Policy', p. 249.
51. Desmond Martin, 'Mongol Army', p. 53, note 2.
52. ibid., p. 52.
53. Marco Polo, *Travels*, trans. Marsden, p. 214.
54. Jagchid and Bawden, 'Horse Policy', pp. 246–64.
55. Desmond Martin, 'Mongol Army', p. 58.
56. Marco Polo, *Travels*, trans. Waugh, p. 62, LXXV.
57. Vernadsky, *Mongols in Russia*, p. 51f.

58. Jagchid and Bawden, 'Horse Policy', pp. 246–64.
59. Vernadsky, *Mongols in Russia*, p. 126f.
60. Rubruck, *Journey*, p. 76.
61. Robinson, *Oriental Armour*, p. 138.
62. Rubruck, *Journey*, p. 24.
63. Desmond Martin, 'Mongol Army', p. 70.
64. Rubruck, *Journey*, p. 261.
65. ibid.
66. ibid., pp. 131–3.
67. ibid., p. 74.
68. Hyland, *Endurance Horse*, p. 75; both incidents were told to me by Lieutenant-Colonel Stephen Jenkins who taught at Ulaanbaatar and knew Adalbish and the student.
69. Marco Polo, *Travels*, trans. Waugh, p. 57.
70. Rashid al-Din, *Successors of Genghis Khan*, p. 34.
71. Marco Polo, *Travels*, trans. Waugh, p. 82ff, XCI, XCII, XCIII, XCIV.
72. Maurice, *Strategikon*, Book XII, section D, p. 165ff.
73. Jankovich, *They Rode into Europe*, p. 64f.
74. Desmond Martin, 'Mongol Army', p. 47.
75. Vernadsky, *Mongols in Russia*, p. 30.
76. Phillips, *The Mongols*, p. 69.
77. Chambers, *Devil's Horsemen*, p. 48f.
78. Vernadsky, *Mongols in Russia*, p. 49. Phillips, *The Mongols*, p. 69.
79. Chambers, *Devil's Horsemen*, p. 70ff.
80. Kalinin, 'Horse Breeding in the Soviet Union', in *Book of the Horse*, ed. Vesey-Fitzgerald, pp. 595–8.
81. Chambers, *Devil's Horsemen*, p. 81.
82. ibid., p. 78.
83. Oman, *Art of War*, p. 328ff.
84. Chambers, *Devil's Horsemen*, p. 99.
85. Oman, *Art of War*, p. 330.
86. ibid. Chambers, *Devil's Horsemen*, pp. 101–3.
87. ibid., p. 108ff. Oman, *Art of War*, p. 332.
88. Rashid al-Din, *Successors of Genghis Khan*, p. 55.
89. ibid., p. 62f.
90. Marco Polo, *Travels*, trans. Marsden, pp. 364–6.
91. Rashid al-Din, *Successors of Genghis Khan*, p. 219.
92. Rubruck, *Journey*, p. 79, note 2.

8. The Importance of the Horse in the Crusades

1. Ibn Battuta, *Travels AD 1325–1354*, p. 478.
2. Hyland, *Equus*, pp. 76, 78, 79. Strabo, *Geography*, 16.2.10.
3. Abou Bekr, *Naceri*, Vol. II, Ch. 2, p. 18.
4. Comnena, *Alexiad*, Book V, Ch. iv, p. 163. F. Gabrieli, *Arab Historians of the Crusade*, trans. (from Italian) E.J. Costello (Routledge & Kegan Paul, London, 1984 [1969]). Ibn al-Athir, in ibid., XII.20–6, p. 187. Ibn al-Qalānisī, in ibid., 297–300 p. 58.
5. See endemic diseases in Chapter 2.
6. I refer to breeds as distinct from types because Europeans came late to purebred breeding.
7. Bertrandon de la Brocquière, from 'The Travels of Bertrandon de la Brocquière' in the *Early Travels in Palestine*, ed. and annotated T. Wright (Henry G. Bohn, London, 1848), pp. 305, 363.
8. Reported to me by the photographer Ron Massey, himself an Arabian breeder.
9. De la Brocquière, in *Early Travels in Palestine*, pp. 305 and 363.
10. A complicated area; see Hyland, *Endurance Horse*, p. 139f, where muscle fatigue is discussed with Dr David Snow from the Equine Research Station at Newmarket, who did the pioneer work in this field.
11. Lady Wentworth, *Authentic Arabian*, Ch. 4, *passim*.
12. William of Malmesbury, *History of the Norman Kings*, 347, p. 82ff.
13. Runciman, *History of the Crusades*, Vol. I, p. 104.
14. 'Franks' is here used collectively to include Urban's immediate audience and other western nations.
15. Runciman, *History of the Crusades*, Vol. I, p. 115.
16. Comnena, *Alexiad*, Book X, Ch. vii, p. 313.
17. William of Tyre, *Deeds*, Vol. I, Ch. 5, p. 123; Ch. 6, p. 124, Ch. 9, p. 128.
18. Comnena, *Alexiad*, Book X, Ch. ix, p. 321.
19. Runciman, *History of the Crusades*, Vol. I, p. 150f.
20. William of Tyre, *Deeds*, Book II, Ch. 12, p. 133.
21. Pryor, 'Transportation' pp. 1, 9–27. Part II: *Chelandia* and *Salandria*, p. 9; *Usari, Uscerii*, pp. 12 and 20; *Dromons*, p. 19; *Tarida/Taride*, p. 18; *Uissiers*, p. 22.
22. ibid., p. 12f.
23. Comnena, *Alexiad*, Book X, Ch. viii, p. 316.
24. Fulcher of Chartres, *A History of the Expedition to Jerusalem, 1095–1127*, trans. F.R. Ryan (Knoxville, 1969), II.6.12, p. 150.
25. ibid., II. 15.2 and II.15.4, p. 239.
26. ibid., I.8.4, p. 76.
27. William of Tyre, *Deeds*, I.X.13, p. 433.
28. Pryor, 'Transportation', p. 18.
29. Villehardouin, Geoffrey of, 'History of the Fourth Crusade', in *Chronicles of the Crusades*, trans. M.R.B. Shaw (Dorset Press, 1985; Penguin, Harmondsworth, 1963), Ch. 2, p. 33.

30. ibid., p. 46.
31. ibid., p. 46f.
32. ibid., p. 46.
33. Joinville, in *Chronicles of the Crusades*, Ch. 3, p. 196.
34 and 35. ibid., p. 196. Also Villehardouin, p. 66.
36. ibid.
37. Pryor, 'Transportation', p. 22.
38. Veterinary information from Russel Lyon, MRCVS.
39. Pryor, 'Transportation', p. 105f.
40. ibid., p. 118f.
41. P. Heiney, *George Soper's Horses* (Houghton Mifflin, Boston, 1991), p. 32.
42. Khusrau was not used in the ridden part as he was being broken in and riding under a low doorway would be dangerous with a green horse.
43. Pryor, 'Transportation', pp. 108–9.
44. Hay needs air circulating round it unless it is hermetically sealed.
45. On azoturia see Chapter 5, note 171. Barley is a very hard grain now never fed whole, unless soaked; usually flaked and/or micronized.
46. Veterinary information from Russel Lyon, MRCVS.
47. Vitamins B.12 and D help counteract stress.
48. Villehardouin, in *Chronicles of the Crusades*, pp. 55ff. The actual feast day is 24 June, according to the Roman Catholic liturgical calendar.
49. *La Règle du Temple* (La Société de l'Histoire de France, par Henri de Curson, Librairie Renouard, Paris, 1886), rule 84.
50. ibid., rule 66.
51. Pryor, 'Transportation', p. 110.
52. ibid., p. 15.
53. Behā ed-Dīn Abu el Mehāsan Yūsuf, *Saladin or What Befell Sultan Yusuf, Salāh ed-Dīn* (Library of the Palestine Pilgrims Text Society), Vol. XIII, *The Life of Saladin, 1137–1193* (Committee of the Palestine Exploration Fund, 1897), CLXIX.
54. William of Tyre, *Deeds*, Book 12, Ch. 7, p. 524.
55. Runciman, *History of the Crusades*, Vol. II, p. 156f.
56. ibid., Vol. II, p. 312f.
57. Ibn al-Athir, in *Arab Historians*, trans. Gabrielli, XI.347–51, p. 114f. 'Imād ad-Din al-Isfahani, in ibid., 18–29, p. 136.
58. *La Règle du Temple* rules 84 and 107.
59. ibid., rule 78.
60. 'Rouncy' changed its meaning. Once used to denote a packhorse, it was later applied to a lower-grade saddle-horse that could be used for war, usually by a man-at-arms. In the Templar context, the latter is meant.
61. *La Règle du Temple,* rule 101.

62. ibid., rule 99.
63. ibid., rule 101.
64. ibid., rule 110.
65. ibid., rule 120.
66. ibid., rule 125.
67. ibid., rule 13.
68. ibid., rules 103 and 169.
69. ibid., rule 77.
70. The phrasing implies four plus a riding animal, but in some cases it is not clear if it was a total of four, or four plus one.
71. *The Rules, Statutes and Customs of the Hospitallers 1099–1310*, trans. E.J. King (Methuen, London, 1934). Statutes of Fr Odo des Pins (1294–6) at Grand Chapters of 1294 and 1295 held at Limassol, p. 96f.
72. *La Règle du Temple,* rule 132.
73. ibid., rule 138.
74. ibid., rule 143.
75. ibid.
76. Behā, *Saladin*, CXXII, p. 302; CXXV, p. 306.
77. *La Règle du Temple,* rule 103.
78. Behā, *Saladin*, CXXVII, p. 310.
79. *La Règle du Temple,* rule 181.
80. ibid., rule 115.
81. ibid.
82. 'Colt' is an entire under 4 years of age, 'foal' applies to both sexes up to weaning age.
83. *La Règle du Temple,* rule 115.
84. ibid., rule 128.
85. ibid., rule 52.
86. ibid., rule 149.
87. ibid.
88. ibid., rule 123.
89. *Rules of the Hospitallers*, Statutes of Fr John de Villiers (1285–94), p. 92, no. 1.
90. *La Règle du Temple,* rule 173.
91. ibid., rule 377.
92. Usāmah Ibn Munqidh, *Memoirs of Usāmah Ibn Munqidh (Kitab al-I'Tibār)*, trans. (from original mss) P.L. Hitti (Princeton University/Columbia University Press, New York, 1929), p. 126.
93. *La Règle du Temple,* rule 140.
94. Overgirths are used today as a safeguard against buckle failure. Western saddles are secured with a flat knot. A horse's ribcage distends markedly on sudden intake of air.
95. *La Règle du Temple,* rule 378.
96. ibid., rule 146.
97. ibid., rule 102.
98. ibid., rule 162.
99. Behā, *Saladin*, LXXVIII.
100. *La Règle du Temple,* rule 66.
101. *Rules of the Hospitallers*, p. 95, no. 5.
102. *La Règle du Temple,* rule 149.
103. ibid., rule 178.
104. ibid., rule 14.

105. ibid., rule 79.
106. ibid., rule 379.
107. ibid., rule 319.
108. Runciman, *History of the Crusades*, Vol. I, p. 237.
109. Raymond of Aguiliers, *Historia Francorum*, Ch. VII, p. 59.
110. Runciman, *History of the Crusades*, Vol. I, p. 246f.
111. ibid., Vol. I, p. 232.
112. Aguiliers, *Historia Francorum*, Ch. IX, p. 63f.
113. Ibn al-Qalānisī, *Damascus Chronicle*, p. 226f.
114. ibid., p. 238f.
115. Usāmah, *Memoirs*, p. 99.
116. ibid., p. 41f.
117. Ibn al-Qalānisī, *Damascus Chronicle*, p. 159f.
118. Oman, *Art of War*, Vol. I, p. 297; Oman gives the date of this battle as 27 June 1119.
119. Usāmah, *Memoirs*, p. 96.
120. *La Règle du Temple*, rule 55.
121. ibid., rule 315; 'amble' is a comfortable two-beat gait.
122. ibid., rule 117.
123. ibid., rule 154.
124. ibid., rule 317.
125. ibid., rule 451.
126. ibid., rules 456 and 596.
127. ibid., rule 600.
128. ibid., rule 610.
129. ibid., rule 606.
130. ibid., rules 614 and 615.
131. *Rules of the Hospitallers*, p. 141.
132. ibid., p. 160. Nos 38, 40, 41 and 59 on p. 166 were horse-related offences.
133. *La Règle du Temple*, rule 167.
134. ibid., rule 301.
135. Behā, *Saladin*, Part I, p. 35.
136. ibid., Ch. CXVII, p. 282.
137. ibid., Chs CII–CXX *passim*.
138. ibid., Ch. CXXI, p. 289ff.
139. ibid., p. 395.
140. *La Règle du Temple*, rule 156.
141. ibid., rule 158.
142. ibid., rule 159.
143. *Rules of the Hospitallers*, p. 68. Chapter-General of 1264 at Acre on 8 September. C. No. 1.
144. Hyland, *Endurance Horse*, see above, note 10, p. 67f.
145. *La Règle du Temple*, rule 160.
146. ibid., rule 161.
147. ibid., rule 162.
148. Bridles often take their name from the type of bit, e.g. snaffle, pelham, double, curb, etc.
149. *La Règle du Temple*, rule 163.
150. ibid.; under rule 99 it is stated that the Seneschal carries the gonfanon, so there were times when this was altered according to circumstances.
151. ibid., rules 164–6.
152. ibid., rules 167–8.
153. No doubt an exaggerated underestimation.
154. Behā, *Saladin*, Ch. LX.
155. In field fights even though horses hurt each other, they keep on fighting and seem to show the pain only after aggression has ceased.
156. Behā, *Saladin*, Ch. CXVII.
157. Usāmah, *Memoirs*, 243F.
158. ibid., p. 225.
159. ibid., p. 67.
160. ibid., p. 67f.
161. ibid., p. 90.
162. ibid.; this phrase occurs several times in Usāmah's work and may be accepted as meaning a horse larger than the average. Camels vary in height but a Mihari, or riding camel, would stand 16 hh plus measured the same way as a horse – at the withers.
163. ibid., p. 126ff.
164. Behā, *Saladin*, Ch. LX.
165. ibid., Ch. CLXVI.
166. Runciman, *History of the Crusades*, Vol. I, p. 339.
167. Joinville, in *Chronicles of Crusades*, p. 202.
168. Villehardouin, in ibid., p. 33.
169. William of Tyre, *Deeds*, Book 3, p. 185.
170. ibid., p. 186.
171. ibid., Book 7, p. 316.
172. Ibn al-Qalānisī, *Damascus Chronicle*, pp. 94f, 117, 152.
173. Usāmah, *Memoirs*, pp. 95, 126, 128; Usāmah often refers to breeds, whereas we refer to strains of the Arabian breed of which there are at least a dozen major ones, and many sub-strains; however, all come under the title *Keheilan*, which means purebred. Interestingly one of the dozen strains is called *Managhi* (or under its alternative spellings, *Munighi* or *Muniqhi*). As the strains take their name from the original breeder who specialized with a nucleus of horses, it would be very interesting to try to trace any link between Usāmah Ibn Munqidh's family and this strain.
174. ibid., p. 94f.
175. Aguiliers, *Historia Francorum*, Ch. XI, p. 83f.
176. ibid., p. 91f.
177. Although the translator of Raymond of Aguiliers' work has put 'thoroughbred' instead of 'Arabian' for the horses Tancred received, this is misleading, a very common error in translation of contemporary sources by historians who often mistake the word 'purebred' for 'thoroughbred'; it is clear from the Arabic sources, especially the *Naceri*, that there was a plain distinction between Faras, Asil, or Keheilan (i.e. pure) and Hedjin, Akadish, or Berdhun (not pure). The

thoroughbred had not even been thought of until modern English flat-racing came on the scene and Wetherbys started registering bloodstock.

178. Aguiliers, *Historia Francorum*, Ch. V.

179. ibid.: pp. 87, 92, 105, gift; pp. 36, 84, purchase; p. 46, theft; p. 91, plundering 2,000 from pasture; pp. 79, 84f, 85f, spoils.

180. ibid., p. 28.

181. ibid., p. 35.

182. ibid., p. 37.

183. ibid., p. 50.

184. ibid., p. 79.

185. ibid., p. 118.

Bibliography

Primary Sources

Abou Bekr ibn Bedr, *Le Naceri*, trans. M. Perron, Ministry of Agriculture of France, Paris, 1860, 3 vols.

Aguiliers, Raymond of, *Historia Francorum Qui Ceperent Iherusalem*, trans., intro. and annotated John Hugh Hill and Laurita L. Hill, American Philosophical Society, Philadelphia, 1968.

Ammianus Marcellinus, *The Later Roman Empire AD 354–378*, trans. W. Hamilton, Penguin, Harmondsworth, 1986.

Anglo-Saxon Chronicles, The, trans. and coll. Anne Savage, William Heinemann, London, 1982.

Anglo-Saxon Wills, ed. and trans. Dorothy Whitlock, Oxford University Press, Oxford, 1930.

Bede, *Bede's Ecclesiastical History of the English People*, ed. Bertram Colgrave and R.A.B. Mynors, Oxford University Press, Oxford, 1969.

Behā ed-Dīn Abu el Mehāsan Yūsuf, *Saladin, or What Befell Sultan Yusuf, Salāh ed-Dīn*, Library of the Palestine Pilgrims Text Society, Vol. XIII, *The Life of Saladin (1137–1193)*, Committee of the Palestine Exploration Fund, 1897.

Beowulf, trans. Kevin Crossley-Holland, Folio Society, London, 1973.

Bökönyi, S., *History of Domesticated Mammals in Central and Eastern Europe*, Akadémiai Kiadó, Budapest, 1974.

Brocquière, Bertrandon de la, 'From the Travels of Bertrandon de la Brocquière' in *Early Travels in Palestine*, ed. and annotated Thomas Wright, Henry G. Bohn, London, 1848.

Caesar, Julius, *The Gallic Wars*, trans. J.J. Edwards, Loeb Classical Library, Heinemann, 1955.

Calkin, V.I., *Drevneje zsivotnovodsztvo plenjon vasztocsnoj Jevropu i szregynyej Azu* [Stockbreeding in Antiquity among East European and Central Asian Tribes], Moscow, 1966.

Cambrensis, Giraldus, *Expugnatio Hibernica*, ed. Frederick J. Furnivall for the Early English Texts Society, Kegan Paul, Trench, Trubner, London, 1896.

Cambrensis, Giraldus, *First Version of the Topography of Ireland*, trans. J.H. O'Meara, Dundalk, 1951.

Cambrensis, Giraldus, 'Description of Wales', in *Gerald of Wales*, trans. and intro. L. Thorpe, Penguin, Harmondsworth, 1978.

Cambrensis, Giraldus, 'The Journey through Wales', in *Gerald of Wales*, trans. and intro. L. Thorpe, Penguin, Harmondsworth, 1978.

Carmen de Hastingal Proelio, in *EHR* (R.H.C. Davies), Vol. 367 (April 1978), pp. 241–51.

Catholic Bible, ed. Revd John P. O'Connell, Virtue/Harwin Press, London, 1956.

Chartres, Fulcher of, *A History of the Expedition to Jerusalem, 1095–1127*, trans. F.R. Ryan, Knoxville, 1969.

Comnena, Anna, *The Alexiad*, trans. E.R.A. Sewter, Penguin, Harmondsworth, 1969; repr. 1979, 1982, 1985, 1987.

Cotton Mss, Cleopatra B.5 and Cleopatra C.VIII, folio 4.v., Department of Mss, British Library, British Museum.

Daily Missal and Liturgical Manual, comp. from the *Missale Romanum*, Laverty, Leeds, 10th edn, 1957.

Dede Korkut, *The Book of Dede Korkut*, trans. G. Lewis, Penguin, Harmondsworth, 1982 (1974).

De Gestis Herewardi Saxonis, trans. Revd W.D. Sweeting, Carter, Peterborough, 1895.

'De Villis' (Capitularies of Charlemagne), in *The Reign of Charlemagne*, ed. H.R. Loyn and J. Percival, Edward Arnold, 1975.

Dio Cassius, *Dio's Roman History*, 9 vols, trans. E. Cary, Loeb Classical Library, Heinemann, 1961–70.

Einhard, 'Life of Charlemagne', in *Two Lives of Charlemagne*, trans. and intro. L. Thorpe, Penguin, Harmondsworth, 1969.

Eschenbach, Wolfram von, *Parsival*, trans. H.M. Mustard and C.E. Passage, Vintage Books, Random House, New York, 1961.

Eschenbach, Wolfram von, *Willehalm*, trans. C.E. Passage, Frederick Unger, New York, 1977.

Fantosme, Jordan, 'Fantosme's Chronicle', in *Contemporary Chronicles of the Middle Ages*, trans. J. Stephenson, Llanerch Enterprises, 1988.

Fitzstephen, William, 'The Life of St Thomas Becket', in *The Plantagenet Chronicles*, ed. Elizabeth Hallam, Guild Publishing, London, BCA edn, 1986.

Froissart, Jean, *Chronicles*, trans. and ed. G. Brereton, Penguin, Harmondsworth, 1983 (1968).

Heliodorus, *Aethiopica*, quoted in M.I. Rostovtzeff, *Excavations at Dura Europus*, 6th season, preliminary report, New Haven, Yale University Press, 1936.

Huntingdon, Henry of, *The Chronicle of Henry of Huntingdon*, ed. and trans. T. Forester, first pub. 1853, facsimile repr. Llanerch Press, 1991.

Herodotus, *The Histories*, trans. A. de Selincourt, Penguin, Harmondsworth, 1974 (1954).

Hexham, Richard of, 'History of the Acts of King Stephen and the Battle of the Standard', in *Contemporary Chronicles of the Middle Ages*, trans. Joseph Stephenson, Llanerch Enterprises, 1988.

Histoire secrète des Mongols, trans. (from Mongolian) P. Pelliot, Librairie d'Amérique et d'Orient, Paris, 1949.

Hywel Dda, *Welsh Medieval Law*, trans. A.W. Wade-Evans, Clarendon Press, Oxford, 1909; Harleian Mss 4353, the British Museum, London.

Ibn al-Athir, see 'Izz ad-Din.

Ibn al-Qalānisī, *The Damascus Chronicle of the Crusades*, ed. and trans. H.A.R. Gibb, University of London Historical Series No. V, Luzac, London, 1932.

Ibn Battuta, *The Travels of Ibn Battuta, AD 1325–1354*, trans. H.A.R. Gibb, issued by the Hakluyt Society, 2nd series, No. CX., 1956, Cambridge University Press, Cambridge, 1958; Vol. II, 1962; Vol. III, 1971.

Ibn Hodeil (Aly Ben Abderrahman Ben Hodeil El Andalusy), trans. Louis Mercier as *La Parure des cavaliers et l'insigne des preux*, Librairie Orientaliste, Paul Geuthner, Paris, 1924.

Ibn Munqidh see Usāmah.

'Imād ad-Din al-Isfahani, see *Arab Historians of the Crusades*, trans. E.J. Costello (from the Italian translation by F. Gabrieli), Routledge & Kegan Paul, London, 1969; pbk, 1984.

Ingulph, *Chronicle of the Abbey of Croyland*, trans. H.T. Riley, Bell, London, 1893.

'Izz ad-Din Ibn al-Athir, see *Arab Historians of the Crusades*, trans. E.J. Costello (from the Italian translation by F. Gabrieli), Routledge & Kegan Paul, London, 1969; pbk, 1984.

Jahiz of Basra (Amr b. Bahr b. Mahbub Abu Othman al-Jahiz), 'Exploits of the Turks and the Army of the Khalifate in General', trans. C.T. Harley-Walker, *JRAS* (1915), pp. 631–97.

Joinville, Jean de, see *Chronicles of the Crusades*, trans. M.R.B. Shaw, Dorset Press, 1985.

Kai Ka'us Ibn Iskander, *Qabus Nama: a Mirror for Princes*, trans. (from Persian) R. Levy, Cresset Press, 1951.

Kalinin, Victor, 'Horse Breeding in the Soviet Union', trans. H.P. Fox, in *Book of the Horse*, ed. B. Vesey-Fitzgerald, Ivor Nicholson & Watson, London and Brussels, 1947.

Liber Quotidianus Contrarotulatoris Garderobae, Anno Regni Regis Edwardi Primi Vicesimo Octavo AD MCCXIX and MCCC, Society of Antiquities, London, 1787.

Malmesbury, William of, *A History of the Norman Kings*, trans. J. Stephenson, first pub. Seeleys in series 'The Church Historians of England', *c.*1860s; facsimile repr. Llanerch Enterprises, 1989.

Malmesbury, William of, 'Historia Novella, or History of His Own Times', in *Contemporary Chronicles of the Middle Ages*, Llanerch Enterprises, 1988.

Marmoutier, John of, 'The Chronicles of the Counts of Anjou', in *The Plantagenet Chronicles*, ed. Elizabeth Hallam, Guild Publishing, London, BCA edn, 1986.

Maurice, *Maurice's Strategikon*, trans. G.T. Dennis, University of Pennsylvania Press, Philadelphia, 1984.

Medieval Muslim Horsemanship, ed. G. Rex Smith, British Library, London, 1979.

Monte, Robert de, *The Chronicles of Robert de Monte*, trans. J. Stevenson, first pub. Seeleys in series 'The Church Historians of England', 1856, facsimile repr. Llanerch Publishers, 1991.

Nithard, 'Nithard's Histories', in *Carolingian Chronicles*, trans. B.W. Scholz with B. Rogers, Ann Arbor Paperbacks, University of Michigan Press, Ann Arbor, 1972.

Notker the Stammerer, 'Charlemagne', in *Two Lives of Charlemagne*, trans. and intro. L. Thorpe, Penguin, Harmondsworth, 1969.

Oppian, *Cynegetica*, trans. A.W. Mair, Loeb Classical Library, Heinemann, London, 1926.

Owen Aneurin, 'Ancient Laws and Institutes of Wales', in *Welsh Medieval Law*, British Museum Harleian mss 4353, trans. A.W. Wade-Evans, Clarendon Press, Oxford, 1909.

Plano Carpini, John of, see Rubruck, William.

Plutarch, *Lives*, trans. W. and J. Langthorne, Chandos Classics, Frederick Warne, 1884, V I and II Roman.

Poitiers, William of, see *The Bayeux Tapestry and the Norman Invasion*, trans. L. Thorpe, Folio Society, London, 1973.

Polo, Marco, (1) *The Travels of Marco Polo*, trans. T. Waugh (from the Italian translation by M. Bellonci) Sidgwick & Jackson, London, BCA edn, 1984,
            (2) *The Travels of Marco Polo*, trans. W. Marsden (from the Italian translation by Remusio) Cox & Bayliss, London, 1818.

Porphyrogenitus, Constantine, *De Administrando Imperio*, trans. R.J.H. Jenkins, (from Greek text ed. Gy Moravcsik), Budapest, 1949.

Procopius, *The History of the Wars*, Vols I–V, trans. H.B. Dewing, Loeb Classical Library, Heinemann, 1914–28.

Procopius, *Secret History*, trans. G.A. Williamson, Penguin, Harmondsworth, 1966; citing 1987 edn.

Psellus, Michael, *Fourteen Byzantine Rulers*, trans. E.R.A. Sewter, Penguin, Harmondsworth, rev. edn, 1966.

Qu'ran, The Holy, trans. A. Yusuf Ali, Sh. Muhammad Ashraf, Lahore, Pakistan, 1975; repr. 1976, 1977.

Rashid al-Din, *The Successors of Genghis Khan*, trans. (from Persian) J.A. Boyle, New York and London, Columbia University Press, 1971.

Règle du Temple, La, Henri de Curzon, Paris, Librairie Renouard, for the Société de l'histoire de France, 1886.

Robertson, A.J. (ed.), *The Laws of the Kings of England from Edmund to Henry I*, trans. A.J. Robertson, Cambridge University Press, Cambridge, 1925.

Royal Frankish Annals, in *Carolingian Chronicles*, trans. B.W. Scholz with B. Rogers, Ann Arbor Paperbacks, University of Michigan Press, Ann Arbor, 1972.

Rubruck, William, *The Journey of William Rubruck to the Western Parts of the World, 1253–55, with two accounts of the earlier journey of John of Plano Carpini*, ed. and trans. W.W. Rockhill, Hakluyt Society, second series, No. IV.

Rules, Statutes and Customs of the Hospitallers, 1099–1310, trans. E.J. King, Methuen, London, 1934.

Strabo, *Geography*, Loeb Classical Library, Heinemann, 1961.

Sturleson, Snorri, *Heimskringla: Sagas of the Norse Kings*, trans. S. Laing, rev. with intro. and notes Peter Foote, Everyman's Library, London, 1961 (1930).

Taybugha al-Baklamishi al-Yunani, *Saracen Archery*, trans. J.D. Latham and W.F. Paterson, Holland Press, London, 1970.

Theodosian Code, The, trans. C. Pharr, Princeton University Press, Princeton, 1952.

Turoldus, *The Song of Roland*, trans. D.L. Sayers, Penguin Harmondsworth, 1988 (1957).

Tyre, William, Archbishop of, *A History of Deeds Done Beyond the Sea*, Vol. I, trans. and annotated E.A. Babcock and A.C. Krey, Columbia University Press, 1943.

'Umar ibn Ibrahim al-Awsī al-Ansarī, *Tafrīj Al Kurūb Fī Tadbīr Al-Hurūb: A Muslim Manual of War*, ed. and trans. G.T. Scanlon, American University at Cairo Press, Cairo, 1961.

Usāmah ibn Munqidh, *Memoirs of Usāmah ibn Munqidh (Kitab al-I'Tibār)*, trans. (from original mss) P.L. Hitti, Princeton University/Columbia University Press, New York, 1929.

Vegetius Publius Renatus, *Digestorum Artis Mulomedicinae*, ed. E. Lommatzsch, Leipzig, 1903.

Villehardouin, Geoffrey of, 'History of the Fourth Crusade', see *Chronicles of the Crusades*, trans. M.R.B. Shaw, Dorset Press, 1985.

Vitalis, Orderic, *Orderici Vitalis ecclesiasticae historiae, libri tredecim*, ed. A. Le Prevost for the Société de l'histoire de France, ed. and trans. M. Chibnall, 1969–81.

Welsh Medieval Law, see Hywel Dda.

Wentworth, Lady, *The Authentic Arabian Horse*, Allen & Unwin, London, 1945.

Worcester, Florence of, *A History of the Kings of England*, trans. J. Stevenson, first pub. Seeleys in series 'The Church Historians of England', *c.* 1860s; repr. Llanerch Enterprises, 1989.

Xenophon, *The Persian Expedition*, trans. R. Warner, Penguin, Harmondsworth, 1986.

Secondary Sources

Allibone, Finch, *In Pursuit of the Robber Baron*, Lennard, 1988.

Altschul, Michael, *A Baronial Family in Medieval England: The Clares, 1217–1314*, Johns Hopkins University Press, Baltimore, 1965.

Ayalon, D., 'Preliminary Remarks on the Mamlūk Military Institution in Islam', in *War Technology and Society in the Middle East*, ed. V.J. Parry and M.E. Yapp, Oxford University Press, Oxford, 1986.

Bachrach, B.S., 'Animals in Warfare in Early Medieval Europe', *Septimane*, Vol. XXXL (1983), pp. 707–64.

Bandung, Channel 4 TV programme with Dr Humphreys, Mongolian Studies, Cambridge University, 26 September 1990.

Barber, R. and Barker, J., *Tournaments, Jousts, Chivalry and Pageants in the Middle Ages*, Boydell Press, Woodbridge, 1989.

Barlow, Frank, *William Rufus*, Methuen, London, 1983.

Baynes, Norman H., 'The Campaigns of Heraclius Against Persia', *EHR*, Vol. 19 (1904), pp. 694–702.

Beeler, John, *Warfare in Feudal Europe 730–1200*, Cornell University Press, Ithaca, NY and London, 1972.

Birley, Eric, *Housesteads Roman Fort* (English Heritage, Historic Buildings and Monuments Commission for England, HMSO, London, 1985; repr. 1986, 1987; first published by the National Trust, London, 1936.

Bishop, M.D., 'Cavalry Equipment of the Roman Army in the 1st Century AD', in Military Equipment and the Identity of Roman Soldiers, *BAR International Series*, 394, 1988.

Bivar, A.D.N., 'The Stirrup and its Origin', *Oriental Art*, new series 1, no. 2 (1955), pp. 61–5.

Bivar, A.D.N., 'Cavalry Tactics and Equipment on the Euphrates Frontier', *Dumbarton Oaks Papers*, no. 26 (1972), pp. 273–91.

Bovill, E.W., *The Golden Trade of the Moors*, 2nd edn, rev. and with add. material R. Hallett, Oxford University Press, Oxford, 1978.

Brehier, L., *Les Institutes de L'Empire Byzantin*, ed. Albin Michel, Paris, 1949.

Brookes, A.J., 'The Percheron Horse in Great Britain', in *The Book of the Horse*, ed. B. Vesey-Fitzgerald, Ivor Nicholson & Watson, London and Brussels, 1947.

Cambridge Enclyclopedia of Archaeology, ed. A. Sherratt, Cambridge University Press, Cambridge, 1980.

Chambers, J., *The Devil's Horsemen*, Weidenfeld & Nicolson, London, 1979, Book Club Associates edn.

Chibnall, M., 'Military Service in Normandy before 1066', *ANS*, Vol. V (1982), pp. 65–77.

Childs, W., *Anglo-Castilian Trade in the Later Middle Ages*, Manchester University Press, Manchester, 1978.

Clark, J., 'Medieval Horseshoes', Department of Medieval Antiquities, Museum of London, Finds Research Group 700–1700, datasheet 4, reproduced and distributed by Coventry Museums.

Connolly, P., 'The Roman Saddle', in *Roman Military Equipment: The Accoutrements of War: Proceedings of the Third Roman Military Equipment Research Seminar*, *BAR International Series*, 336, 1987.

Contamine, P., *War in the Middle Ages*, trans. Michael Jones, Basil Blackwell, Oxford, 1984.

Coulston, J.C., 'Roman Archery Equipment' in *The Production and Distribution of Roman Military Equipment: Proceedings of the Second Roman Military Equipment Research Seminar*, ed. M.C. Bishop, *BAR International Series*, 275, 1985.

Creel, H.G., 'History of the Horse in China', *AHR*, Vol. LXX, no. 3 (April 1965), pp. 647–72.

Curle, J., *A Roman Frontier Post and its People*, James Maclehouse, Glasgow, 1911.

Davis, R.H.C., 'The Warhorses of the Normans', *ANS*, Vol. X (1987), pp. 67–82.

Dent, A., contribution to *Encyclopedia of the Horse*, Octopus, London, 1977.

Douglas, D.C., *William the Conqueror*, University of California Press, 1964.

Dykes Shaw, R., 'The Fall of the Visigothic Power in Spain', *EHR*, Vol. XXI, no. 82 (April 1900), pp. 209–28.

Fauber, L.H., *Narses, Hammer of the Goths*, Alan Sutton, Stroud, 1990.

Fleming, George, *Horseshoes and Horseshoeing*, Chapman & Hall, London, 1869.

Frere, S., *Britannia*, Guild Publishing/Routledge & Kegan Paul, London, BCA edn, 1987.

Gabrieli, F., *Arab Historians of the Crusades*, trans. (from Italian) E.J. Costello, Routledge & Kegan Paul, London, 1984 (1969).

Glover, R., 'English Warfare in 1066', *EHR*, Vol. LXVII, no. 262 (January 1952), pp. 1–18.

Glubb, J.B., *The Great Arab Conquests*, Hodder & Stoughton, Sevenoaks, 1963.

Grant, M., *Dawn of the Middle Ages*, Weidenfeld & Nicolson, London, 1961.

Hayes, H.M., *Veterinary Notes for Horseowners*, Stanley Paul, London, 1976 edn.

Heiney, P., *George Soper's Horses*, Houghton Mifflin, Boston, 1991.

Hewitt, J., *Ancient Armour and Weapons in Europe*, John Henry and James Parker, Oxford and London, 1855.

Hill, D.R., 'The Role of the Camel and the Horse in the Early Arab Conquests', *War Technology and Society in the Middle East*, ed. V.J. Parry and M.E. Yapp, Oxford University Press, Oxford, 1986.

Hollister, C.W., *Anglo-Saxon Military Institutions*, Clarendon Press, Oxford, 1962.

Hsiao, Dr Ch'i-Ch'ing, *The Military Establishment of the Yuan Dynasty*, Council on East Asian Studies, Harvard University Press, Cambridge, Mass., 1978.

Hyland, A., *The Appaloosa*, J.A. Allen, London, 1990.

Hyland, A., *The Endurance Horse*, J.A. Allen, London, 1988.

Hyland, A., *Equus*, Batsford, London, 1990.

Hyland, A., *Training the Roman Cavalry from Arrian's Ars Tactica*, Alan Sutton, Stroud, 1993.

Jagchid, S. and Bawden, C.R., 'Some Notes on the Horse Policy of the Yuan Dynasty', *CAS*, Vol. 10 (1965), pp. 246–65.

Jankovich, Miklos, *They Rode into Europe*, trans. A. Dent, Harrap, London, 1971.

Keller, W., *The Bible as History*, trans. William Neil, Hodder & Stoughton, Sevenoaks, BCA edn, 1956.

Leake, W.M., *The Edict of Diocletian, AD 303*, John Murray, London, 1826.

Loch, S., *The Royal Horse of Europe*, J.A. Allen, London, 1986.

Lot, F., *L'Art militaire et les armées au moyen âge en Europe et dans le proche orient*, Vol. I, Payot, Paris, 1946.

Loyn, H.R. and Percival, J.R., *The Reign of Charlemagne*, Edward Arnold, 1975; includes 'De Villis'.

Macartney, C.A., *The Magyars in the Ninth Century*, Oxford University Press, Oxford, 1930; repr. 1968.

Mann, J.G., 'Notes on the Armour of the Maximilian Period and the Italian Wars', *Archaeologia*, Vol. 79 (1929), pp. 217–44.

Marshall, C., *Warfare in the Latin East 1192–1291*, Cambridge University Press, Cambridge, 1992.

Martin, H. Desmond, 'The Mongol Army', *JRAS* (April 1943), pp. 46–85.

Merwin, M.S., contribution to *The Horse through Fifty Centuries of Civilization*, pr. A. Dent, Phaidon Press, 1974.

Montgomery Watt, W., *A History of Islamic Spain*, Edinburgh University Press, Edinburgh, 1965.

Morgan, D.O., 'The Mongol Armies in Persia', *Der Islam*, Vol. 56 (1979), pp. 81–96.

Museum of London Catalogues, No. 7, Medieval Catalogue, HMSO, London, 1940.

Nicolle, D., 'The Impact of the European Couched Lance on Muslim Military Tradition', *Journal of the Arms and Armour Society*, Vol. X (1980), pp. 7–39.

Oakeshott, E., *A Knight and his Horse*, Lutterworth Press, London, 1962.

Obolensky, D., *The Byzantine Commonwealth*, Weidenfeld & Nicolson, London, 1974; Cardinal, Sphere Books, 1974.

Oman, C., *A History of the Art of War in the Middle Ages*, Vol. I, Burt Franklin, rev. edn 1924.

Phillips, E.D., *The Mongols*, Thames & Hudson, London, 1969.

Pryor, J.H., 'Transportation of Horses by Sea during the Era of the Crusades, eighth century to AD 1285', Parts I and II, *Mariner's Mirror*, no. 68 (1982), pp. 9–27, 103ff.

Rabie, H., 'The Training of the Mamlūk Fāris' in *War, Technology and Society in the Middle East*, ed. V.J. Parry and M.E. Yapp, Oxford University Press, Oxford, 1986.

Ridgeway, William, *The Origin and Influence of the Thoroughbred Horse*, Cambridge Biological Series, Cambridge University Press, Cambridge, 1905.

Rivet, A.L.F. and Smith, C., *The Place-Names of Roman Britain*, Batsford, London, BCA edn, 1981.

Robinson, R., *Oriental Armour*, Herbert Jenkins, London, 1967.

Roche, R., *The Norman Invasion of Ireland*, Anvil Books, 1970.

Roolvink, R., *The Historical Atlas of the Muslim Peoples*, Djambatan, Amsterdam, 1957.

Ross, D.J.A., 'L'Originalité de "Turoldus": le maniement de la lance', *Cahiers de civilisation Médiévale*, Vol. VI (1963), pp. 127–38.

Rudenko, S.I., *The Frozen Tombs of Siberia*, Dent, London, 1970.

Runciman, S., *A History of the Crusades*, 3 vols, Cambridge University Press, Cambridge, 1925; Pelican, Harmondsworth, 1971.

Runciman, S., *The First Crusade*, abr. edn, Cambridge University Press, Cambridge, 1980.

Saggs, H.W.F., *The Might that was Assyria*, Sidgwick & Jackson, London, 1984.

Sinor, D., 'The Inner Asian Warriors', *JAOS*, Vol. 101 (1981), pp. 133–44.

Sinor, D., 'Horse and Pasture in Inner Asian History', *Oriens Extremus*, Vol. 19 (1972), pp. 171–83.

Sitwell, N.H.H., *The World the Romans Knew*, Hamish Hamilton, London, 1984.

Smail, R.C., *Crusading Warfare*, Cambridge University Press, Cambridge, 1956.

Smith, G.R., *Medieval Muslim Horsemanship*, British Library, London, 1979.

Talbot, Rice, T., *The Seljuks*, Thames & Hudson, London, 1961.

Trevelyan, C.M., *English Social History*, Longmans Green, 1942; Pelican, Harmondsworth, 1967; repr. 1970, 1972.

Vernadsky, G., *The Mongols and Russia*, New Haven, Yale University Press, 1953.

Vernam, G.R., *Man on Horseback*, Harper & Row, New York, 1964.

Vesey-Fitzgerald, B. (ed.), *Book of the Horse*, Ivor Nicholson & Watson, 1947 edn.

Vyronis, S., *Byzantium and Europe*, Thames & Hudson, London, 1967.

Wade Evans, A.W. (trans.) *Welsh Medieval Law*, British Museum Harleian mss 4353, Clarendon Press, Oxford, 1909.

Warren, W.L., *Henry II*, Methuen, London, 1973, repr. 1991.

Webster, G., *The Roman Army*, Grosvenor Museum, Chester, rev. edn 1973.

Wentworth, Lady, 'The World's Horse', in *Book of the Horse*, ed. B. Vesey-Fitzgerald, Ivor Nicholson & Watson, London and Brussels, 1947.

White, L., Jr, *Medieval Technology and Social Change*, Clarendon Press, Oxford, 1962.

Index of Horse Related Subjects

General Index

Some places and peoples are repeated so frequently that each individual reference is not listed. Instead the first mention, or ones with a particular relevance appear in the index. Horse related subjects, including breeds and types, can be found in the specialized index.